THE PRESBYTERIAN CONFLICT

Dedicated to the memory of J. Gresham Machen,
who played the leading role in The Presbyterian Conflict.
Drawing by Leo Mielziner

THE PRESBYTERIAN CONFLICT

by
Edwin H. Rian, A.M., Th.B.

The Committee for the Historian of the
Orthodox Presbyterian Church
Philadelphia • *1992*

Reprinted 1992 by
The Committee for the Historian of
the Orthodox Presbyterian Church
303 Horsham Road, Suite G
Horsham, Pennsylvania 19044

Cover Photo (June 15, 1936): At the height of the presbyterian conflict, the Rev. David Freeman leads worshippers to a new place of worship, after leaving Grace Presbyterian Church, Philadelphia (PCUSA). Some sources say that the group adjourned to Oakford Street and the home of Helen Hollenbach, the church organist. Later this group organized an Orthodox Presbyterian congregation.

The Machen drawing first appeared accompanying his article "My Idea of God" in the December, 1925 issue of the Woman's Home Companion.

Library of Congress Cataloging in Publication Data

Rian, Edwin H.
THE PRESBYTERIAN CONFLICT
    1. Church History — Presbyterianianism
    2. American Denominations — The Orthodox Presbyterian Church
    I. Title   II. Presbyterian Church
ISBN   0-934688-67-2

Book designed and typeset by Eric D. Bristley
Olive Tree Graphics
Set in Goudy Old Style
Printed in the United States of America

Contents

Preface to the 1992 Edition

The *Presbyterian Conflict*, originally published by William B. Eerdmans in 1940, is a monument to a cause that continues beyond Edwin H. Rian's involvement with it. To many it remains the classic inside look at the valiant effort to preserve Presbyterian orthodoxy and ecclesiastical integrity.

The figure of J. Gresham Machen, the man so revered and relied upon by Mr. Rian in those days, stands behind the work. The book itself, therefore, pays tribute to this remarkable servant of Jesus Christ. However, it sets before us more than the reputation of one man. In it we confront the issues that demand reflection and repentance from the twentieth-century church if she is to be true to her Savior.

The Committee for the Historian of the Orthodox Presbyterian Church reissues *The Presbyterian Conflict* to the glory of God. We make no further comment but to encourage you, the reader, to allow this outstanding work to speak for itself.

The book has been reset. Changes in capitalization and punctuation, together with the reformatting of a number of quotations and footnotes, are the only improvements we offer to the text. Some additions have been made to the index.

Charles G. Dennison,
Historian for the Orthodox Presbyterian Church
January 1, 1992

Preface

THE STARTLING EVENTS which have occurred in the past decade within the Presbyterian Church in the USA are illustrative of what has taken place in most of the large Protestant churches since the turn of the century. No one with an open mind and an honest judgment of the situation within the so-called evangelical churches can ignore the fact that, for the most part, they have turned away from historic Christianity. There are individual ministers within these communions who believe and preach the Christianity of the Bible, but the vast majority of the churches in their corporate testimony are witnessing to another gospel which one might designate as "Modernism," "Liberalism," or by one of several other titles. Dr. Harry Emerson Fosdick of New York City is right when he makes the assertion that modernism has won a sweeping victory in the Protestant churches. One thing, however, is certain: this new gospel is not the Christianity which the Bible teaches, and which was revived by the Protestant Reformation. It is another attenuated gospel which is predicated upon the assumption that man can and must work out his own salvation. It denies the supernatural basis of Christianity and substitutes for it a social and moral naturalism. The final authority of the Bible for faith and life is replaced by that nebulous and uncertain standard, human experience. Such is the essential nature of so-called modernism which is a present day version of unbelief.

This historical sketch of the conflict within the Presbyterian Church in the USA is written with these facts in view. There are many who have little interest in the struggles of a particular denomination, but when it is seen that this single conflict is merely a portrayal of what has taken place to a great extent within the Protestant church as a whole, then the seriousness of the situation becomes apparent. It should make every clear right-thinking Protestant ask himself the question, "Whither Protestantism?" And when he has squarely faced that enigma he might further ask himself, "What can be done about it?"

Frankly this book is written from the standpoint of one who believes whole-heartedly in historic, biblical Christianity even though some of his theological studies were pursued at the universities of Marburg and

3

Berlin where modernism was most ably presented. Furthermore, it is true that the author was one of those involved in the Presbyterian conflict, but it is his hope that this historical survey is a fairly dispassionate exposition of the events in that struggle. While a participant may be somewhat prejudiced in his opinion, it is also true that a firsthand witness knows more of the facts. It is the author's hope that the following presentation of a particular church's theological dispute will help to awaken the Protestant world to the real situation within its gates.

The author desires to express his gratitude to the Rev. Paul Woolley, professor of church history at Westminster Seminary and Mr. Thomas R. Birch, managing editor of the *Presbyterian Guardian*, for reading the manuscript and for many valuable suggestions. He also wishes to thank professors John Murray and Cornelius Van Til, members of the faculty at Westminster Seminary, for their suggestions with respect to certain points in chapters one and fifteen.

Edwin H. Rian
Philadelphia, Pennsylvania
March 15, 1940

1

The Beginnings of Unbelief

IN ORDER TO appreciate properly the significance of the theological struggle which has just ended within the Presbyterian Church in the USA, it is essential at the outset that an historical perspective be gained. It is important to realize that this conflict which resulted in the formation of the Presbyterian Church of America in June, 1936, now known as the Orthodox Presbyterian Church, was not a controversy over some trivial matter or a difference between certain individuals but the culmination of many years of doctrinal defection. The real basic issue was a clash between two divergent points of view in doctrine, one conservative or orthodox and the other liberal or modernist. The struggle had been in evidence for a generation or more, but it had been kept subdued. A study of the history of the Presbyterian Church in the USA will show how true this is.

The Presbyterian Church in the USA was organized largely by Presbyterians from the British Isles. These Presbyterians of the Puritan type settled in New England, New York, New Jersey, Maryland, Delaware, Pennsylvania, the Carolinas, and Virginia, where they established churches under the guidance and encouragement of Presbyterians in England, Scotland, and Ireland. At first they existed as separate congregations, but finally in 1706 the Presbytery of Philadelphia was formed and later on the Presbyterian Church in the USA was organized into synods and a general assembly until it reached its present constituency of approximately two million members.

The creed which was adopted by the Synod of Philadelphia in 1729 was the Westminster Confession of Faith with the Larger and Shorter Catechisms, which documents had been completed by the great divines at the Westminster Assembly 1643–49. It is not possible here to discuss all of the doctrines of the Westminster Confession of Faith nor is it necessary, but one thing is certain—the doctrines of the confession, as admitted by all, are based on the assumption that the Bible is true and the sole authority in religion, and that the articles of the confession are a systematic presentation of what the Bible teaches. While the confession necessarily contains dogmas which are distinctive to Presbyterianism and taught in the Bible, there also appear doctrines such as the virgin birth, the bodily resurrection of Christ, his atonement for sin, his miracles, and the full trustworthiness of the Bible, which have been regarded as essential by all branches of Christendom. It is rather important to keep this fact in mind throughout the discussion because the main contention of this survey is that the Presbyterian Church in the USA has departed in practice from these doctrines.

There are several dates which one might mark as the beginning of doctrinal impurity in the church. For example, in 1801 the General Association of Connecticut and the general assembly of the Presbyterian Church in the USA adopted a plan of union in order to avoid competition. By the terms of this plan a Presbyterian minister could serve in a Congregational church and vice versa, but the congregation was to conduct its discipline according to the form of government obtaining, either Presbyterian or Congregational.[1] Some material growth and prosperity resulted from this merger, but with it came the inroads of Hopkinsianism, which originated in New England and which denied that man is depraved and separated from God because of his relationship to Adam. Two ministers, the Rev. Albert Barnes, pastor of the First Presbyterian Church of Philadelphia, and Dr. Lyman Beecher, professor at Lane Theological Seminary in Cincinnati, Ohio, were tried for heresy on this point. While Dr. Barnes was acquitted by the general assembly and Dr. Beecher's case was not carried to the general assembly, it was not due to a lack of heresy but mostly because Hopkinsianism was growing in strength and could control the general assembly at times.

The controversy between the Old School and the New School theologies, which ended in a division into the Old School assembly and the New School assembly in 1837, was the result of doctrinal unsoundness in certain presbyteries of the church. When the general assembly met in 1837 in Philadelphia, the Old School was in a majority and it decided to abrogate the Plan of Union of 1801. A "Testimony and Memorial" was addressed to the assembly exhibiting the doctrinal errors

---

1   *The Presbyterian Digest*, Vol. 2 (1938), 50.

and lapses in the church. The Old School leaders were determined to rid the church of heresy so that a true Presbyterian body would result. While the constitutionality of the Plan of Union of 1801 was also attacked, it was the doctrinal divergence from the Westminster Confession of Faith which motivated the Old School party in seeking the rescinding of the Plan of Union. These doctrinal errors consisted mainly in a wrong view of man's guilt in Adam, of the atonement, of election, and of regeneration.[2]

After much debate the Synods of Western Reserve, Utica, Geneva, and Genesee were exscinded because they were the most affected by the New England theology. A strong protest signed by one hundred and three ministers, among whom was Horace Bushnell, a leading liberal theologian of that day, was entered against the abrogation of the union.[3] This action by the Old School party was a bold step, but it was the only real solution to the differences in doctrine between the two groups in the church.[4] The Old School was truly Presbyterian in doctrine and polity, while the New School was tainted with anti-scriptural beliefs.

If the division into Old School and New School had continued, it is very likely that the doctrinal controversy which resulted in the formation of the Presbyterian Church of America would never have occurred. But the Civil War produced new issues which made these two parties forget their differences, and a union was effected in 1869.[5] That union should never have taken place, for it brought together two parties who disagreed fundamentally as to doctrine. It was one of the tragic events in Presbyterian history.

There are other events which illustrate the disagreement between the two doctrinal factions within the church, but the most important controversy was the one which led to a revision of the Westminster Confession of Faith in 1903. It is this dispute which shall be examined in detail as it demonstrates how much the New School theology had permeated the church. In 1788, chapters XX, XXIII, and XXXI of the Confession of Faith concerning the powers of synods, councils, and civil magistrates were amended and, in 1886-87, the clause forbidding marriage with a deceased wife's sister was stricken from chapter XXIV,

---

2   *Minutes of the General Assembly of the Presbyterian Church in the U.S.A.* 1837, Part 1, 420-22.
3   *Ibid.*, 454.
4   *Ibid.*, 444.
5   *The Presbyterian Digest*, Vol. 2 (1930), 42.

section 4 of the Confession of Faith, but this did not affect the Calvinistic system of doctrine of the confession. The amendments in 1903, on the other hand, vitally altered the emphasis of the confession.

The agitation to revise the Confession of Faith began in 1889 when fifteen presbyteries overtured the general assembly asking that some change be made in the doctrinal standards of the church. A committee appointed by the assembly brought in a report which was later adopted to the effect that the matter be referred to the presbyteries under two questions: 1. Do you desire a revision of the Confession of Faith? 2. If so, in what respects and to what extent?[6] When the general assembly met in 1890 it was learned that 134 presbyteries had voted in the affirmative. This was a sufficient majority to warrant the assembly appointing a committee of fifteen ministers and ten elders who were instructed to consider the whole matter and to report to the next assembly, but they were specifically told that the Calvinistic aspect of the confession must not be impaired.[7]

When the general assembly convened in 1891 the committee on revision proposed changes involving many chapters of the confession and questions in the Larger and Shorter Catechisms.[8] The changes which the assembly of 1892 finally sent to the presbyteries for discussion and a vote concerned not only the chapters which the committee had recommended for revision, but additional ones. These proposed changes failed to receive the affirmative vote of a two-thirds majority of the presbyteries and so the efforts to revise the confession failed at that time.[9]

Two reasons in the main caused the defeat of the revisions: the strong opposition of the men at Princeton Theological Seminary like Francis L. Patton and B. B. Warfield, and the heresy trial of Dr. Charles A. Briggs, professor at Union Theological Seminary, New York City. It is perhaps true that the heresy trial of Dr. Briggs was the stronger reason because it dramatized the doctrinal viewpoint of some who favored revision.

Dr. Briggs held to a belief in the errancy of holy Scripture, the sanctification of the soul after death, and the sufficiency of human reason and the church as adequate guides in the matter of salvation. At the

---

6   *Minutes of the General Assembly* 1889, 79.
7   *Minutes of the General Assembly* 1890, 85-86.
8   *Minutes of the General Assembly* 1891, 22-37.
9   *Minutes of the General Assembly* 1892, 130ff.

general assembly in 1893 Dr. Briggs was declared guilty and suspended from the ministry of the Presbyterian Church in the USA.[10]

After these attempts at revision had failed, comparative quiet obtained in the church, but those who believed in a modified Calvinism and a less strict interpretation of the Bible continued their fight to revise the standards of the church. Many in the church were firm believers in the New School theology and were not to be discouraged so easily.

Again in 1900 twenty-three presbyteries overtured the general assembly to establish a new and shorter creed, while fifteen presbyteries asked for a revision of the Confession of Faith and a new creed.[11] Such demand by so many presbyteries could not be ignored, so a committee of fifteen—eight ministers and seven elders—was appointed to study the matter and asked to report to the next general assembly. Through two successive assemblies certain changes were considered, and in 1903 modifications were made by adding a declaratory statement as to chapter III and chapter X, section 3; and changes were made in chapters XVI, section 7, XXII, section 3, XXV, section 6; and chapter XXXIV on the Holy Spirit and chapter XXXV on the Love of God and Missions were added. These revisions were less extensive than those proposed in 1890, yet they meant a victory for the New School party and a definite toning down of the Calvinistic emphasis of the Confession of Faith.[12]

Several doctrines distinctively Calvinistic or Reformed were involved in these changes, but the one which is paramount is the doctrine of election and its consistent application to the doctrine of the atonement. This is seen in the declaratory statement which deals with chapter III and chapter X, section 3, of the confession, and is also seen in chapter XXXV on the Love of God and Missions.

In commenting on chapter III the declaratory statement says,

> With reference to chapter III of the Confession of Faith: that concerning those who are saved in Christ, the doctrine of God's eternal decree is held in harmony with the doctrine of His love to all mankind, His gift of His Son to be the propitiation for the sins of the whole world, and His readiness to bestow His saving grace on all who seek it.

It is, of course, biblical to say that God loved the world (John 3:16) and that Christ is the propitiation for the sins of the whole world (I John

---

10   *Minutes of the General Assembly* 1893, 166.

11   *Minutes of the General Assembly* 1900, 35, 46.

12   *Minutes of the General Assembly* 1903, 124-128.

2:2). Such expressions must, however, be understood in their biblical sense. The declaratory statement gives to such expressions a turn that distinctly tends to obscure the particularism of God's redemptive love and universalizes the design of Christ's atoning work. It is the contention of the Reformed faith that God's redemptive love as set forth in the Bible is coextensive with the extent of the atonement, and that Christ did not die to save all men but only the elect.

The effort to tone down this particularism of the gospel is also seen in chapter XXXV, "Of the Love of God and Missions." Let it be said with emphasis that Calvinists are staunch believers in and supporters of missions. In fact, they are among the most zealous for preaching the gospel to the lost. But in chapter XXXV there is no mention made of the fact that God not only loves all in a general benevolent way, but that he loves some unto salvation. There is also an omission in this chapter of the efficacious grace of the Holy Spirit which makes salvation real to some. In other words, that particularism of the gospel which is so precious to lovers of the Bible and so offensive to the enemies of the cross is studiously avoided. A statement which seeks to declare the teaching of the confession on the love of God and omits the fact that God has elected some to salvation is not true to nor consistent with the whole of the confession.

There are those who contend that such an interpretation of the Confession of Faith would eliminate the love of God from the confession entirely.[13] It is true that the confession and the Bible do not include the love of God as preached by those who hold to the general fatherhood of God and the brotherhood of man. It is also true that the confession and the Bible do not warrant the teaching that God loves all unto salvation. As Dr. Ned B. Stonehouse pointed out in discussing this subject,

> It is not true, however, that the Westminster Confession of Faith drops the Biblical doctrine of the love of God. At the heart of the Bible, at the heart of Christianity and the gospel, and so at the heart of Calvinism, is the doctrine of the particular saving love of God for His people. This doctrine of redeeming love avoids the one-sided preaching of the love of God, which is so common today, with its consequent passing over the righteousness and holiness of God and the radical sinfulness of man.[14]

---

13   *The Christian Century* 53 (November 25, 1936), 1548.
14   Ned B. Stonehouse, "Have We Dropped the Love of God ?" *Presbyterian Guardian* 3 (December 26, 1936), 119.

The very same weakness is seen in the declaratory statement concerning chapter X, section 3, on elect infants. The declaratory statement is right when it says, "With reference to chapter X, section 3, of the Confession of Faith, that it is not to be regarded as teaching that any who die in infancy are lost." This leaves the question of the extent of the salvation of infants dying in infancy open to various opinions. In fact, on this point the Scriptures are not definite. But the declaratory statement goes farther by saying, "that all lost in infancy are included in the election of grace and are regenerated and saved by Christ through the Spirit, who works when and where and how He pleases." According to the Word of God and the Confession of Faith, no one has a right to make such a statement because revealed truth is not clear on the subject. The extent of infant salvation has been left a mystery in the Bible and that is where it must be left. One of the glories of the Confession of Faith is the fact that it includes all that the Scriptures teach but no more; it does not speculate. In dealing with this question professor John Murray makes it clear that there have been various convictions concerning the salvation of infants dying in infancy.

> There have been Reformed theologians of the highest repute who held to the position expressed in the Declaratory Statement. Dr. Charles Hodge for example [*Systematic Theology* 1, 26-27] is unambiguous in his argument for the salvation of all infants dying in infancy. Other Reformed theologians of equal distinction scrupulously refrained from taking any such position. It is apparent, therefore, that there is surely room for difference of judgment in the matter. Our objection to the Declaratory Statement is that it incorporates into the creed of the church what is, to say the least, a highly debatable position, and therefore a position that should never be made part of creedal confession.[15]

A perusal of the discussions concerning these amendments in the Presbyterian Church in the USA between 1889 and 1903 will show that the Calvinists were on one side of the debate and those with Arminian and anti-scriptural tendencies were on the other.

Dr. Grier, editor of *The Presbyterian* in 1889, wrote with almost prophetic insight,

> The General Assembly has by one of its acts just passed opened up the sluices of debate in the church for the coming years. It has put its Standards in question before the Presbyteries and invited their suggestions as to the revision of the

---

15 John Murray, "Shall We Include the Revision of 1903 in Our Creed?" *Presbyterian Guardian* 2 (September 26, 1936), 251.

Confession of Faith. This is a movement which may have immense consequences in the future, and largely determine the position of the body in the circle of the Churches, in the time to come, and its own stability and unity as well.[16]

In fact, this act of the assembly not only opened up the "sluices of debate," but the ultimate revisions in 1903 gave comfort and impetus to those who wished the New School theology to control the church. As it turned out, the stability and the unity of the church were mightily affected, since the child of New School theology, which is known as modernism, does dominate that church today, and the unity of the church is only in name.

Dr. B. B. Warfield, of Princeton Theological Seminary, entered into the discussion against revision with vigor and helped measurably to delay action until 1903. In commenting on chapter X which deals with "Effectual Calling," he wrote,

> The chapter, as a whole, comes out of the Committees' hands a fair model of what a Confessional statement ought not to be—obscure and ambiguous where certainty and clearness are not only attainable but had already been attained in the original statement, dogmatic where the Scriptures are silent or even opposed, and not without both omissions and insertions which can be made to play into the hands of error.[17]

Of the report as a whole he wrote,

> Theologically, the report as a whole exhibits a decided tendency to lessen the sharpness and precision of the doctrinal statement of distinctive Calvinism. . . . To all the clamorous proclamation of false doctrine about us—yes in our midst—against which the Church needs protection, the Committee has been deaf. To all the demands thus made on it for progress in the doctrinal statement of our orthodox truth in relation to present-day needs, it has been blind. Turning its back on it all, its whole doctrinal work is comprised in requesting the Church to lower its voice in telling the world the truth![18]

When Dr. Warfield was asked to serve on the committee for revision in 1900, he refused on the ground that to revise the standards as was indicated would be to lower the testimony of the church to the truth.

Abraham Kuyper, that eminent Dutch theologian, was concerned and wrote a long article on the general subject of revision and its perils. He

---

16   *The Presbyterian* 59 (June 1, 1889), 3.
17   Benjamin B. Warfield, "The Final Report of the Committee on Revision of the Confession," *The Presbyterian and Reformed Review* 3 (1892), 323.
18   Ibid., 329-330.

pictured the danger in that day of toning down the Calvinistic emphasis of the Confession of Faith instead of enriching and unfolding it. He concluded his article by stating,

> These are the reasons why the author, hearing of the revision proposed in America, and realizing what its consequences might be for the Dutch Churches, would feel in duty bound in the sight of God to dissuade from such revision in the most positive manner, if it were proposed in his own country.[19]

It is significant that Dr. Briggs, who was suspended from the ministry of the church for holding beliefs contrary to the Confession of Faith, which are known today as modernism, was one of the most vigorous proponents of revision. He argued that the people, the elders of the church, and the ministers desired relief from the antiquated elements of the confession. He ended his discussion by saying, "Biblical critics will not much longer tolerate persecution on the part of a contra-Confessional majority."[20]

Dr. Henry Van Dyke, who was chairman of the Committee on Revision, was also in favor of the amendments. It is revealing to note that it was he who ceased attending the First Presbyterian Church in Princeton, New Jersey, in 1924 because he could no longer tolerate the orthodox Christianity which Dr. J. Gresham Machen was preaching while stated supply of the church.

On the whole it is clear that those who stood for revision wanted more than a modified Calvinism; they desired a liberalizing of the confession. Their victory was only partial, but nevertheless it was a definite step toward the ultimate goal which they hoped to achieve, that of broadening the doctrinal standards of the church.

There may be some who will contend that the revisions of 1903 did not modify the Calvinism of the confession, but the union of the Cumberland Presbyterian Church with the Presbyterian Church in the USA in 1906 is testimony to the fact that a denomination was convinced that they did. The Cumberland Presbyterian Church was a strange mixture of Arminianism and Calvinism. Its creed was an attempt to strike a middle ground between the two points of view, and, as a result, it was more Arminian than Calvinistic. In fact, it was the Calvinism of the confession which was one of the dominant factors in leading certain

---

19   Abraham Kuyper, "Calvinism and Confessional Revision," *The Presbyterian and Reformed Review* 2 (July 1891), 399.

20   *The Presbyterian* 59 (August 10, 1889), 6-7.

ministers of the Presbyterian Church in the USA to separate themselves from the church and to form the Cumberland Presbyterian Church in 1810. But when the revisions of 1903 were a part of the standards of the Presbyterian Church in the USA, immediately the Cumberland Presbyterian Church began to make overtures looking toward union. The Cumberland people felt that the Westminster Confession had been modified sufficiently to remove all substantial doctrinal differences between these two churches. Accordingly, a union was effected between the two bodies in 1906.[21]

The result of this union was to weaken the testimony of the Presbyterian Church in the USA to the Bible and the Calvinism of the confession. It helped further to entrench the position of those who wanted the confession and the church modernized.

Another attempt to effect a union with other churches which demonstrated that the doctrinal defection in the Presbyterian Church in the USA had gained a strong foothold was the proposal to unite with other Protestant bodies in 1918. In that year thirty-five presbyteries overtured the general assembly meeting in Columbus, Ohio, to consider a proposal to merge eighteen Protestant churches into one evangelical church. The plan as finally presented by a council composed of representatives from these organizations contained stipulations as to government as well as doctrine, but it is the doctrinal basis which is most significant.[22]

The preamble to the doctrinal section of the plan reads:

> Whereas: We desire to share, as a common heritage, the faith of the Christian Church, which has, from time to time, found expression in great historical statements; and whereas: We all share belief in God our Father; in Jesus Christ, His only Son, our Saviour; in the Holy Spirit, our Guide and Comforter; in the Holy Catholic Church, through which God's eternal purpose of salvation is to be proclaimed and the Kingdom of God is to be realized on earth; in the Scriptures of the Old and New Testaments as containing God's revealed will, in the life eternal.[23]

In none of these vague statements is there an attempt to make clear the doctrines concerning God, Jesus Christ, the Holy Spirit, the church, salvation, the Scriptures, or eternal life. Practically anyone, whether orthodox or liberal, could subscribe to such a creed because each could

---

21   *The Presbyterian Digest* (1938), Vol. 2, 59-68.
22   *Minutes of the General Assembly* 1918, Part 1, 153-154.
23   *Minutes of the General Assembly* 1920, Part 1, 118.

read into the statements what he desires. Such a state of indifference and doctrinal disintegration becomes all the more significant when it is realized that 100 presbyteries of the Presbyterian Church in the USA voted for this organic union. It demonstrates graphically how formidable had become the number and influence of those who no longer considered sound doctrine as essential to the church. Fortunately, the majority of the presbyteries voted against the plan of union so that it was defeated in 1920.[24]

While this attempt at organic union with many other so-called evangelical bodies on a vague doctrinal basis proved unsuccessful, nevertheless it demonstrated the temper of a large portion of the Presbyterian Church in the USA. In fact, to those who could discern the trend it showed how rapidly the spirit of compromise and doctrinal indifference had spread. To those who were awake to the true situation, the next important step in the process of doctrinal defection was no surprise but an expected conclusion.

These evidences of unbelief in the church were only the beginning. During each succeeding crisis those who advocated modernism added to their power and prestige, and when the next bold move of this group was launched in the issuance of the "Auburn Affirmation," which will be discussed in the next chapter, they not only enlisted a large following but succeeded finally in controlling the church.

---

24   *Minutes of the General Assembly* 1921, Part 1, 41 ff.

2
The Auburn Affirmation

THE SERMON, "Shall the Fundamentalists Win?" preached by the Rev. Harry Emerson Fosdick, D.D., in the First Presbyterian Church, New York City, May, 1922, was the signal for a new and public outbreak of the conflict between the forces of historic Christianity and modern liberalism within the Presbyterian Church in the USA. While many look upon this event as the first real skirmish between liberals and conservatives in the church, it is more accurate to consider it as a continuance of the struggle. On the other hand, it is correct to point to the publication of this sermon as the immediate cause for the conflict which eventually led to the formation of the Orthodox Presbyterian Church. As a matter of fact, the ensuing events show that the trend toward modernism, not only in the Presbyterian Church in the USA but also in many other Protestant churches, was very pronounced and that in many cases this form of religion dominated the situation.

In 1918 three churches in lower New York City united to form the First Presbyterian Church. The Rev. George Alexander, D.D., was called as pastor and the Rev. Harry Emerson Fosdick, D.D., a Baptist, was invited to become associate minister. The officers of the church believed that this arrangement of a pastor and an associate would solve the problems of a downtown church in a most acceptable fashion. They realized that it was extraordinary to ask a Baptist to act as associate minister in a Presbyterian church so they secured the permission of the Presbytery of New York to sanction the arrangement. Under this plan church attendance increased, and the fame of Dr. Fosdick as a preacher spread throughout the nation.[1]

On Sunday morning, May 21, 1922, Dr. Fosdick preached the now famous sermon, "Shall the Fundamentalists Win?" Without his

---

1   *The First Presbyterian Church of New York and Dr. Fosdick* (New York: n.p., [1925]).

knowledge, so Dr. Fosdick claims, Mr. Ivy Lee had the sermon reprinted, an introduction added, and the title changed to, "The New Knowledge and the Christian Faith."[2] He then proceeded to send copies of the sermon throughout the country, some of which came into the hands of Presbyterian ministers in Philadelphia.

The Presbytery of Philadelphia then had a large majority of conservatives with the Rev. Clarence E. Macartney, D.D., pastor of the Arch Street Church, as the acknowledged leader. Informal discussions concerning the presence of a Baptist minister in a Presbyterian church who did not believe in the doctrines of the Westminster Confession of Faith were held by members of Philadelphia Presbytery. It was finally decided by this group to introduce the following overture to the Presbytery of Philadelphia so that the matter would be brought to the attention of the general assembly. The overture was adopted on October 16, 1922, by an overwhelming majority—seventy-two to twenty-one.[3] Part of it follows:

> The Presbytery of Philadelphia hereby respectfully overtures the General Assembly to direct the Presbytery of New York to take such action as will require the preaching and teaching in the First Presbyterian Church of New York City to conform to the system of doctrine taught in the Confession of Faith.[4]

The sermon, "Shall the Fundamentalists Win?" contrasts the conservative and radical views on the virgin birth, the inspiration of the Scriptures, the atonement, and the second advent of Christ and pleads for a tolerance of both views within the Christian church. In a letter to Dr. Macartney, Dr. Fosdick claimed that he had been misunderstood and that the burden of his sermon was tolerance and not necessarily liberalism.[5] But in 1923 Dr. Fosdick gave the Lyman Beecher Lectures on Preaching before the Yale Divinity School, which were published under the title, "The Modern Use of the Bible," and in which he upheld completely the modern "higher critical" views of the books of the Bible as to date and authorship. In fact, in his letter to Dr. Macartney he admitted that he represented the liberal view. Dr. Fosdick's theological position ever since that time has been well-known and no attempt has been made on his part to conceal the fact that he has advocated modernism as the religion for this day and generation.

---

2   *The Presbyterian* 92 (December 7, 1922), 6.
3   *The Presbyterian* 93 (April 26, 1923), 4.
4   *The Presbyterian* 92 (October 26, 1922), 6-7.
5   *The Presbyterian* 92 (December 7, 1922), 6.

When the general assembly met in May, 1923, the most important issue before it was the overture from Philadelphia concerning the presence of Dr. Fosdick in the pulpit of the First Presbyterian Church in New York City. Agitation in all of the Presbyterian papers on this point had aroused the church so that sympathizers with the overture and opponents of it were well represented among the commissioners. The issue was far greater than the Philadelphia overture; actually it involved not only doctrines peculiar to Presbyterianism, but the fundamental doctrines of historic Christianity. The Rev. David S. Kennedy, D.D., editor of *The Presbyterian*, stated,

> The center of the contention lies between supernaturalistic evangelicalism on the one side, and naturalistic rationalism on the other. It is a contention between two spirits and two convictions which are mutually exclusive and destructive; one or the other must prevail, and the one which prevails will determine the character and future of the Presbyterian Church in the U.S.A., and will have an important influence upon the testimony of the whole evangelical church.[6]

There were two leading candidates for the position of moderator of the general assembly at the meeting in Indianapolis, May, 1923: the Rev. Charles F. Wishart, D.D., president of the College of Wooster, and the Honorable William Jennings Bryan, former Secretary of State under President Wilson. Dr. Wishart represented those in the church who stood for unity and inclusivism rather than a division on doctrinal grounds, while Mr. Bryan represented those who wanted a church pure in doctrine and true to the historic interpretation of Christianity and the Westminster Confession of Faith. His followers were regarded as the militant wing of the church, although the nominating speeches stressed the orthodoxy of both candidates. Dr. Wishart won by a majority of only twenty-four.[7]

After the election of the moderator, the disposition of the Philadelphia overture became the paramount concern of the commissioners. In fact, overtures of a similar nature were before the assembly from nine other presbyteries.[8] As is customary, this overture was placed in the hands of the assembly's Committee on Bills and Overtures, of which the chairman was the Rev. Hugh K. Walker, D.D., of Los Angeles, who was appointed to this position by the moderator. The usual procedure is for the moderator to proffer this important office to the defeated moderatorial

---

6   *The Presbyterian* 93 (May 17, 1923), 4.
7   *The Presbyterian* 93 (May 24, 1923), 12-13.
8   *Minutes of the General Assembly* 1923, Part 1, 23.

candidate, which would have been Mr. Bryan, but it is rather indicative of the feeling between the two camps in that assembly that this custom was not followed.

The Committee on Bills and Overtures brought in a report rejecting the Philadelphia overture and recommending that the Presbytery of New York be allowed to conduct its own investigation and report to the 1924 assembly, especially since the presbytery had already appointed a committee to institute such an investigation. The majority report signed by twenty-one of the twenty-two members of the committee was roundly scored for its straddling of the issue and for its pusillanimous compromise.[9]

The Rev. Gordon A. MacLennan, D.D., of Philadelphia, brought in a minority report signed only by himself, yet it was adopted by the assembly by a vote of 439 to 359.[10] It called upon the assembly to direct the Presbytery of New York to require the preaching and teaching at the First Presbyterian Church in New York City to conform to the Bible and the Westminster Confession of Faith. It also asked the assembly to reaffirm its faith in the infallibility of the Bible, in the virgin birth of Jesus Christ, in his substitutionary atonement on the cross, in his bodily resurrection, and in his mighty miracles as essential doctrines of holy Scripture and the Westminster Confession of Faith.

The majority report was championed by the Rev. Hugh K. Walker, D.D., chairman of the committee, Nolan R. Best, editor of *The Continent*, and by the moderator. Those in favor of the minority report were led by the Rev. Gordon A. MacLennan, D.D., William Jennings Bryan, and the Rev. C. E. Macartney, D.D. The debate was limited to ten-minute speeches, and a closing argument of fifteen minutes was allowed for each side.

In presenting the minority report, Dr. MacLennan said,

> It is with the firm conviction that this General Assembly will answer the questions of our church in a definite and concrete form that I present this minority report. Shall not our Assembly give answer to these questions declaring its absolute faith in the virgin birth, in the inspiration of the Scriptures and the vicarious death on Calvary, and the bodily resurrection of Jesus Christ

---

9   *The Presbyterian* 93 (May 31, 1923), 10-11.
10   *Minutes of the General Assembly* 1923, Part 1, 253.

from the dead, and in the mighty miracles which He wrought while here on earth?[11]

In closing the debate for the minority report Dr. Macartney asserted,

> I wish I could pay tribute to the majority report. But I cannot. It is a masterpiece of whitewash, and the man who wrote it ought to seek employment as an exterior decorator. . . We take our stand upon the New Testament and the Confession of Faith. . . . What you have heard here this afternoon is but the "sound of a going in the tops of the mulberry trees." The storm is coming, and you cannot stop it with any pusillanimous compromise.[12]

Those who argued in favor of the majority report contended that the matter of pulpit supplies in the First Presbyterian Church of New York City rested with the Presbytery of New York. This presbytery had already appointed a committee to investigate the situation, so that it would be discourteous and unpresbyterian to interfere in the matter.

Following the assembly, the editor of *The Continent* wrote, "Men who insist that these and other theological formulas are vital to the perpetuation of Christianity are without exception men who have mistaken religion's first definition—Christianity is not a dogma but a life."[13] The Rev. Alexander MacColl, D.D., pastor of the Second Presbyterian Church, Philadelphia, was quoted as having said,

> Let us be quite clear that the advocates of this materialistic philosophy, which robs life of all its glory and its beauty, have their chief allies today in those religious teachers whose expression of spiritual realities is always in material terms, whose perpetual emphasis is upon physical facts, upon a physical birth, physical blood, a physical ascension and coming again; the letter of a book.[14]

This decision of the general assembly was hailed by the orthodox as a great victory for historic Christianity and "the faith which was once delivered unto the saints." But the rejoicing was to be short-lived. The liberals were thoroughly aroused and determined to do everything to bring the corporate witness of the church into conformity with their point of view. While the Rev. George Alexander, D.D., pastor of the First

---

11   A. Gordon MacLennan, "Notes from the Speech Presenting the Minority Report of the General Assembly," *The Presbyterian* 93 (June 7, 1923), 7.

12   "Excerpts from Dr. Macartney's Closing Argument at the Assembly," *The Presbyterian* 93 (June 7, 1923), 8.

13   *The Continent* 54 (July 5, 1923), 849.

14   *The Philadelphia Public Ledger*, 26 May 1923.

Presbyterian Church of New York City, said that he would attempt to carry out the mandate of the assembly, the leaders of New York Presbytery displayed little intention to comply. As soon as the action was taken by the assembly, a protest was filed with the assembly disapproving of the decision because it was not substantiated by evidence, because it passed judgment upon a matter not rightly before the assembly, and because it imposed doctrinal tests upon office-bearers not allowed by the constitution of the church.[15]

When the Presbytery of New York met on June 11, 1923, it proceeded to ignore the intent of the assembly's action, which was to rid the church of false doctrine, by licensing two young men, Henry P. Van Dusen and Cedric O. Lehman, who refused to affirm their faith in the virgin birth—one of the doctrines which Dr. Fosdick had attacked. A group of ministers and elders in New York Presbytery, led by the Rev. Walter D. Buchanan, D.D., filed a protest with the presbytery against the action. This protest or complaint was carried to the general assembly in 1924, but the Permanent Judicial Commission of the assembly ruled that the complaint must first be remitted to the Synod of New York. At a later date Mr. Van Dusen was not only ordained by New York Presbytery, but he also became a professor at Union Theological Seminary, an outstanding modernist institution.[16]

At the same meeting of New York Presbytery the action of the general assembly with respect to Dr. Fosdick was referred to the special committee of three ministers and two elders who had been appointed by the presbytery on April 9, 1923, in answer to a request from the Harlem-New York Church to investigate matters at the First Presbyterian Church.[17]

On October 1, 1923, and on January 14, 1924, the committee reported to the presbytery and on February 4, 1924, its recommendations were adopted. The committee came to four major conclusions and recommendations: (1) they were convinced that the doctrines of grace were being proclaimed in the pulpit of the First Church, (2) they expressed their confidence and loyalty in the session of the First Church, (3) they expressed their readiness to receive more reports on the subject in general, and (4) they affirmed their faith in the Bible. They also reported that the sermon, "Shall the Fundamentalists Win?" was perhaps

---

15   *Minutes of the General Assembly* 1923, Part 1, 338.
16   *Minutes of the General Assembly* 1924, 194.
17   *Presbyterian Church of New York and Dr. Fosdick*, 7.

ill-advised and that it had been distributed without the knowledge of the session of the First Church.[18]

This action was not at all satisfactory to the conservatives in the Presbytery of New York, who immediately drew up a complaint to be presented to the general assembly meeting in Grand Rapids in 1924. The Permanent Judicial Commission of general assembly held in Grand Rapids ruled that the presbytery and its committee had obeyed the mandate of the assembly, but that the situation at the First Church would be clarified if Dr. Fosdick would express his purpose as to whether he intended to enter the ministry of the Presbyterian Church in the USA or to remain a minister of the Baptist denomination.

> We therefore recommend that the Presbytery of New York be instructed, through its committee or through the session of the First Presbyterian Church, to take up with Dr. Fosdick this question to the end that he may determine whether it is his pleasure to enter the Presbyterian church and thus be in a regular relationship with the First Presbyterian Church as one of its pastors.[19]

The New York Presbytery's committee to deal with this matter addressed a letter to Dr. Fosdick asking him to define his relationship to the First Presbyterian Church of New York City, and to state his intentions with reference to ministerial membership in the Presbyterian Church in the USA. Dr. Fosdick replied in a letter to the Rev. Edgar W. Work, D.D., chairman of the presbytery's committee, in which he refused to unite with the Presbyterian Church in the USA because of his unwillingness to subscribe to any confession of faith on the ground that it would violate his conscience. In the same letter he mentioned his intention to resign as associate minister of the First Church.[20]

The First Church accepted Dr. Fosdick's resignation as associate minister to take effect in March, 1925, but also extended an invitation to him to preach for them "when not otherwise engaged."[21]

Both the action of the general assembly and that of the First Presbyterian Church of New York were strongly assailed by the conservatives of the church at large. The editor of one religious weekly called the assembly's decision "A Monstrous Suggestion."

---

18   *Ibid.*, 28-29.
19   *Minutes of the General Assembly*, 1924, Part 1, 196.
20   *Presbyterian Church of New York and Dr. Fosdick*, 38-42.
21   *Ibid.*, 50.

It seems almost incredible that anyone should even suggest that the disturbance over Dr. Fosdick has been occasioned by the fact that he is not a Presbyterian minister. The disturbance arose from the belief—in our judgment a well-grounded belief—that his teachings not only openly deny the essential doctrines of the Presbyterian Church, but they are "subversive of the truth of Christianity as received, confessed, held and defended by the Christian church of all ages."[22]

In commenting on the invitation of the First Presbyterian Church of New York City to Dr. Fosdick to preach for them "when not otherwise engaged," Dr. Macartney wrote, "We cannot think, either, that the special preacher could lend himself to this plan to evade the will of the Presbyterian Church."[23] In spite of this opposition and in spite of the apparent evasion of the assembly's action, the First Church of New York City continued to have Dr. Fosdick fill the pulpit as a supply until March 1, 1925.[24]

In this connection it is interesting and informing to read the comment of the Rev. Albert C. Dieffenbach, D. D., then editor of the Unitarian weekly, *The Christian Register,*

> I have the profoundest respect for a man who is consistently a fundamentalist, or for a man who is consistently a Roman Catholic, but I have no respect for the attitude of Dr. Fosdick. . . . When he goes to Cambridge he speaks in terms of liberalism and when he comes to New York he says, "I am an evangelical Christian!"[25]

While this controversy between Dr. Fosdick and the Presbyterian Church in the USA was continuing, the conflict between modernists and conservatives in the church at large became more and more stormy. On October 30, 1923, at a gathering in New York City sponsored by the Rev. Walter D. Buchanan, D.D. and attended largely by ministers and elders of New York City and vicinity, Dr. J. Gresham Machen, then assistant professor of New Testament at Princeton Theological Seminary, and Dr. Macartney spoke of the need of contending for the faith. Dr. Macartney stressed the importance of being loyal to the creed of the church and Dr. Machen showed that the neo-Christianity preached by the liberals was not a perversion of Christianity but a new and different religion.

---

22   *The Presbyterian* 94 (June 5, 1924), 5.
23   *The Presbyterian* 94 (October 30, 1924), 22.
24   *Presbyterian Church of New York and Dr. Fosdick,* 60.
25   *The Presbyterian* 94 (November 6, 1924), 12.

Two large mass meetings were held on December 10 and 14, 1923, in New York City and Philadelphia, both of which were addressed by the Rev. Maitland Alexander, D.D., a former moderator of the general assembly and then pastor of the large and influential First Presbyterian Church in Pittsburgh, on the subject, "The Maintenance of the Reformed Theology."[26] Dr. Alexander not only pointed out the faithfulness of the Westminster standards to the New Testament, but he also emphasized the importance of ordaining ministers and elders who would be true to the standards of the church, and of electing members to the boards and agencies of the church who would maintain the Reformed faith.

It was during this height of the controversy in the Presbyterian Church in the USA that the small but significant book, *Christianity and Liberalism*, by J. Gresham Machen, appeared. This book, which was much discussed and was accepted as the best statement of the issue between modernism and historic Christianity, compelled the public to recognize Dr. Machen as the intellectual leader of those who believed in the Christianity of the Bible. He demonstrated quite conclusively that the religion of liberalism or modernism was not even a perversion of Christianity, like Roman Catholicism, but rather a new and different religion. Walter Lippmann, the well-known publicist, characterized the book as follows: "For its acumen, for its saliency, and for its wit this cool and stringent defense of orthodox Protestantism is, I think, the best popular argument produced by either side in the current controversy."[27]

The modernists were also much stirred over the turn of events. A committee of 150 Presbyterian ministers with headquarters at 10 Nelson Street, Auburn, New York, issued a document on December 26, 1923, in answer to the action of the general assembly concerning the Philadelphia overture. This document is commonly called the "Auburn Affirmation," and requires detailed study because it has profoundly affected the course of the Presbyterian Church in the USA.[28]

The contention of the Affirmation is twofold: first, that the general assembly has no constitutional right to elevate the five doctrines mentioned as special tests for ordination to the ministry, unless the constitution be changed by a vote of the presbyteries; and secondly, that the five

---

26   Maitland Alexander, "The Maintenance of the Reformed Theology," *The Presbyterian* 93 (December 27, 1923), 6-9.
27   Walter Lippmann, *A Preface to Morals* (New York: Macmillan Co., 1929), 32.
28   See Appendix, note 1.

doctrines enumerated in the assembly's action are non-essential to the system of doctrine taught in the holy Scriptures and are merely theories of those facts and doctrines.

There have been opinions expressed by many Presbyterians of high repute relative to the constitutionality of the doctrinal deliverance of the 1923 General Assembly. Two conservatives like Dr. D. S. Kennedy and Dr. J. Gresham Machen differed on this question. Dr. Kennedy maintained that "The whole structure of the Form of Government and Book of Discipline makes the interpretation of the courts binding and the interpretation of the general assembly as final."[29] On the other hand, Dr. Machen argued in favor of the constitutionality of the deliverance, not because the general assembly has a right to demand allegiance to these five doctrines as part of the constitutional questions for ordination, but on the ground that these five doctrines are taught in the word of God. Those who agreed with Dr. Kennedy contended that every candidate for ordination must answer the question, "Do you sincerely receive and adopt the Confession of Faith of this church as containing the system of doctrine taught in the Scriptures?" and that every one of the five doctrines mentioned in the deliverance is essential to the system of doctrine taught in the Scriptures.

The weight of the law seems to be on the side of the Auburn Affirmation. There are already certain questions asked of a candidate for the ministry in the Presbyterian Church in the USA, and if further and special tests for ordination are to be given, an overture to this effect would have to be sent down to the presbyteries for ratification. It is altogether likely that the general assembly does not have the power to bind the presbyteries to "any essential and necessary articles" unless the presbyteries have so voted. The matter of the constitutionality of the deliverance is not important to the main issue. As a matter of fact, if the question of constitutionality were the only point, it would hardly be worth discussing. It is the second contention of the Affirmation with respect to the essential nature of the five doctrines which makes the subject of historical significance.

There have been three ways in which the vow, "Do you sincerely receive and adopt the Confession of Faith as containing the system of doctrine taught in the Scriptures?" has been interpreted: (1) the candidate assents to every proposition in the Confession of Faith, (2) the candidate

---

29   *The Presbyterian* 94 (January 17, 1924), 9.

accepts the Confession of Faith as containing the "substance" of the doctrine taught in the Bible, and (3) the candidate receives the confession as containing the "system" of doctrine taught in the Bible.[30]

Very few have held the position that every article in the Confession of Faith must be accepted as essential to the system of truth. In fact, the Presbyterian Church in the USA has never officially maintained that every article in the Confession of Faith is essential to the system of doctrine. For example, the chapter on Marriage and Divorce recognizes that "such willful desertion as can no way be remedied by the church or civil magistrate, is cause sufficient of dissolving the bond of marriage."[31] There are many ministers in the church who recognize that there is only one biblical ground of divorce, namely, adultery. The Presbyterian Church in the USA has never refused ordination to anyone for differences on this point as well as others nor has it held this as vital to the system of doctrine.

The signers of the Auburn Affirmation expressed their agreement with the second interpretation, that the Confession of Faith contains the "substance" of the doctrine taught in the Bible. They argued that the Synod of Philadelphia in the Adopting Act of 1729 had declared,

> All the ministers of this Synod or that shall hereafter be admitted into this Synod, shall declare their agreement in and approbation of the Confession of Faith with the Larger and Shorter Catechisms of the Assembly of Divines at Westminster, as being, in all the essential and necessary articles, good forms of sound words and systems of Christian doctrine, and do also adopt the said Confession and Catechisms as the confession of our faith.[32]

They maintained that this Act gives great liberty in assuming the ordination vow and has never been abrogated.

Those who were opposed to this interpretation pointed to the fact that an Act Explaining the Adopting Act was passed by the Synod of Philadelphia in 1736, in which it is stated specifically that, with the exception of chapters twenty and twenty-three, the Confession of Faith is to be regarded as the faith of the church.[33] Furthermore, the Act explained that if anyone did not subscribe to certain articles, the members

---

30   Charles Hodge, *The Church and its Polity* (London: Thomas Nelson and Sons, 1879), 317-35.
31   *Confession of Faith, Presbyterian Church in the U.S.A.*, chapter XXIV, section VI.
32   *The Presbyterian Digest* Vol. 2 (1938), 4.
33   *Ibid.*, 6.

of the synod were to decide whether those articles were essential to the
system of doctrine or not.

> . . . and in case any minister of this Synod, or any candidate for the ministry,
> shall have any scruple with respect to any article or articles of said Confession
> or Catechisms, he shall at the time of his making said declaration declare his
> sentiments to the Presbytery or Synod, who shall, notwithstanding, admit him
> to the exercise of the ministry within our bounds, and to ministerial commis-
> sion, if the Synod or Presbytery shall judge his scruple or mistake to be only
> about articles not essential and necessary in doctrine, worship or government.[34]

In other words, no such latitudinarian principle of interpretation of the
confession as that advocated by the Auburn Affirmation was to be
allowed. If such an interpretation were permitted, the conservatives
maintained, and each individual could determine just what is essential
to the system of truth, it is conceivable that even the doctrine of the Trinity
might be omitted, thereby making the confession meaningless.[35]

The third interpretation is the one which the Presbyterian Church in
the USA has always employed, namely, that the candidate receives the
Confession of Faith as containing the "system" of doctrine taught in the
Bible. This means more than acceptance of certain individual articles or
isolated sections; rather, it involves a well-defined plan of redemption
with its doctrines of God, man, sin, and salvation, which has come to
be known as the "Reformed theology" or "Calvinism," and which is set
forth in the Scriptures. Dr. Charles Hodge, the famous Princeton
theologian, was very emphatic on this point.

> If the question, "What is the system of doctrine taught by the Reformed
> Churches?" be submitted to a hundred Romanists, to a hundred Lutherans, to
> a hundred members of the Church of England, or to a hundred skeptics, if
> intelligent and candid, they would all give precisely the same answer. There is
> not the slightest dispute among disinterested scholars as to what doctrines do,
> and what do not belong to the faith of the Reformed. And, therefore, any man
> who receives these several classes of doctrine, (viz.: those common to all
> Christians, those common to all Protestants, and those peculiar to the Reformed
> Churches) holds in its integrity the system of doctrine contained in the
> Westminster Confession.[36]

The five doctrines enunciated in the Deliverance of the 1923 General
Assembly, however, are not peculiar to the Reformed theology nor even

---

34   *Ibid.*, 4-5.
35   Clarence E. Macartney, "The Creed of Presbyterians," *The Presbyterian*
      93 (July 12, 1923), 8-10, 26.
36   Hodge, *Church Polity*, 333-4.

to Protestantism, but are common to all Christians, Protestants, Roman Catholics, and Greek Orthodox alike. Consequently, the real issue is not the technical point of the constitutionality of the deliverance nor even the question of the system of doctrine peculiar to Presbyterianism, but rather whether or not these five doctrines are taught in the Bible and essential to any system of doctrine which calls itself Christian. A study of each doctrine will show how true this is.

The first doctrine mentioned by the General Assembly of 1923 reads, "It is an essential doctrine of the Word of God and our standards that the Holy Spirit did so inspire, guide and move the writers of Holy Scripture, as to keep them from error." With respect to this, the Auburn Affirmation states,

> There is no assertion in the Scriptures that their writers were "kept from error"! The Confession of Faith does not make this assertion; and it is significant that this assertion is not found in the Apostles' Creed or the Nicene Creed or in any other of the great Reformation confessions. . . . The doctrine of inerrancy, intended to enhance the authority of the Scriptures, in fact impairs their supreme authority for faith and life, and weakens the testimony of the church to the power of God unto salvation through Jesus Christ.

In answer the conservatives maintained that each minister must give an affirmative reply to the question, "Do you believe the Scriptures of the Old and New Testaments to be the Word of God, the only *infallible* rule of faith and practise?"

The Confession of Faith, chapter I, section V, which treats "Of the Holy Scripture" does not employ the phrase, "kept from error," but it does contain such expressions as, "the entire perfection thereof" and "our full persuasion and assurance of the infallible truth" which imply and connote inerrancy. Furthermore, they argued, in 1893 the general assembly suspended the Rev. Charles A. Briggs, D.D., professor at Union Theological Seminary, New York City, because he believed in the errancy of holy Scripture.[37] In other words, the church had already interpreted the constitution with respect to the inspiration of the Bible and exactly as the Deliverance of 1923 had stated. What is more, it is clear that the other branches of the Christian church—the Roman Catholic Church as expressed in the Council of Trent, and the Greek

---

37   *Minutes of the General Assembly* 1893, Part 1, 166.

Orthodox Church as expressed through its confessions and catechisms—
believe in the full truthfulness of the Bible. The Council of Trent
describes the books of the Bible as having come down to the church,
"the Holy Ghost dictating."[38] The Greek Orthodox Church doctrine, as
expressed in "The Confession of Dositheus," is that the inerrancy and
infallibility of the church's judgment is based upon the absolute inerrancy
of the Bible.[39] In other words, this doctrine of an infallible Bible has
been the belief of the Christian church these many centuries.

The second doctrine contained in the deliverance reads, "It is an
essential doctrine of the Word of God and our standards that our Lord
Jesus Christ was born of the Virgin Mary." Concerning this statement
the Auburn Affirmation affirms,

> We all believe from our hearts . . . that Jesus Christ was God manifest in the
> flesh. . . . But we are united in believing that these [five doctrines] are not the
> only theories allowed by the Scriptures and our standards as explanations of
> these facts and doctrines of our religion, whatever theories they may employ to
> explain them, are worthy of all confidence and fellowship.

It is plain from this assertion that the Auburn Affirmation regards the
virgin birth as a theory of the incarnation. The narratives in Matthew
and Luke, on the other hand, are very explicit in their description of the
birth of Jesus Christ. He was conceived by the Holy Ghost in the womb
of the virgin Mary (Matt 1:20, Luke 1:34-35). That statement of an
historical event in the external world in the two gospels is either true or
false. It is not a theory, for to make such a claim would be to reduce the
gospel story to an absurdity and to make nonsense of the language.
Furthermore, it is beyond dispute that the Roman Catholic Church, the
Greek Orthodox Church, and the various branches of Protestantism
clearly teach a belief in the virgin birth of Christ.

The statement of the deliverance with reference to the atonement of
Christ for sin reads, "It is an essential doctrine of the Word of God and
our standards that Christ offered up Himself a sacrifice to satisfy divine
justice and to reconcile us to God." The Auburn Affirmation states, "that
God was in Christ reconciling the world unto Himself, and through Him
we have our redemption."

---

38   Philip Schaff, "The Canons and Dogmatic Decrees of the Council of
      Trent, A.D. 1563, " in *Creeds of Christendom* (New York: Harper &
      Brothers, 1931), 2:80.
39   *Ibid.*, 403.

No one can object to the statement of the Auburn Affirmation about the atonement because it is a partial quotation from the Bible (II Cor 5:19), but when the assertion of the deliverance is referred to as a theory of the atonement and that other theories which may be employed to explain the doctrine are worthy of all confidence, then an entirely different situation obtains and the question of anti-scriptural views comes into consideration. The Confession of Faith uses practically the same language as the deliverance to describe the sacrifice of Christ.

> The Lord Jesus, by his perfect obedience and sacrifice of himself which he through the eternal Spirit once offered up unto God, hath fully satisfied the justice of his Father.[40]

Officially, the Presbyterian Church in the USA has never taught any other view of the atonement than that expressed in the deliverance. In fact, its essential features are common to the Latin, Lutheran, and Reformed churches. In discussing the various theories of atonement, Dr. Charles Hodge wrote,

> The first is that which has been for ages regarded as the orthodox doctrine; in its essential features common to the Latin, Lutheran, and Reformed churches. . . . According to this doctrine the work of Christ is a real satisfaction, of infinite inherent merit, to the vindicatory justice of God; so that He saves his people by doing for them, and in their stead, what they were unable to do for themselves, satisfying the demands of the law in their behalf, and bearing its penalty in their stead; whereby they are reconciled to God, receive the Holy Ghost, and are made partakers of the life of Christ to their present sanctification and eternal salvation.[41]

The fourth statement of the deliverance reads:

> It is an essential doctrine of the Word of God and of our standards concerning our Lord Jesus Christ, that on the third day He arose again from the dead with the same body with which He suffered, with which He also ascended into heaven, and there sitteth at the right hand of His Father, making intercession.

In opposition to this view of the deliverance, the Auburn Affirmation states, "that having died for our sins He rose from the dead and is our everlasting saviour." The proper implication of this statement is that the resurrection of Christ was not necessarily a bodily one, especially since the Auburn Affirmation claims that the bodily resurrection is only one

---

40   *Westminster Confession of Faith*, chapter VIII, section V.
41   Charles Hodge, *Systematic Theology* (New York: Charles Scribner's Sons, 1895), 2:563-64.

of many theories. With reference to this doctrine the deliverance quoted directly from the Confession of Faith.[42]

If the bodily resurrection of Christ is only a theory, then the fifteenth chapter of 1 Corinthians is mistaken, because it is devoted almost exclusively to a discussion and proof of the resurrection of Christ and the assertion that the resurrection was a bodily one. It also makes of no meaning the claim of Christ to Thomas, "Handle me, and see; for a spirit hath not flesh and bones, as ye see me have" (Luke 24:39). In fact, no other theory of the resurrection is taught or implied in the Scripture. In addition, all branches of Christendom in their creeds teach the bodily resurrection of Christ. Of that there can be no question. So again the fact becomes clear that the issue raised by the Auburn Affirmation concerns the fundamental basis of Christianity, and not doctrines peculiarly Presbyterian.

The fifth doctrine of the deliverance reads,

> It is an essential doctrine of the Word of God as the supreme standard of our faith that our Lord Jesus showed His power by working mighty miracles. This working was not contrary to nature, but superior to it.

The Auburn Affirmation states, "that in His earthly ministry He wrought many mighty works."

Here the attempt is made by the Auburn Affirmation to undermine the entire supernatural element in the works of Christ and to make them to appear as mighty, but explainable to this generation by natural causes. The Confession of Faith reads, "God, in his ordinary providence, maketh use of means, yet is free to work without, above, and against them, at his pleasure."[43] At this point the tendency toward naturalism in the Affirmation becomes more evident, and the real underlying difference between it and historic Christianity is clear. It is here that the contention between two spirits, two convictions, and two conceptions of Christianity becomes most plain, and anyone who would understand this conflict correctly must honestly recognize that fact. The essential nature of the miraculous is evident not only in the works of Christ but in the whole of the New Testament. Eliminate that or try to distinguish between miraculous and non-miraculous Christianity, and no Christianity remains. What is more, no informed person would question the asser-

---

42   *Westminster*, chapter VIII, section IV.
43   *Westminster*, chapter V, section III.

tion that the Roman Catholic Church and the Greek Orthodox Church believe in the supernatural character of Christ's miracles.

It is obvious to any honest, clear-thinking man that there exists a world of difference concerning the essential nature of Christianity between the Deliverance of the 1923 Assembly and the Auburn Affirmation. The deliverance holds to a supernatural religion which comes as a revelation from a personal God, while the Affirmation supports the view that the Bible may be a revelation from God but no one can be sure of it, and that the miraculous aspects of Christianity are to be questioned and perhaps explained on a naturalistic basis. As Dr. Machen so ably argued many times, the religion of the Affirmation is a new and different religion, separate and distinct from historic Christianity.

The issuance of the Auburn Affirmation called forth a veritable flood of articles for and against it. These articles dealt with the constitutionality of the deliverance, but more especially with the doctrinal questions raised by the Affirmation. It became evident that this issue would be one of the main considerations at the general assembly in May, 1924.

When the assembly met at Grand Rapids in May, 1924, the following overture from the Presbytery of Cincinnati concerning the Affirmation was presented and, according to custom, sent to the Committee on Bills and Overtures of which the Rev. Maitland Alexander, D.D., was chairman.

> The Presbytery of Cincinnati would respectfully place in your hands the accompanying pamphlet, entitled, "An Affirmation," that you may be "well advised" of its contents and purposes and that your venerable body may exercise intelligently, under the guidance of the Divine Spirit, its "powers of deciding in all controversies respecting doctrine; of reproving, warning, or bearing testimony against error in doctrine, or immorality in practice, in any church, Presbytery or Synod;" "and of repressing schismatical conventions and disputation."[44]

The Committee debated this overture as well as several others of a similar nature for five days, and then recommended that no action be taken.[45]

Since Dr. Clarence E. Macartney, an outstanding conservative leader in that assembly, was elected moderator, and since Dr. Maitland Alexander and William Jennings Bryan, both of whom were well-known conservatives, were members of the Committee on Bills and Overtures,

---

44 *Form of Government* XII, section 5; John Vant Stephens, "An Affirmation," 27-28.

45 *Minutes of the General Assembly* 1924, Part 1, 202.

the question has often been asked, "Why was not some action taken against the Auburn Affirmation and its signers?" Dr. Alexander and elder A. Marshall Thompson have partially answered that question in their letters to *The Presbyterian*,[46] by stating that the committee was dominated by liberals thirteen to nine, so that every report coming from the committee represented the liberal point of view. Dr. Alexander further states that the general assembly laid the matter on the table on motion of Dr. Mark A. Matthews, and that by unanimous vote. The fact remains that as far as the record is concerned, there was no protest and no dissenting vote. It is also surprising that very little or no comment is made concerning this overture in the report of the proceedings of the general assembly in such a magazine as *The Presbyterian*, which was then the most aggressive organ for the faith. The statute of limitations which outlaws action against individuals one year after an offense has been committed, did not apply because only six months had elapsed since the issuance of the Auburn Affirmation in December, 1923.[47]

There seems to be no sound explanation of this action and attitude of the conservatives except that they made a grave mistake. No advice was given to the church concerning the Auburn Affirmation and, as a result, the matter has troubled the church ever since. One editor asked the rhetorical question, "What has become of 'An Affirmation,' signed by 150 ministers of the Presbyterian church, which number, through the labors and at the expense of Union Seminary, New York, was increased to twelve hundred?" Then he answered his own question, "It is dead."[48] But the church was to discover to its regret that the Affirmation was far from dead.

On the other hand, large mass meetings were held in several cities, deploring the doctrinal decadence in the Presbyterian Church in the USA as evidenced by the Auburn Affirmation. One such gathering took place in Cincinnati under the leadership of the Rev. Frank H. Stevenson, D.D., then pastor of the Church of the Covenant of Cincinnati, and one of the founders of Westminster Theological Seminary. In fact, the situation in the church became so acute that the 1925 General Assembly appointed a committee of fifteen with the following instructions,

---

46   *The Presbyterian* 106 (January 23, 1936), 22.
47   *The Book of Discipline* (1909), chapter XII, section 17 .
48   *The Presbyterian* 94 (September 4, 1924), 3.

> That a Commission of fifteen members be appointed to study the present
> spiritual condition of our Church and the causes making for unrest, and report
> to the next General Assembly, to the end that purity, peace, unity and progress
> of the Church may be assured.[49]

No Auburn Affirmationist was appointed to the commission, nor was
any out-and-out member of the orthodox wing of the church. It was
evident that this commission was appointed to still the voice of objection
which the Auburn Affirmation had created.

The commission made reports to the 1926 and 1927 General
Assemblies, both of which were adopted. As a whole, the reports dealt
with church polity, the powers of the general assembly and presbyteries,
ordination, licensure, essential and necessary articles of faith, and many
other kindred subjects, but failed completely to point out the "causes
making for unrest" in the church, which was the main purpose of the
commission. It hid behind a barrage of technicalities, most of which were
according to the constitution of the church, but made no adequate
proposals "to the end that purity, peace, unity and progress of the Church
may be assured," and recognized no deep-seated doctrinal difference
among the ministers in the church, but rather urged brotherly consideration and fair play. A short quotation from the reports will demonstrate
the spirit of doctrinal inclusivism of the members and their attitude
toward the great doctrinal issues involved in the conflict.

> Two controlling factors emerge. One is, that the Presbyterian system admits
> of diversity of view where the core of truth is identical. Another is, that the
> Church has flourished best and showed most clearly the good hand of God
> upon it, when it laid aside its tendencies to stress these differences, and put the
> emphasis on its unity of spirit.[50]

It is a matter of great sorrow that no attempt whatsoever was made at
the time to bring individual signers of the Auburn Affirmation to trial.
This method would have been the proper one, for when heresy exists
among ministers in the Presbyterian Church in the USA, charges must
be filed against a particular minister with the presbytery. The orthodox
ministers of the church wrote many pamphlets and made many speeches
against the Auburn Affirmation, but no individual signer of that document was charged with heresy. This grave error caused irreparable harm
in the church and furthered the cause of the modernists in the church.
The Presbyterian League of Faith was organized in 1931 as a direct

---

49   *Minutes of the General Assembly* 1925, Part 1, 88.
50   *Minutes of the General Assembly* 1926, Part 1, 78.

testimony against the Auburn Affirmation, and its constitution was signed by about twelve hundred ministers, but this did not result in any action against signers of the Affirmation (see chapter fourteen).

One attempt was made to bring the Auburn Affirmationists to trial in the Presbytery of Philadelphia in October, 1934, when the Rev. H. McAllister Griffiths and elders Murray Forst Thompson and Gordon H. Clark lodged six charges against the eleven signers of the Affirmation in the Presbytery of Philadelphia for violation of their ordination vows.[51] Through questionable methods and technical maneuvers the Affirmationists in the presbytery succeeded in keeping the charges from being filed. In addition, the legal difficulty imposed by the Book of Discipline in the statute of limitations, which requires charges to be filed within one year after an offense has been committed, would have militated against the success of this move. Yet the initiators of the charge felt morally obligated to start this suit in order to show the church that they regarded the signers of the Affirmation as heretics. When the Auburn Affirmation was issued in 1923, Mr. Griffiths was not a minister of the Presbyterian Church in the USA and Messrs. Thompson and Clark were not elders.

So the episode of the Auburn Affirmation ended, with the modernists scoring a decisive victory as shown by their success in restraining the church from admitting doctrinal heresy, at least in an official manner, and in keeping signers of the Affirmation in positions of great power in the church. It is very revealing to study the membership lists of the boards and agencies of the Presbyterian Church in the USA. In 1927, when the commission of fifteen made its last report, many signers of the Affirmation were on those boards. The Board of Foreign Missions had four, the Board of National Missions seven, the Board of Christian Education three, and the Permanent Judicial Commission of the general assembly, which is practically the final arbiter of doctrine in the church, had two. Dr. D. S. Kennedy, editor of *The Presbyterian* in 1924, said that the Auburn Affirmation was dead; subsequent events prove that its signers were more alive than ever and that its spirit dominated the church. The following chapters will attempt to prove that fact.

---

51   *Christianity Today* 5 (November 1934), 141-43.

3

The Reorganization of Princeton Theological Seminary

PRINCETON Theological Seminary prior to 1929 was regarded by theologians of all shades of opinion as the citadel of historic Christianity. Such great scholars as Charles Hodge, William Henry Green, Francis L. Patton, B. B. Warfield, and Geerhardus Vos had made the theology at Princeton the standard presentation of orthodoxy in the Christian world. In the last years Robert Dick Wilson and J. Gresham Machen were among the best known professors, and carried the fame of the institution as a contender for the faith to every land where Christianity is taught. It was to this seminary that students came to receive instruction for the ministry so that they would be able to give "a reason for the hope" that was in them, while others entered in order to discover whether orthodoxy had a reasonable case and could be accepted as true in the modern world. The young men emerged from the institution strengthened in the faith and convinced of the truthfulness of the Bible.

Princeton Seminary was known not only as an institution which defended historic Christianity, but as one which stood firmly for the propagation and defense of the Reformed faith or the Calvinistic system of doctrine that is set forth in the Westminster Confession of Faith and is taught in the Bible. In 1929, however, a change took place in the administration of the seminary and from that time a different and new theological emphasis became effective. The administration of the institution by a board of directors which controlled the educational program, and a board of trustees which held the real property in trust, was altered so that a single board of trustees was placed in charge of the seminary. With this new arrangement a radical change took place in the educational program which has shifted the theological emphasis from historic

Calvinism to twentieth-century Barthianism. A brief review of the conflict which produced the change will reveal this fact.

The Plan for the Theological Seminary of the Presbyterian Church in the USA, commonly called Princeton Theological Seminary, was adopted by the general assembly of the church in 1811.[1] It provided for a board of directors which had immediate control of the seminary, subject to the approval of the assembly. Every board member was asked to subscribe to the following pledge:

> Approving the Plan of the Theological Seminary of the Presbyterian Church in the U.S.A., I solemnly declare and promise in the presence of God and of this Board, that I will faithfully endeavor to carry into effect all the articles and provisions of said Plan, and to promote the great design of the Seminary.[2]

Each professor was required to agree to the following formula:

> In the presence of God, and of the directors of this Seminary, I do solemnly and *ex animo* adopt, receive, and subscribe to the Confession of Faith and Catechisms of the Presbyterian Church in the U.S.A., as the confession of my faith, or as a summary and just exhibition of that system of doctrine and religious belief, which is contained in Holy Scripture, and therein revealed by God to man for his salvation; and I do solemnly, *ex animo*, profess to receive the Form of Government of said Church, as agreeable to the inspired oracles. And I do solemnly promise and engage not to inculcate, teach, or insinuate anything which shall appear to me to contradict or contravene, either directly or impliedly, anything taught in the said Confession of Faith or Catechisms, nor to oppose any of the fundamental principles of Presbyterian Church government, while I remain a professor in this seminary.[3]

In 1870 the general assembly adopted changes in the plan of the seminary which added greatly to the power of the board of directors by allowing the board to fill its own vacancies, and to fix the salaries of professors, the first of which powers was subject to veto by the general assembly.[4]

The property of the seminary was first held by the trustees of the general assembly, but in 1822 the legislature of New Jersey passed "An Act for Incorporating Trustees of the Theological Seminary of the

---

1   *The Presbyterian Digest*, Vol. 2 (1930), 435.
2   *Ibid.*, 440.
3   *Ibid.*, 441.
4   See *Reports Relating to Princeton Theological Seminary before the General Assembly of the Presbyterian Church in the U.S.A., St. Paul, Minnesota, May, 1929*, reprinted from the Blue Book, 220.

Presbyterian Church, at Princeton, in the State of New Jersey," and so the trustees of the seminary became the custodians of the property under state law.[5]

Accordingly, from that time on two boards were in control of the institution: a board of directors which was entrusted with the task of directing the educational program, subject to the approval of the general assembly, and a board of trustees which was responsible for the real property held in trust by them for the seminary.

The institution had no president until 1902, when the general assembly added an article to the plan of the seminary providing for an election of a president by the board of directors, subject to the approval of the assembly.[6] The duties of the president are described as follows,

> Such president shall, by virtue of such election, be the president of the faculty. He shall be inaugurated in such manner and form as the Board of Directors may prescribe, and at his inauguration shall make the subscription and declaration required of a professor; he shall be subject to the regulations made by the Board of Directors and to the prescriptions of the Plan of the Seminary with regard to professors. He shall be the representative of the Seminary before the Church; he shall be the administrative agent of the Seminary in matters of order and discipline, he shall give instruction to the students in such departments as the Board of Directors may direct or the General Assembly may order. Such president shall, by virtue of his election, as aforesaid, become and be a member of the Board of Directors during his continuance in office, and a member, *ex officio*, of all Committees of the Board.[7]

Prior to 1902, a chairman of the faculty had been elected by the faculty, usually the senior member, whose duties were to preside at the faculty meetings, but in no way was the chairman superior to his colleagues.[8] The move to create the office of president originated in the relationship which Dr. Francis L. Patton had maintained with the seminary since 1880. While Dr. Patton had been president of Princeton University, he had been a lecturer at the seminary, but in 1902 he resigned as president of the university so that there was much agitation to make him a full professor at the seminary. The fact that Dr. Patton had been president of the university made some feel that a full professorship at the seminary

---

5   *The Presbyterian Digest* (1930), 451-52.
6   Ibid., 438.
7   Ibid.
8   *Charter and Plan of the Theological Seminary of the Presbytyerian Church, Princeton, N. J.* (Somerville: Press of the Unionist–Gazette Association, 1927), 28.

was not enough to offer him, and so the board of directors decided to inaugurate him the first president of the theological seminary. After his installation as president, Dr. Patton carried on in this office much in the same way as the former chairmen of the faculty had done as *unus inter pares,* or perhaps as *primus inter pares.* In no way did he assume the full responsibilities or duties of a president in the accepted sense of that office. On the other hand, he did become a member of the board of trustees and the board of directors, in which he exercised great influence mostly because of his strong personality and brilliance. In 1913 he retired and the task of choosing a successor became a very important and difficult one.[9] After considering many candidates and after much discussion, in fact after balloting several times, the Rev. J. Ross Stevenson, D.D., LL.D., pastor of the Brown Memorial Presbyterian Church in Baltimore, Maryland, was elected by the board of directors to the position by a majority of one vote. Several on the faculty and board of directors were not at all pleased by the election.[10] Dr. Stevenson was inaugurated in 1914, and made a member of the board of trustees, and became a member *ex officio* of the board of directors and all of its committees.

Dr. Stevenson, a graduate of McCormick Theological Seminary of Chicago, and later a professor there, had served in some of the leading churches of the Presbyterian Church in the USA, the most notable of which was the Fifth Avenue Presbyterian Church, New York City. He came to Princeton not appreciating fully its theological position and emphasis, and at the same time accepting the office of president on the terms set forth in the plan of the seminary which he interpreted in the plain sense, but which interpretation had never been enforced at the institution.

In fact, his spirit of doctrinal inclusivism and his great zeal for church union, even when based upon vague and meaningless theological statements, marked his whole career at Princeton and brought an alien viewpoint to the institution. It was plain to any objective observer that Dr. Stevenson and most of the faculty were far apart in their understanding of Princeton's place in the Christian world. The conflict between the two viewpoints was a logical result which men like Dr.

---

9   *Minutes of the General Assembly* 1913, Part 1, 226.
10   See William Courtland Robinson, *Princeton Theological Seminary: Its Troubles as Viewed by Amicus* (n.p., [1927]).

Warfield foresaw and which made them so reluctant to welcome Dr. Stevenson's appointment as president.

From the standpoint of administration, Dr. Stevenson conceived of his position as that of the real head of the institution who was to have a leading part in forming its policies, choosing its professors, inviting men to address the students and representing the seminary before the church. One who did not know the history of Princeton and its administrative policy would be likely to accept that interpretation of the president's position from a reading of the plan of the seminary. On the other hand, the faculty had always believed that the president was little more than a presiding officer who, together with his colleagues, decided on the entire educational program for the institution. This had been the practice of Dr. Patton as president and of the chairmen of the faculty before him.

Doctrinally there was also a divergence of opinion between the president and the majority of the members of the faculty. Dr. Stevenson was convinced that the institution existed to represent the whole Presbyterian Church in the USA, since it was under the direct control of the general assembly.[11] On the other hand, the majority of the faculty were fully convinced that the seminary could not possibly represent the whole church and be true to its charter and history.[12] Princeton was organized to uphold the Westminster Confession of Faith and the Larger and Shorter Catechisms, maintained the faculty, and by no standard of judgment could anyone say that all the ministers or officers of the church held to the truths of these documents in their historic meaning. Princeton must represent the Old School tradition in the church, they said, if it were to carry out the design of the founders.

Dr. J. Gresham Machen wrote,

> Never has Dr. Stevenson given any clear indication, by the policy that he has followed as President of the Seminary, that he recognizes the profound line of cleavage that separates the two opposite tendencies within the Presbyterian church, and the necessity that if Princeton Seminary is to be true to its great heritage and true to the moral obligations involved in the distinctive basis upon which it has always appealed for support, it must, in this great contention, definitely and unequivocally take sides.[13]

---

11   *Ibid.*, 60.
12   *Ibid.*, 75-80.
13   J. Gresham Machen, *The Attack upon Princeton Seminary: A Plea for Fair Play* (Princeton: J. Gresham Machen, 1927), 9.

Dr. William Park Armstrong, professor of New Testament at Princeton Seminary, made the assertion on behalf of the faculty,

> We do not believe that Princeton Seminary can be made a Seminary of the
> whole Church, i.e., representing the whole Church doctrinally, even under the
> constitution of the Church, without departing from its historical position,
> because of the prevailing latitude in interpretation of our doctrinal standards.[14]
> . . . The majority of the Faculty maintain that the Institution has been historically
> affiliated with that doctrinal point of view in the Church known as the Old
> School.[15]

On the other hand, Dr. Stevenson maintained,

> We [Princeton Seminary] are the agency of the combined Old School and New
> School and my ambition as President of the Seminary is to have it represent
> the whole Presbyterian Church and not any particular faction of it.[16]

So the president and the faculty clashed on the matter of administration
and doctrinal viewpoint. The president's stand for an inclusive doctrinal
policy as opposed to the faculty's demand for an exclusive one became
evident as soon as Dr. Stevenson assumed the presidency.

The first major clash between the president and the faculty came in
1920 over a Plan of Organic Union of Evangelical Churches, as
introduced in the general assembly by Dr. Stevenson, vice-chairman of
the Committee on Church Cooperation and Union.[17] The plan, and
particularly its unevangelical preamble, as set forth in chapter one of this
book, was opposed by professors Allis, Davis, Greene, Hodge, Machen,
and Warfield, as being contrary to the Westminster Confession of Faith
and inimical to the life of the church and its witness to the truth of the
Bible. On the other hand, Dr. Charles R. Erdman, professor of practical
theology, was a member of the Committee on Church Cooperation and
Union which prepared the plan and strongly favored its adoption.[18] In
other words, Dr. Stevenson had the support of at least one member of
the faculty in this issue, which showed the majority of the professors were

---

14   *Report of the Special Committee to Visit Princeton Theological Seminary to
      the General Assembly of the Presbyterian Church in the U.S.A., San
      Francisco, California, May, 1927* (Philadelphia: Office of the General
      Assembly, 1927), 75.
15   *Ibid.*, 68.
16   *Ibid.*, 72.
17   *Minutes of the General Assembly of the Presbyterian Church in the U.S.A.*
      1920, Part 1, 98.
18   *Ibid.*, 448.

opposed vigorously to the union on doctrinal grounds. There could be no mistake that at least the attitude toward the importance of doctrine and a real concern for the integrity and purity of the church's witness to the Reformed faith were at the basis of this difference between the president and the faculty.

The divergence of opinion on the importance of doctrine and the need for defending it arose again during the General Assembly of 1924 when Dr. Erdman, a member of the faculty, and Dr. Macartney, a member of the board of directors, were candidates for the position of moderator of the assembly. As has been seen already in the preceding chapter, Dr. Erdman, even though he was personally evangelical, was regarded as the candidate of those who wanted a union of all the forces in the church, and on this basis the liberals in the assembly supported him. Dr. Macartney, on the other hand, was considered the candidate of the conservatives. Dr. Stevenson supported Dr. Erdman, while the majority of the faculty were staunch allies of Dr. Macartney and his stand for the faith.[19] This contributed to the breach between Dr. Stevenson and the faculty.

In the fall of 1924 the conflict between historic Christianity and liberalism which had been disturbing the peace of the Presbyterian Church in the USA, became a live issue among the students on the Princeton Seminary campus. A delegation of students had been sent to the conference of the Middle Atlantic Association of Theological Seminaries at Drew Theological Seminary in Madison, New Jersey. On October 21, 1924, these men gave their report to the Students' Association meeting, in which they made it abundantly clear that some of the speakers and students at the conference had expressed their doubt about the necessity and truthfulness of such doctrines as the final authority of the Bible, the deity of Christ, and the virgin birth.[20] After much debate and consideration, the Students' Association decided to sever its relationship with the Middle Atlantic Association of Theological Seminaries and to form an organization of seminaries which would be committed to the great truths of the Bible. On April 4, 1925, in the city of Pittsburgh, Pennsylvania, twelve representatives from six theological institutions met

19   *Report of the Special Committee*, 1927, 62.
20   *Minutes of the Students' Association of Princeton Theological Seminary*, October 21, 1924.

and formed what is known as the League of Evangelical Students.[21] The doctrinal basis was indicated in the constitution of the league, in which certain dogmas such as the infallibility of the Bible, the Trinity, the virgin birth, the bodily resurrection, the substitutionary atonement, and the coming again of Jesus Christ were declared essential to the Christian religion.[22] Since that time the league has grown to large proportions, having chapters in fifty-eight theological seminaries, universities, and Bible schools.

The establishment of the League of Evangelical Students brought the president of the seminary at Princeton and the majority of the faculty into sharp disagreement over its advisability and necessity. The president maintained that the league dissociated Princeton from the seminaries of the Presbyterian Church in the USA, because most of them refused to join the league. In the second place, he declared that the league allowed Bible schools to become members and so the firm stand at Princeton, "that religion without sound learning must ultimately prove injurious to the church," would be undermined. He further stated, "shall this institution now be permitted to swing off to the extreme right wing so as to become an interdenominational Seminary for Bible School-premillennial-secession fundamentalism?"[23]

The majority of the faculty had an entirely different conception of the need and influence of the league on the campus of the seminary and in the world at large. Their general feeling is perhaps best expressed by Dr. Machen when he wrote,

> It [a spiritual advance] has been signally manifested at the institution which I have the honor to serve. The morale of our theological student body had been becoming rather low: there was a marked indifference to the central things of the faith: and religious experience was of the most superficial kind. But during the academic year, 1924–25 there has been something like an awakening. . . . Controversy, in other words, has resulted in a striking intellectual and spiritual advance. Some of us discern in all this the work of the Spirit of God. And God grant that his fire be not quenched.[24]

---

21   *The Modern Conflict and the League of Evangelical Students of America*, 3.
22   *Constitution of the League of Evangelical Students*, article III, section 1.
23   *Report of the Special Committee*, 1927, 57.
24   J. Gresham Machen, *What is Faith?* (New York: Macmillan Co., 1925), 42.

The majority of the faculty, while they did not enter into the affairs of the student body directly, nevertheless by their teaching and general attitude encouraged the students to continue their testimony among seminary and college students. So once again the difference in attitude toward doctrine between the president and faculty and the need for contending for the faith became clear.

In the spring of 1925 the question of the election of a faculty student adviser came before the cabinet of the Students' Association of the seminary. The president, W. C. Wright, was personally in favor of asking Dr. Erdman to continue in this office which he had held for twenty years, although other members of the cabinet preferred some other faculty member. Acting on his supposed prerogative in this regard, Mr. Wright asked Dr. Erdman to accept the office, which Dr. Erdman did. The cabinet called a special meeting, revoked Mr. Wright's appointment, and voted to ask the faculty to appoint an adviser from among its members. This resulted in the election of Dr. Robert Dick Wilson. The faculty felt obliged to make this selection because sympathy with the plans of the Students' Association was necessary, and Dr. Erdman had declared himself as opposed to the League of Evangelical Students which had been recently organized. In all of this controversy over the student adviser, Dr. Stevenson was much opposed to the majority of the faculty.[25]

The attitude of the majority of the faculty and of Dr. Stevenson toward the report of the commission of fifteen which had been appointed by the General Assembly of 1925 to "study the present spiritual condition of our Church and the causes making for unrest" differed sharply. Dr. Macartney, a member of the board of directors and Dr. Allis, a member of the faculty, voiced their serious indictment of the report. Dr. Macartney characterized it as a victory won by a "coalition of modernists, indifferentists and pacifists,"[26] while Dr. Stevenson found in the report a source of much satisfaction.[27]

The differences between Dr. Stevenson and the faculty assumed a personal note when Dr. Machen was nominated to the chair of apologetics and Christian ethics by the faculty on May 10, 1926.[28] This nomination was placed before the general assembly in May, 1926, for

---

25   *Report of the Special Committee*, 1927, 64-65, 72.
26   *Ibid.*, 59.
27   *Ibid.*
28   *Minutes of the General Assembly* 1926, Part 1, 266.

approval, at which time Drs. Stevenson and Erdman opposed it vigorously on the ground of Dr. Machen's alleged temperamental unfitness
for the position. The assembly took no action on Dr. Machen's nomination.[29] This attitude and action on the part of the president widened the
breach still more.

During this heated discussion and debate between Dr. Stevenson and
the majority of the faculty, Dr. Erdman accused the majority of the faculty,
and especially Dr. Machen, of labelling him as one who was strengthen-
ing the "forces of rationalism" when he accepted the pastorate of the First
Presbyterian Church, Princeton, New Jersey. The basis for Dr. Erdman's
assertion was an editorial in *The Presbyterian*, January 15, 1925, which
commented upon Dr. Henry Van Dyke's return to the First Presbyterian
Church, Princeton, New Jersey, from which he had departed in 1924 as
a protest against Dr. Machen's preaching. *The Presbyterian* stated,

> In a recent notice of the installation of Dr. Erdman, the inquiry was raised as
> to the significance of attempting to unite the rationalism of the university,
> represented by Drs. Van Dyke and Hibben, with the evangelicism of the
> seminary, represented by Dr. Erdman. Does this action of Dr. Van Dyke signify
> that the rationalists have gained an important advantage from the combination?
> If so, the situation and the new combination is threatening sacred interests.

To this comment Dr. Erdman replied with considerable agitation,

> Allow me to reply, that I repudiate your insinuations as unfounded, unwar-
> ranted, unkind and un-Christian. . . . .You intimate that a division exists in the
> seminary faculty. No such division exists on points of doctrine. Every member
> of the faculty is absolutely loyal to the standards of our church. The only division
> I have observed is as to spirit, methods or policies. This division would be of
> no consequence were it not for the unkindness, suspicion, bitterness and
> intolerance of those members of the faculty who are also editors of *The
> Presbyterian*.[30]

Since Dr. Machen was the only member of the faculty who was also
an editor of *The Presbyterian*, this rather abusive characterization could
only refer to him. Dr. Machen immediately explained,

> I do not remember having contributed a line to the paper which has not
> appeared under my own name, and I was quite unacquainted beforehand with
> the reference to my former relation and Dr. Erdman's present relation to the
> First Presbyterian Church of Princeton, to which he takes special exception.

---

29   *Ibid.*, 175.
30   "Dr. Erdman Speaks in Self Defense," *The Presbyterian Advance* 30
      (January 22, 1925), 24.

> . . . With regard to Dr. Erdman's letter, I desire to say two things. In the first place, I regret the personal tone in which the letter is couched. . . . But in what do our differences consist? That question brings me to the second thing that I desire to say in answer to the letter.
>
> Dr. Erdman says that no division exists in the faculty of Princeton Seminary on "points of doctrine." That assertion I hold to be not altogether correct. There is between Dr. Erdman and myself a very serious doctrinal difference indeed. It concerns the question not of this doctrine or that, but of the importance which is to be attributed to doctrine as such. . . . Dr. Erdman does not indeed reject the doctrinal system of our church, but he is perfectly willing on many occasions to keep it in the background. I, on the other hand, can never consent to keep it in the background.[31]

This personal equation which entered into the debate only aggravated the differences between Dr. Stevenson and the faculty still more, and caused Dr. Stevenson in May, 1925, to appeal to the board of directors to appoint a committee to adjust the problems within the faculty.[32] A committee of seven was appointed but no real accomplishment was forthcoming, mostly because the underlying disagreement was so profound that no discussion could heal the breach; rather, it required a change of doctrinal viewpoint which was highly unlikely to take place in either party.

This clash between Dr. Stevenson and the faculty, which had caused considerable agitation in the church at large, compelled the trustees and a minority of the board of directors of the seminary in May, 1926, to make a request of the general assembly through its Standing Committee on Theological Seminaries to appoint a special committee to investigate matters at Princeton Seminary. On June 2, 1926, the general assembly took the following action,

> That the Assembly appoint a Committee of three ministers and two elders to make a sympathetic study of conditions affecting the welfare of Princeton Seminary and to cooperate responsively with seminary leaders in striving to adjust and harmonize differences and to report to the next Assembly.[33]

---

31 *The Presbyterian* 95 (February 5, 1925), 20-21.

32 *Report of the Special Committee*, 1927, 16.

33 *Minutes of the General Assembly* 1926, Part 1, 174. The Rev. W. O. Thompson, D.D., LL.D., was made chairman of the committee and he named the Rev. G. N. Luccock, D.D., Wooster, Ohio, the Rev. W. L. Whallon, D.D., Newark, New Jersey, the Honorable Thomas E. D. Bradley, Chicago, Illinois, and the Honorable R. P. Ernst, Covington, Kentucky, as the other members of the committee.

The committee visited the Princeton campus and had conferences with the faculty, the board of directors, the board of trustees, the alumni, and the students. In every one of these bodies they found the same division as was manifest in the faculty, namely, one party which believed that Princeton was founded to teach and to defend, in its purity and integrity, the Westminster Confession of Faith as the system of doctrine taught in the Bible, and that an aggressive stand should be taken against the encroachment of unbelief in the church; and a second party which contended with Dr. Stevenson, the president, that the seminary should represent the whole church, that the disagreement between him and the faculty was administrative, and that certain members of the faculty, of whom Dr. Machen was the chief offender, were disturbers of the peace of the institution.

The majority of the board of directors, the faculty, and the students agreed that the issue was doctrinal and that the attitude toward doctrine was important. On the other hand, the president, a majority of the trustees, and many alumni felt strongly that if the two boards could be merged into one, the difficulties at the institution would be eliminated, because in their judgment the real trouble was administrative.[34]

The findings of the committee which were given to the following assembly can be summarized in this one sentence from their report, "The root and source of the serious difficulties at Princeton and the greatest obstacle to the removal of these difficulties, seem to be in the plan of government by two boards."[35] The committee presented recommendations which were adopted by the 1927 General Assembly.[36]

They urged the appointment of a committee of eleven with power to recommend amendments to the charter of the seminary in order to establish a single board of control. They also asked that the appointments of the Rev. O. T. Allis and the Rev. J. Gresham Machen as full professors be not confirmed until the reorganization had been effected.

The Rev. Samuel G. Craig, D.D., a director of the seminary and a representative of the majority on the board of directors, made a very able

---

34   *Report of the Special Committee,* 1927, 49.
35   *Ibid.,* 47.
36   *Minutes of the General Assembly* 1927, Part 1, 133-34. See Appendix, note 2.

criticism of the report of the committee of five. His main contention was that the committee exceeded its instructions and authority in making its recommendations.[37] Dr. Craig further accused the committee of misrepresenting the faculty and the board of directors and of issuing a report which was essentially an *ex parte* document. He also pointed out what the majority of the faculty and of the board of directors had frequently maintained, namely, that the question of one or two boards was beside the point.[38]

At the general assembly in 1928 the committee of eleven presented recommendations calling for a single board of control of thirty-three members, certain necessary charter amendments, and enlarged powers for the president of the seminary.[39]

The report of the committee of eleven was not unanimous, however, since the Rev. Ethelbert D. Warfield, D.D., brought in a minority report of one in which he made several criticisms of the majority report, the most important of which stated that "the report and its recommendations give no ground for hope that they will terminate or allay the discord in the Seminary and the Church."[40]

At the same general assembly a petition containing the signatures of over ten thousand ministers and elders of the church representing more than thirty synods asked, "We, therefore, the signers of this Petition, earnestly pray you to reject the reorganization of the Seminary recommended to the General Assembly of 1927 by the Special Committee to visit Princeton, and thus to leave the control of this great institution where it now resides."[41]

The Rev. W. P. Armstrong, D.D., professor of New Testament at Princeton, made a thorough study of the proposed charter amendments,

---

37 Samuel G. Craig, "The Report of the Princeton Seminary Committee: a Criticism," reprinted from *The Presbyterian* (May 19, 1927), with some additions (1927), 3.

38 *Ibid.*, 16.

39 *Minutes of the General Assembly* 1928, 212-46.

40 *Ibid.*, 249.

41 *A Petition Presented to the 140th General Assembly of the Presbyterian Church, U. S. A., Meeting at Tulsa, Oklahoma, May, 1928* (The Princeton Committee of One Thousand), 6.

in which he demonstrated that some of these were illegal and others unnecessary.[42] There will be no attempt here to enter into a study of these amendments because that discussion is not essential to the main purpose of this book.

The majority and minority reports were ordered placed on the docket of the 1929 General Assembly, and the board of directors of Princeton was instructed to attempt to compose differences at the seminary and to make a report to the next assembly.[43] The board of directors attempted to carry out these instructions, but the division in the board became apparent when a minority and a majority report was presented to the 1929 Assembly. The majority report, signed by seventeen, practically agreed with the recommendations of the committee of eleven, while the minority of ten stated that the main cause of the trouble at Princeton was the ambition of president Stevenson, who desired to shift the historic doctrinal position of the seminary from the Old School theology to an inclusive doctrinal position. "It is here that we find the main cause of the serious differences at Princeton Seminary."[44] The minority recommended only slight changes in the original plan of the seminary, all of which tended to limit the power of the president so that his actions would be subject to the advice of the board of directors in cooperation with the faculty. The president was also eliminated as a member of the board of directors.[45]

In spite of these pleas by the ten thousand ministers and elders and the minority on the board of directors, the report of the special committee of eleven was adopted by the 1929 Assembly.[46] The report called for one board of trustees of thirty-three members, one-third from the old board of trustees, one-third from the old board of directors, and one-third from the church at large, and the enlargement of the powers of the president.

---

42   W. P. Armstrong, *Certain Legal Aspects of the Proposal to Amend the Charter of the Trustees of Princeton Theological Seminary* (n.p., May 12, 1928).

43   *Minutes of the General Assembly 1928*, 59.

44   *Reports Relating to Princeton Theological Seminary before the General Assembly of the Presbyterian Church in the U.S.A.*, St. Paul, Minnesota, May, 1929, Reprinted from the Blue Book, 224.

45   *Ibid.*, 230-31.

46   *Minutes of the General Assembly 1929*, 80-110.

The temporary board of trustees, which was approved as the permanent board of trustees by the 1930 General Assembly,[47] made the Rev. W. L. McEwan, D.D., chairman. The Rev. Clarence E. Macartney, D.D., declined to serve on the board, and the Rev. Robert Dick Wilson, Ph.D., D.D., the Rev. J. Gresham Machen, D.D., the Rev. Oswald T. Allis, Ph.D., D.D., and the Rev. Cornelius Van Til, Ph.D., refused to continue as members of the teaching staff under the new board of trustees. And so, with these drastic alterations in management and faculty, the reorganization of Princeton Seminary became a reality.

This has been only a rapid survey of the tremendous changes which took place at Princeton in 1929, but a description of the many public meetings, articles, and debates which occurred, and the bitterness, animosities, and heartaches which were created have been purposely omitted in order to keep the account as factual as possible.

With the completion of the reorganization of Princeton Seminary the question naturally arises: Were the fears of the minority of the board of directors, the faculty, the students, and many alumni fulfilled, and was the historic doctrinal position of the institution changed from Old School theology or biblical Christianity to twentieth-century Barthianism and modernism? It is safe to assert without hesitation that those fears were fulfilled. A few facts as evidence will prove that statement.

Upon this new board of trustees were placed two ministers, the Rev. W. Beatty Jennings, D.D., and the Rev. Asa J. Ferry, D.D., who had signed the Auburn Affirmation, which, as was pointed out in chapter two, declared that the belief in the infallibility of holy Scripture, the substitutionary atonement, the virgin birth, the bodily resurrection of our Lord, and the miracles of Jesus Christ is non-essential to the Christian faith, and that the doctrine of the infallibility of the holy Scripture is harmful. The Rev. J. Ross Stevenson, D.D., LL.D., the president of the seminary, and the Rev. W. L. McEwan, D.D., chairman of the board of trustees, put their stamp of approval upon these signers of the Auburn Affirmation on the board, and so upon the attitude which the document advocated, in the letter which they jointly signed and addressed to the "Alumni, Students and Friends of Princeton Theological Seminary" in September, 1929, and in which they claimed that the new board of trustees was worthy of the church's confidence and

---

47   *Minutes of the General Assembly* 1930, 36-42.

qualified to direct the educational policies of the seminary, and that the entire faculty was loyal to the Bible.[48] Anyone acquainted with the Princeton of the Hodges, Warfield, Greene, and Machen could not conceive of its approval of men on the board of directors who held such anti-Reformed and modernist ideas.

At the present time only two professors of the regime prior to 1929 remain: the Rev. F. W. Loetscher, Ph.D., D.D., and the Rev. W. P. Armstrong, D.D., as all of the other professors who did not resign in 1929 are retired or dead. In 1936 Dr. J. Ross Stevenson was retired as president and the Rev. John A. Mackay, Ph.D., D.D., was elected to fill that office.[49] Dr. Mackay has carried the institution much more to the left. The professors who have been asked to serve at Princeton at his invitation have, for the most part, been men who hold to Barthianism in some form. In fact, Dr. Mackay himself embraces this theology.[50]

Wherein does Barthianism, or the theology of crisis, differ from the historic position of Princeton? someone might ask. The difference lies chiefly in two matters: first, concerning the authority of the Bible, and second, the conception of history. The Barthian school of theology does not believe in the infallibility of holy Scripture, while the old Princeton was noted for its insistence on this doctrine. As Charles Hodge once wrote,

> On this subject the common doctrine of the Church is, and ever has been, that inspiration was an influence of the Holy Spirit on the minds of certain select men, which rendered them the organs of God for the infallible communication of his mind and will. They were in such a sense the organs of God, that what they said God said.[51]

Emil Brunner, guest professor of systematic theology at Princeton 1938–1939, on the other hand, believes that the Bible is the Word of God, but only in a very restricted sense. He uses the illustration of the phonograph record. The voice of Caruso comes forth from the megaphone but there also is heard the scratchings of the needle, which are comparable to the human errors and mistakes in the Bible.[52]

---

48   *The Presbyterian* 99 (September 19, 1929), 3-4.
49   *Minutes of the General Assembly* 1936, 312.
50   John A. Mackay, "Historical and Superhistorical Elements in Christianity," *The Journal of Religion* 17 (January 1937), 1-8.
51   Hodge, *Systematic Theology*, 1:154.
52   Emil Brunner, *Our Faith* (London: Charles Scribner, 1936), 10.

When the final authority of the Bible is rejected, one is compelled to fall back on an authority in religion which is the church or some form of human experience. The Barthians do not accept the church as the final authority, as do the Roman Catholics, but rather in the last analysis must resort to an authority which is to be found in fallible human experience. And this they do.

It is the Scripture's testimony to itself as being from God, "God-breathed" and the Word of God, which must be the ultimate judge of the kind of inspiration. If the testimony of the Bible to itself as the Word of God is not to be accepted, how can one trust the authority of the Bible for faith and conduct? The belief in the full trustworthiness of the Bible is the "impregnable rock" of Christianity and is the only consistent and logical position which a Christian can maintain. It is the doctrine of historic Christianity. Most assuredly, it was the doctrine of the old Princeton.

Such a theology as Barthianism is essentially modernist because upon Barth's premises every doctrine and practice must inevitably find its authority in the experience of man as the determining factor. At heart this theology will destroy the true genius of Protestantism, which looks to the revelation of God in the Bible as the final arbiter of faith and conduct.

The same tendency to emphasize experience rather than the Bible as the norm for Christian life is manifest in Dr. Mackay's endorsement of Buchmanism, a movement which includes men and women of all shades of thought and belief and which judges the validity of a person's religion by the quality of his "changed life" experience.[53] In opposition to this point of view the Princeton of old fought, and fought vigorously, to show the vagaries of human experience in all of its subtleties and to demonstrate that human experience, instead of being a guide in religion, must itself be tested and judged by the Bible.

The Barthian conception of history also destroys the very foundation of Christianity. Historic Christianity declares that the virgin birth and the bodily resurrection of Jesus Christ are events in history, but many Barthians claim that these facts are only pointers to the real events which take place in "supra-history." Such a contention not only makes the narratives in Matthew and Luke concerning the virgin birth and the account in I Corinthians 15 describing the bodily resurrection mean-

---

53   *Rising Tide* (1937), 28.

ingless, but the historical foundation of Christianity is utterly demolished. It is upon such events in the external world as the birth, death, and resurrection of Jesus Christ that Christianity is built. If these are not to be regarded as actual historical facts in the plain sense, then Christianity as revealed in the Bible loses all meaning. When Barthianism is examined closely, it is clear that this attempt to place these events in the category of the "supra-historical" is only a subtle way of trying to avoid the conflict between the miraculous in Christianity and modern scientific ideas. Barthianism's unwillingness to accept the historical events of redemption as they are revealed in the Bible and as real events in time, sets it in opposition to biblical Christianity.

In order to demonstrate further what little regard the new president has for the old Princeton, that is, the Princeton prior to 1929, and its defense and exposition of historic Christianity, notice should be taken of the fact that the Rev. L. R. Farmer, D.D., LL.D., a signer of the Auburn Affirmation, was visiting professor of homiletics during the academic year 1937–38.[54] This is the first time in the history of the institution that any one has been on the faculty who has declared in a public document, or in any other way, that the five doctrines mentioned in the Affirmation are only theories, and that the belief in an infallible Bible weakens the testimony of the five doctrines enumerated.

In another way and in a way more discernible to those not theologically trained, the new Princeton has made its position abundantly clear. Before 1929, the professors at Princeton were very audible in their protest against unbelief not only in the world at large, but also in the Presbyterian Church in the USA itself. The men at Princeton assumed the leadership in attempting to keep the Presbyterian Church in the USA loyal to the Westminster Confession of Faith. Without question the seminary was the citadel of orthodoxy. Now the lack of protest against the evident modernism among the ministers in that church is almost eloquent in its silence. When the amendments to the Confession of Faith were proposed at the turn of the century, it was the faculty at Princeton, led by Warfield, who protested against them because of their tendency to weaken the testimony of the church to the truth. It was the Princeton faculty who wrote and spoke against the proposed union with the eighteen churches in 1918 on the ground of its unevangelical doctrinal

---

54   *The Princeton Seminary Bulletin*, Fall Conference Number, vol. XXXI, (November 1937), Number 3, 37.

basis. In fact, whenever a voice was needed to warn the church of unbelief, the men at Princeton were ready to raise their voices in behalf of the Bible. Now where are the one-time champions of the faith at Princeton? They are not there. Princeton has changed—and changed radically.

The modernists themselves have noticed this radical change. Once *The Christian Century*, the leading modernist religious weekly in America, ridiculed the antiquated and obscurantist theology at Princeton, while now it has taken Dr. Mackay to its bosom[55] and finds space available for members of the faculty at Princeton, which formerly was not at their disposal save for an occasional article in some series of theological debate. The Princeton Seminary of Hodge, Warfield, and Machen is no more, and the world knows it.

One of two things has happened since 1929: either the Presbyterian Church in the USA has become entirely free from modernism and anti-scriptural tendencies so that the Princeton professors have no occasion for protest, or else Princeton Seminary has fallen in line with the temper of the day and has become more liberal in its theological program and attitude. The following chapters will attempt to show that the Presbyterian Church in the USA, instead of becoming more loyal to the Westminster Confession of Faith, has succumbed more and more to the inroads of modernism. The only possible conclusion is that Princeton has been definitely liberalized, as shown not only by the writings of the professors, but also by the lack of defense of historic Christianity within the councils of the church.

The editors of *The Boston Evening Transcript* wrote,

> One cannot say what will happen at Princeton Theological Seminary, but one hopes that the house will stand. Clearly the battle at Princeton has a significance reaching far beyond its local scene. Its forces, its bitterness, give strong indication that the issues there in contest, as in other parts of the United States, are the dominant issues of the religious thought of our times. Certainly with regard to the Protestant denominations, it now seems clear that upon the outcome of the warfare, whether for weal or woe, the future character of Protestant Christianity depends.[56]

Princeton Seminary did not stand as it stood before. Its influence is now exerted in the direction away from historic Christianity, and that defec-

---

55   *The Christian Century* 54 (September 29, 1937), 1189.
56   *The Boston Evening Transcript*, as quoted by Frank H. Stevenson, "A Pastor Looks at Princeton," *The Presbyterian* 98 (January 12, 1928), 6.

tion has profoundly affected not only the Presbyterian Church in the USA, but also the complexion of Protestantism in America.

4
Westminster Theological Seminary

WHEN THE general assembly of the Presbyterian Church in the USA made the reorganization of Princeton Seminary final in June, 1929, certain former directors and faculty members of the seminary and a group of Presbyterian laymen and ministers, mostly from Philadelphia and vicinity, met to discuss the launching of another theological institution, Presbyterian in doctrine and of high scholarship, which would carry on the traditions of Princeton Seminary before its reorganization. The initial meeting took place on June 17, 1929, in New York City at the University Club by invitation of the Rev. Walter D. Buchanan, D.D., pastor of the Broadway Presbyterian Church, New York City. Presbyterians from five or six presbyteries who were present at this meeting passed the following resolution:

> Resolved, That this group will support the loyal members of the former Board of Directors of Princeton Theological Seminary in any step they may see fit to take (1) Toward preventing by legal means the misuse of the Seminary's funds; or (2) Toward the formation of a new seminary if they decide that it is necessary.[1]

It was the Rev. Charles Schall, D.D., pastor of the Presbyterian Church, Wayne, Pennsylvania, who first conceived of the idea of a new seminary after the destruction of Princeton and started influences which made the idea a reality. He had luncheon with two elders in Philadelphia, T. E. Ross and F. M. Paist, and discovered that they and many other elders in Philadelphia were willing and eager to launch a new seminary in the fall of 1929 if that were possible. At the Arts Club in Philadelphia eight elders and Drs. Wilson, Machen, and Allis met for luncheon and discussed curriculum, professors, location, and a budget for the proposed seminary. Sufficient funds were pledged at that meeting for the first year's

---

1   *The Presbyterian* 99 (October 3, 1929), 8.

expenses to encourage further efforts to make the plans an actuality. Following this luncheon seventy-eight men, composed of former Princeton directors, faculty, and students, and Presbyterian ministers and elders, met at the central YMCA, Philadelphia, July 18, 1929, at which time a temporary executive committee was formed and the seminary was definitely launched.[2]

The executive committee chosen consisted of ministers: Maitland Alexander, Roy T. Brumbaugh, Walter D. Buchanan, Samuel G. Craig, Charles Schall, and Frank H. Stevenson, and elders: Roland K. Armes, Edgar Frutchey, Frederic M. Paist (chairman), James L. Rankin, T. Edward Ross, James F. Schrader, John L. Steele, and Morgan H. Thomas, with Drs. Robert Dick Wilson, J. Gresham Machen, and Oswald T. Allis in an advisory capacity. Westminster Theological Seminary was selected as the name for the new institution.

Among those who later joined the board of trustees, the name of the Rev. Clarence E. Macartney, D.D., a former moderator of the general assembly of the Presbyterian Church in the USA, is the most prominent, although many others who were well-known pastors of large Presbyterian congregations and laymen of influential positions in the professional and business world also consented to serve. Westminster Seminary began its first academic year on September 25, 1929, with an enrollment of fifty students.

This meager description of the founding of the institution does not portray the faith, courage, work, and real heroism of that small band of men who actually launched the seminary in less than four months after the reorganization of Princeton. Drs. Wilson, Machen, and Allis spent the entire summer in speaking, writing articles, preparing the curriculum, securing professors, and carrying on a large correspondence in order to secure the opening of the institution in September of that year. The Rev. Paul Woolley, registrar, labored tirelessly in preparing the student rooms and the classrooms at 1528 Pine Street (which had been placed at the disposal of the school, rent free, by Dr. Allis), and in answering multitudinous questions about the new seminary. The laymen on the executive committee also did yeoman service, particularly in securing funds.

No report of the organization of Westminster would be proper without special mention of the tremendous work which was accomplished by the

---

2   See Appendix, note 3.

Rev. Frank H. Stevenson, D.D., who became president of the board of trustees, and who was the guiding spirit in the administrative policies of the seminary. His large experience as an executive served to prepare him in a peculiar way for the task of steering the ship through the rough seas of the worst financial depression that this country has ever seen, and which overtook America only one month after Westminster was founded. Much credit must be given to him for guiding the seminary in a remarkable way, so that the infant institution remained free of debt. It was he who had published the article, "A Pastor Looks at Princeton," which was one of the most incisive and well-written discussions of the entire controversy. He had been a member of the board of directors at Princeton and before that of Lane Theological Seminary in Cincinnati, as well as the successful pastor of the Church of the Covenant, Cincinnati. He came to his position as president of the board of trustees of the new seminary bearing the scars of battle and prepared for the task which confronted him. His untimely death at the age of fifty-one in 1934 was a severe blow to the young and struggling institution.

The faculty at Westminster Seminary was composed of four professors from Princeton: Robert Dick Wilson, who was chosen chairman of the faculty, J. Gresham Machen, Oswald T. Allis, and Cornelius Van Til; the Rev. R. B. Kuiper, who had been a graduate student at Princeton under B. B. Warfield, and a pastor in Reformed churches for nearly a quarter of a century, and three recent graduates of Princeton: Allan A. MacRae, Ned B. Stonehouse, and Paul Woolley, who had pursued graduate studies in Europe. A year later Mr. John Murray, who had taught at Princeton Seminary, joined the faculty.

Professor Robert Dick Wilson was considered to be an outstanding scholar in the Old Testament, especially in Semitic studies, and a great defender of the faith. Dr. J. Gresham Machen had come to be regarded as one of the leading exponents of historic Christianity. He, more than any one else, was the central figure of the controversy at Princeton and the theological leader of the conservatives. Dr. O. T. Allis had been the editor of the scholarly *Princeton Theological Review*, and in this position had gained an international reputation for his exact and thorough grasp of orthodox Christianity. Dr. Cornelius Van Til, who had taught only a year at Princeton in the department of apologetics, has since attained a place of prestige in that field of theology. Professor R. B. Kuiper now holds the chair of practical theology, and from his abundant experience in the pastorate and his unique gifts as a preacher, is teaching the young men to become faithful ministers of the Word of God. The four young men who were added to the faculty were brilliant students at Princeton and give promise of a large future in theological scholarship. Two others, the Rev. Edward J. Young and the Rev. John H. Skilton, were later made members of the faculty in the departments of Old and New Testament respectively.

Westminster Seminary is independent of ecclesiastical control, but it is not interdenominational or nondenominational in character, for it is committed to the Westminster Confession of Faith as the system of doctrine taught in the Bible and to the Presbyterian form of church government. Yet it welcomes students from many church bodies, and since the seminary was founded they have come from thirty-four different denominations.

Why was Westminster Theological Seminary founded? The catalogue of the institution states,

> Westminster Theological Seminary was founded in 1929 to carry on and perpetuate the policies and traditions of Princeton Seminary as that institution existed prior to its reorganization by the General Assembly of the Presbyterian Church in the U.S.A.
>
> The need for the new seminary is due ultimately to a long process of defection from the Christian faith which has been going on in the Protestant churches of the world during the past one hundred years; but the special occasion was found in certain recent events in the Presbyterian Church in the United States of America.[3]

In an address at the opening exercises of Westminster, September 25, 1929, Dr. Machen said among other things,

> No, my friends, though Princeton Seminary is dead, the noble tradition of Princeton Seminary is alive. Westminster Seminary will endeavor by God's grace to continue that tradition unimpaired; it will endeavor, not on a foundation of equivocation and compromise, but on an honest foundation of devotion to God's Word, to maintain the same principles that old Princeton maintained. We believe, first, that the Christian religion, as it is set forth in the Confession of Faith of the Presbyterian Church, is true; we believe, second, that the Christian religion welcomes and is capable of scholarly defense; and we believe, third, that the Christian religion should be proclaimed without fear or favor, and in clear opposition to whatever opposes it, whether within or without the church, as the only way of salvation for lost mankind.[4]

---

3   *Catalogue of Westminster Theological Seminary*, 1937-38, 14.

4   J. Gresham Machen, "Westminster Theological Seminary: Its Purpose and Plan," *The Presbyterian* 99 (October 10, 1929), 8-9.

In this pronouncement Dr. Machen laid down the platform upon which the seminary appeals for support and upon which the professors teach.

Westminster Seminary, in other words, is more than a protest against the trend toward modernism at Princeton Seminary; more than an institution set for the defense of the gospel; and even more than a seminary to carry on the traditions and policies of the old Princeton. It is a lighthouse of Christian learning. The seminary and its graduates are fired with a zeal to teach and to preach that men must believe in the God of the Bible if they are to know God as their heavenly Father, and if they are to have a consistent, logical, and reasonable view of the world. The seminary assumes the offensive in the warfare against paganism in its many forms. It is not content to find a way of escape from intellectual difficulties in religion by succumbing to the modern day emphasis upon individual experience as the norm for Christian thinking and living. On the other hand, by painstaking, accurate, and thorough scholarship it ventures to maintain that the Bible is true, that the Christian gospel is the power of God unto salvation, and that the Christian position is the only intellectually honest one.

The seminary's short history has demonstrated that the founders were determined to keep the institution devoted to the Westminster Confession as the system of doctrine taught in the Bible and to the Presbyterian form of church government. The professors have always taught the students to preach the gospel and to be equally vigilant in maintaining it in the councils of the church. As a result of this consistent teaching, the seminary has been much attacked, and two crises have developed within its board of trustees and faculty.

When the seminary came into being, much was said and written about the main conflict between paganism and Christianity, and little by comparison was stated concerning the Presbyterian character of Westminster and the need for upholding the full and consistent view of Christianity as set forth in Calvinism. Men like Dr. Machen made it abundantly plain that Westminster was not only orthodox, but definitely Reformed in its doctrinal basis. On the other hand, the general defense against modernism placed the conflict on a broader basis, and the distinctively Calvinistic character of Westminster was not strongly emphasized. A glance at the past ten years of Westminster Seminary will show that the failure to keep foremost the high biblical stand of the institution as a seminary of the Reformed persuasion led to serious misunderstandings.

When Westminster was organized three different groups of men were appointed to the board of trustees. No one knew at the time that this situation obtained, but the ensuing events have made it evident.

First, there were thorough-going Presbyterians who were resolved to maintain true doctrine regardless of cost. These men were ministers and laymen of the Presbyterian Church in the USA who felt the need of making a good witness for the gospel, not only from the pulpits of the church but also in the meetings of presbyteries, synods, and general assemblies. They were aware of the presence of ministers in the church who controlled much of its ecclesiastical life and who were opposed to the Westminster Confession of Faith. Consequently, the seminary had been formed, at least in one respect, with the hope of sending consecrated and courageous young men into the ministry of the Presbyterian Church in the USA to stem the rising tide of unbelief. This group of trustees, as well as members of the faculty, was convinced that if that course failed, true Presbyterianism must be preserved in some other way.

A second group in the board of trustees and faculty, also ministers and laymen of the Presbyterian Church in the USA, was equally determined to supply loyal ministers for the church, but, as it developed, they were not willing to pay the price of pursuing another course of continuing a true witness to the Reformed faith if the first method of reforming the church failed.

A third group in the board of trustees was composed of ministers and laymen of the same church who were opposed to modernism in the church and wanted to train faithful ministers of the Word of God. These members were non-denominational in their convictions rather than definitely Presbyterian. At the outset all members of the Board appeared to be of the same mind with the first group, but the two crises which developed required decisions, and the above divisions appeared.

Efforts were made in 1933, particularly by certain members of the faculty of whom Dr. Machen was the leader, and members of the board of trustees of the seminary, to reform the Board of Foreign Missions of the Presbyterian Church in the USA.[5] When these efforts failed, a mission society, independent of ecclesiastical control and named the Independent Board for Presbyterian Foreign Missions, was formed. Three members of the faculty and nine members of the board of trustees of the seminary became members of that mission society. The general

---

5   See chapter six for details.

assembly of the Presbyterian Church in the USA issued a mandate in 1934 ordering members of the Presbyterian Church in the USA to resign from the Independent Board or suffer discipline. The members of the seminary faculty and board of trustees refused to resign from the Independent Board. This created dissension within the seminary family because some of the seminary board and one member of the faculty, led by Dr. Samuel G. Craig, felt that the Independent Board and Westminster Seminary should continue as separate institutions, and that sympathy with the seminary did not mean agreement with the establishment of the Independent Board. On the other hand, men like Dr. Machen were convinced that while the seminary and Independent Board were separate and distinct organizations, nevertheless the seminary's whole life and purpose were in hearty agreement with the attempt to reform the church and with the establishment of the Independent Board. In fact, Dr. Machen and the others argued that to take any other position would be to defeat the very reason for the organization of the seminary. If the seminary did not stand like a flint against the encroachments of modernism and unbelief in the church and was not willing to encourage its graduates to take the consequences of such a position, then the institution had no reason to exist.

The Rev. Samuel G. Craig, D.D., was editor of *Christianity Today*, which journal had been launched in May, 1930, when *The Presbyterian*, of which Dr. Craig had been editor, asked him to resign because of his vigorous protests against the reorganization of Princeton Seminary. The masthead of the first issue of *Christianity Today* declared it as "A Presbyterian Journal Devoted to Stating, Defending and Furthering the Gospel in the Modern World," and the editorial in the same issue stated among other things as its conviction, "that it is the duty of Christians to bear clear-cut witness to the Christian faith against all who oppose it, whether within or without the church." Contrary to this avowed purpose, so it seemed to Dr. Machen and many others, the paper had later on vigorously opposed the work of reformation within the Presbyterian Church in the USA, as represented by the Independent Board and the Presbyterian Constitutional Covenant Union.[6] Consequently, the seminary had to make its position clear as to which group, Dr. Craig and his followers or the faculty, represented the seminary's attitude in the church crisis.

---

6   See chapter twelve.

At the regular fall meeting of the board of trustees held on October 22, 1935, the faculty presented a resolution asking the board to declare its position: was the seminary to continue in the vanguard of the gospel and the fight against modernism, or was it to lag in the rear of the battle and carry on the struggle in word only? The board finally upheld the faculty and voted to urge all those on the board opposed to the faculty to resign in order to allow the institution to continue.[7]

It is evident from this unique and generous resolution that it was the desire of those members of the board of trustees who were opposed to the faculty to preserve the witness of the seminary, rather than to have their opinion prevail and force most of the faculty to resign. Dr. O. T. Allis, a member of the faculty, was out of agreement with the other members of the faculty and resigned, stating, "I am taking this step voluntarily in the hope that the Seminary may be saved or at least be enabled to continue."[8]

Dr. Craig was the only member of the board of trustees who opposed this action in a vigorous way, and in order to make his protest formal he sent a long letter to each member of the board setting forth his reasons for disagreeing with the faculty. He presented five considerations which led him to vote against Dr. Macartney's resolution and that of the faculty. (1) It misstates the occasion and purpose of the establishment of Westminster Seminary. (2) It misstates the cause of the division that has been introduced into the affairs of the seminary. (3) It misrepresents the present editorial policy of *Christianity Today* and the present attitude of its editor. (4) It demands that the seminary identify its interests with those of the Independent Board and the Presbyterian Constitutional Covenant Union. (5) It contains a threat to wreck the seminary unless the demand just referred to is granted.[9]

At a specially called meeting of the board on January 7, 1936, thirteen members of the board and Dr. O. T. Allis of the faculty presented their resignations, and a statement was adopted by the board for release to the

---

7   See Appendix, note 4.
8   A letter by Dr. Allis to members of the board of trustees, October 28, 1935.
9   A letter addressed to the members of the board of trustees of Westminster Theological Seminary by Dr. Craig, October 26, 1935.

papers, which declared that the seminary would pursue its original purpose and policy of teaching and defending the Word of God.[10]

The Alumni Association of the seminary came to the defense of the institution and at its annual meeting on May 11, 1936, passed without a dissenting vote the resolution: "The Alumni Association hereby records its hearty approval of the present administration and policy of Westminster Theological Seminary."[11]

The departure of these thirteen members of the board of trustees and one member of the faculty was a serious loss to the seminary. It is a matter of regret that these men, some of whom were the conservative leaders of the Presbyterian Church in the USA and men of large abilities, were unwilling to go the whole way in the attempt to reform the church. It is to be hoped that they will eventually see their mistake and once more support the seminary in a wholehearted fashion.

This ended the first great crisis in the life of Westminster and stamped it as an institution which would brook no compromise with modernism, and which was resolved to instill in the students a militant and aggressive attitude against unbelief in the councils of the church as well as from the pulpit. The original purpose of the seminary had been upheld and its consistent testimony to the truth had been kept clear.

A second crisis within the board of trustees and the faculty occurred in 1937. This time it concerned the question of the distinctively Presbyterian character of the institution. Was it to be only a generally evangelical seminary, or was it to continue its original principles and stand for Presbyterianism, or Calvinism, as the system of doctrine taught in the Bible?

Mr. John Murray, professor of systematic theology at the seminary, began a series of articles on the general theme, "The Reformed Faith and Modern Substitutes," in the December 16, 1935, issue of the *Presbyterian Guardian*. In this series, which extended over a number of months, he dealt with such subjects as "The Limited Atonement," "Arminianism," "Total Depravity," and "Modern Dispensationalism." In considering the last named topic, he attempted to prove that dispensationalism of the Scofield Reference Bible type contradicts the teaching of the Westminster Confession of Faith. He exposed the false distinction between the kingdom of God and the kingdom of heaven in the New Testament

---

10   See Appendix, note 5.

11   *Presbyterian Guardian* 2 (June 1, 1936), 107.

made by Dr. Lewis Chafer, which implies that entrance into the kingdom of God is by the new birth, while entrance into the kingdom of heaven is by works. Mr. Murray made it plain that premillennialism as such was not under discussion, but simply some of the errors which had become attached to it.[12]

Dr. O. T. Allis, a member of the faculty, also wrote an article on this subject in *The Evangelical Quarterly* for January, 1936, defending the same point of view as that expressed by Mr. Murray. Another article added to the emphasis on this subject. After the First General Assembly of the Presbyterian Church of America, now the Orthodox Presbyterian Church, professor R. B. Kuiper wrote a description of the formation of the church for *The Banner* (Christian Reformed), which was reprinted in the *Presbyterian Guardian*, in which he stated,

> The General Assembly had the privilege of examining several graduates of Westminster Seminary for licensure and ordination. It would have warmed the cockles of the heart of any Christian Reformed minister to hear how closely they were questioned about the two errors which are so extremely prevalent among American fundamentalists, Arminianism and the Dispensationalism of the Scofield Bible. The assembly wanted to make sure that these prospective ministers were not tainted with such anti-reformed heresies.[13]

These articles brought protests from certain members of the board of trustees of the seminary and a number of good people who had supported Westminster under the impression that it was a non-denominational institution. In fact, it was the knowledge that the thoroughgoing Calvinistic principles of the seminary were not sufficiently well-known which prompted the articles to be written by Mr. Murray. The criticisms which followed revealed only too clearly that the fears of the seminary leaders were well-grounded.

Another issue, quite irrelevant to the whole question and which obscured the real basic differences of doctrine, was the subject of Christian liberty, particularly concerning the drinking of fermented beverages, and the discussion of the so-called separated life, which sets up certain man-made standards apart from the Bible and judges a Christian's spirituality by his conformity to these norms.[14]

---

12   John Murray, "The Reformed Faith and Modern Substitutes," *Presbyterian Guardian* 2 (May 18, 1936; August 17, 1936), 77-79, 210-212; 3 (January 9, 1937), 139-141.

13   R. B. Kuiper, *Presbyterian Guardian* 2 (September 12, 1936), 225-27.

14   See chapter twelve for a full discussion of these subjects.

Professor Allan A. MacRae, Ph.D., assistant professor in charge of the department of Old Testament at the seminary, sympathized strongly with these criticisms and sent in his resignation to the board of trustees, in which he stated that the teaching at Westminster Seminary was now directed against fundamentalism and premillennialism instead of modernism, that the faculty vigorously defended the use of fermented beverages, that the students were being taught to accept views in opposition "to the great stream of Reformed, Evangelical Christianity in this country,"[15] and that the seminary had "passed into the hands of a small alien group." Ministers Roy Talmage Brumbaugh and Harold S. Laird, and elders Roland K. Armes and F. M. Paist resigned from the board of trustees for the same reasons.[16]

In protest, the above-named trustees and the Rev. Carl McIntire, with Dr. MacRae as chairman of the faculty, formed Faith Theological Seminary at Wilmington, Delaware, in September, 1937, which seminary is wedded to premillennialism and the so-called separated life. The seminary claims to be committed to Presbyterian doctrine, but the presence on the board of trustees of one Baptist, the Rev. David Otis Fuller, D.D., of Grand Rapids, Michigan, and one independent fundamentalist, the Rev. William R. McCarrell, D.D., of Cicero, Illinois, makes it clear that the institution is an inter-denominational one.[17]

The unwarranted attack by Dr. MacRae brought a quick response from the faculty and the students of Westminster Seminary, both of whom denied the allegations of intemperance at the institution and the statement that the seminary denied liberty of view with respect to the second coming of Christ.[18]

This division in the board of trustees and the faculty resulted in the Presbyterian and biblical witness of the seminary being firmly maintained. Fortunately, the seminary weathered the storm and continued on its course as an institution devoted to the Westminster Confession of Faith as the system of doctrine taught in the Bible, and more determined than ever to pursue its original purpose of teaching young men to insist

---

15   Letter by Dr. MacRae to the Rev. Harold S. Laird, secretary of the board of trustees of Westminster Theological Seminary, April 26, 1937.

16   *Minutes of the Meeting of the Board of Trustees of Westminster Theological Seminary*, May 11, 1937.

17   *Catalogue of Faith Theological Seminary*, 1938-1939, 3, 10.

18   See Appendix, note 6.

upon loyalty to the Word of God in the administration of the church, as well as in proclaiming it each Sunday from the sacred desk.

The attack on Westminster Seminary from without was more bitter and very widespread. The hierarchy of the Presbyterian Church in the USA exerted tremendous efforts to still the voice of the institution. On August 1, 1934, the general council of the Presbyterian Church in the USA sent a letter to all ministers and sessions of that church, signed by the moderator of the preceding general assembly, and stating among other things that "The Independent Board for Presbyterian Foreign Missions is a continuation of a divisive movement in the Presbyterian Church which five years ago resulted in the establishment of an independent seminary and which, if not stayed, will result in the formation of other independent Presbyterian agencies." The import of this is evident: Westminster Seminary is a harmful divisive movement which is threatening the future of the Presbyterian church.

This official letter is moderate in comparison with other and more drastic measures which were taken to suppress Westminster. For example, Mr. Calvin Cummings, a graduate of the seminary, was denied licensure in the Presbyterian Church in the USA because he refused to pledge blind allegiance to the official Board of Foreign Missions. There is nothing in the constitution of the church which requires such a vow for licensure, yet the Presbytery of Baltimore demanded that pledge. Advice that it should do this had been given by the stated clerk of the general assembly. No other interpretation of this action is possible than that a pope had suddenly appeared among Presbyterians who was bent on crushing the evangelical cause in the Presbyterian Church in the USA.

The Rev. Henry W. Coray, a graduate of Westminster Seminary and the pastor of the Presbyterian Church in West Pittston, Pennsylvania, applied several years before for appointment as a missionary under the official board of the Presbyterian Church in the USA, but he was denied this privilege. He then applied to the Independent Board for Presbyterian Foreign Missions and was appointed to go to China. What happened? The Presbytery of Lackawanna refused to dissolve the pastoral relationship between Mr. Coray and his church because he was being sent out by the Independent Board, and declared that if he persisted his name would be erased from the roll of presbytery, which is equivalent in this case, as far as the Presbyterian Church in the USA is concerned, to excommunication. His name was actually erased from the roll of presbytery on November 12, 1934. In other words, a Presbyterian minister was not to be allowed to preach Christ unless he would become a slave of the hierarchy of the church. There were many other cases of high-handed methods. The reaction to this kind of propaganda and tactics resulted in sympathy for the seminary and an increased resolution on the part of the professors and the board of trustees to go straight on in the endeavor to teach the truth, no matter what persecution should arise.

A great and unexpected blow fell upon the seminary on January 1, 1937, when its leader, the Rev. J. Gresham Machen, D.D., Litt.D., passed away while on a missionary trip to North Dakota to present the cause of the Bible against modernism in the Presbyterian Church in the USA. He died as he had lived, fighting for the faith without compromise.[19] Prior to this, two of the founders of the seminary had died: in 1930 the Rev. Robert Dick Wilson, Ph.D., D.D., LL.D., a member of the faculty, and in 1934 the Rev. Frank H. Stevenson, D.D., the first president of the board of trustees.

After the death of Dr. Machen, the J. Gresham Machen Memorial Fund was announced in March, 1937, in order to raise funds for the purchase of a campus and buildings, and to secure the necessary $500,000 endowment, which sum is usually required by the state of Pennsylvania before an institution can grant theological degrees.[20] Up to this time the seminary had been housed in rented quarters at 1526 and 1528 Pine Street, Philadelphia. As a result of this campaign a beautiful twenty-two acre estate, located on the edge of Philadelphia and containing five buildings, was purchased in June, 1937, as the seminary campus. The main building was dedicated as the J. Gresham Machen Memorial Hall at the opening exercises on September 29, 1937.[21]

In 1938 the board of trustees approached the State Council of Education asking the council to recommend that the state courts give Westminster Seminary degree-granting power even though the half-million dollar endowment was not at hand. The state council made a thorough investigation of the seminary's academic standards and found them very high and fully warranting the power to grant degrees. The council voted unanimously to approve Westminster's application to grant the Th.B. degree, and the court approved the recommendation and the necessary charter amendments. Ordinarily the endowment is neces-

---

19   See chapter eight.
20   Edwin H. Rian, "The Machen Memorial Fund: its Objectives," *Presbyterian Guardian* 6 (May 1939), 89.
21   *Presbyterian Guardian* 4 (November 1937), 197.

sary but under certain circumstances, when an institution is receiving financial support equivalent in value to the endowment from members and congregations of religious organizations, this may be substituted for the endowment. Westminster Seminary satisfied the State Council of Education of Pennsylvania that such financial support was being received. At the tenth anniversary celebration and commencement exercises on May 9, 1939, nearly 100 of the 162 graduates of the past ten years who held the regular certificate of the seminary received their Th.B. degree. This brought to a successful conclusion the aims of the Machen Memorial Fund, and served as a fitting climax to the tenth anniversary celebration and a proper memorial to such a great theologian and Christian statesman as Dr. Machen.

This recital of the essential facts of the history of Westminster Theological Seminary must have impressed the reader with the unique character of the institution and with its exceptional resiliency. Few institutions have been subjected to such abuse, criticism, and vigorous attacks both from within and without. It places in bold relief the utter devotion of the seminary to the Bible regardless of persecution, and also the enduring qualities of the truth of Christianity under the most adverse circumstances.

Controversy in behalf of the truth against the trend of the times in the church as well as in the world has sharpened the knowledge of the gospel among the followers of the seminary, and has better prepared all those associated with the cause to fight the good fight of faith and to preach the gospel of the Lord Jesus Christ. For the past three years the unity of purpose among the board of trustees, the faculty, and the students of the institution gives promise of a large place of usefulness in the future.

The seminary's reputation as an institution which is committed to the Westminster Confession of Faith is now firmly established, and its scholarly presentation of the truths of the Bible has attracted students not only from many states, but from a number of foreign countries as well. Its graduates are located in twenty-three states and ten foreign lands where they are ministers, professors, and missionaries.

While Westminster's course has been rough and stormy, yet throughout the past ten years it has always held to the conviction that the Bible is true, that salvation is only by the grace of God apart from the works of man, and that the Christian conception of life is the only logical, consistent, and reasonable one. The uncertainty, doubt, and anxiety in the world today makes such a seminary a ray of hope, for from its halls come ministers of the gospel who preach not their own philosophies, but speak the authority of the Word of God, "Thus saith the Lord!"

5
Union Movements

MANY ATTEMPTS at organic union between the Presbyterian Church in the USA and other church bodies have been made, three of which have already been discussed, but so far only three unions, one with the Associate Synod in 1822, one with the Cumberland Presbyterian Church in 1906, and one with the Welsh Calvinistic Methodist Church in 1920, have been consummated. Friendly correspondence has been maintained with several churches of the Reformed persuasion, but in most instances little progress has been made toward actual union.

In 1903 the general assembly adopted the following vague resolution concerning relationships with other churches:

> The Presbyterian Church holds Christian fellowship with all who confess and obey Jesus Christ as their Divine Saviour and Lord, and acknowledges the duty of all Churches that recognize Him, as the only Head of the Church universal, to work together in harmony and love, for the extension of His kingdom and the good of the world; and this Assembly earnestly desires to commend and promote this Christian cooperation, and also practically to advance the cause of Church union by confederation, and, where possible, by consolidation among the Churches of the Reformed Faith, which are most nearly akin in doctrine and organization.[1]

Three movements in particular require detailed consideration because they have occupied the attention of the Presbyterian Church in the USA for many years, and because they represent serious possibilities for organic union. These attempts also show the doctrinal laxity in the church and its growing indifference to doctrine.

In 1907 the general assembly of the Presbyterian Church in the USA received overtures from 113 presbyteries requesting that action be taken with a view to effecting organic union with the United Presbyterian

---

1   *Minutes of the General Assembly* 1903, 90-91.

Church of North America.[2] From that date on, friendly correspondence with the United Presbyterian Church continued, with overtures for union emanating from both bodies. But it was not until 1930, when the general assembly of the Presbyterian Church in the USA received the following message from the committee on correspondence of the United Presbyterian general assembly, "United Presbyterian General Assembly by practically unanimous vote adopted report of Committee on Presbyterian Unity authorizing committee to begin conferences with committees of other Presbyterian and Reformed Churches on plans for Organic Union,"[3] that the movement for union became a definite possibility.

The Department of Church Cooperation and Union under the chairmanship of the Rev. J. Ross Stevenson, D.D., then president of Princeton Theological Seminary and the chief protagonist of church union in the Presbyterian Church in the USA, was authorized to enter into negotiations with other Presbyterian and Reformed churches in order to complete plans or a plan for organic union with any one or all of these bodies.[4] The United Presbyterian Church was the most receptive, so that several meetings between committees of the two churches were held. In 1932 a was presented to both general assemblies. The name proposed for the united church was "The Presbyterian Church of America." A pamphlet entitled, "Documents Relating to the Proposed Organic Union of the Presbyterian Church in the USA and the United Presbyterian Church of North America," was issued by the Joint Committee on Organic Union and widely distributed among the ministers of both churches. This pamphlet included the doctrinal basis for the union as well as the provisional form of government, book of discipline, and directory for worship.

Much criticism was centered about the doctrinal basis of the union, especially the confessional statement of 1925 of the United Presbyterian Church and the brief statement of the Reformed faith adopted by the 1902 General Assembly of the Presbyterian Church in the USA, both of which were included in the doctrinal basis. The strong objections to these statements, on the ground that they toned down the Calvinism of the Westminster Confession of Faith, compelled the joint committee to include these in the Plan of Union only as "historical interpretative

---

2   *Presbyterian Digest*, Vol. 2 (1938), 129.
3   *Ibid.*, 136.
4   *Minutes of the General Assembly* 1930, Part 1, 257.

statements." The Scriptures of the Old and New Testaments were to be regarded as the supreme standard, the only infallible rule of faith and practice. The subordinate standards were to be the Westminster Confession of Faith, together with the amendments adopted in 1903 by the Presbyterian Church in the USA, and the Larger and Shorter Catechisms, all of which were recognized as agreeable to and founded upon the Scripture.[5]

Dr. J. Gresham Machen assumed a leading role in opposition to this proposed Plan of Union. He voiced no objection to a union between the two churches as such because they represented a common Reformed tradition, but he was against this proposed union for several reasons.[6] First, he contended that the proposed form of government for union practically destroyed the rights of the local congregation. The Plan of Union made it possible for a presbytery to take over the affairs of a local church without any judicial process and use the resources and holdings of the local congregation contrary to its desires.[7]

Secondly, the Plan of Union made giving a tax and not a matter of free-will.

> If any person of known pecuniary ability fails in giving of his substance, the session should point out his obligation as revealed in the Word of God and the blessing attending its faithful discharge. If he still withhold from the treasury of the Lord, the session may deal with him as an offender.[8]

But a real central objection by Dr. Machen concerned the 1925 confessional statement of the United Presbyterian Church, even though it was to be regarded only as an "historical interpretative statement." He argued that although the Westminster Confession of Faith, the Larger and Shorter Catechisms, subject to the holy Scriptures, are to be the final authority in matters of doctrine,[9] a document like the "1925 Confessional Statement" actually interprets away the purport of the Westminster

---

5   *The Presbyterian Digest*, Vol. 2, (1938), 13.

6   J. Gresham Machen, "Stop, Look, Listen: Why the Plan of Organic Union Should be Opposed," *Christianity Today* 4 (April 1934), 4-7.

7   *Plan of Union Providing for the Organic Union of the Presbyterian Church in the U.S.A. and the United Presbyterian Church of North America*, (Philadelphia: Joint Committee on Organic Union, 1934), 66.

8   *Ibid.*, 165.

9   *Ibid.*, 9.

Confession of Faith and so destroys its original meaning. For example, the confessional statement maintains that the holy Scriptures are "an infallible rule of faith and practice and the supreme source of authority in spiritual truth."[10] This article, he contended, makes a false distinction between historical truth and spiritual truth and so gives comfort to the central error of the day. On the other hand, a Christian believes that the Bible is true throughout; and therefore events in the external world, like the bodily resurrection of Jesus Christ, must be true.

In addition, the same article states that the writers of the Bible "though moved by the Holy Spirit, wrought in accordance with the laws of the human mind." This sentence, continued Dr. Machen, denies the supernaturalness of the Bible. "What is in accordance with the laws of the human mind or with any others of the laws of nature is natural, what is not in accordance with the laws of the human mind or any of the others of the laws of nature is supernatural."[11]

Another main objection to the Plan of Union concerned the formula of creed-subscription. The formula read, "Do you believe and acknowledge the system of doctrine professed by this Church as contained in the Westminster Confession of Faith, the Larger and Shorter Catechisms, as taught in the Word of God, and do you engage to adhere to and maintain its truths?"[12] Dr. Machen attacked this formula as undermining the faith of the church at the most vital point:

> According to the proposed new formula of creed-subscription the Bible may teach any number of systems and the system contained in the Westminster Confession of Faith may be held to be only one of them. . . . If the Bible contains various contradictory systems of doctrine, then the "infallibility" of the Bible spoken of in the first question of the formula of creed-subscription can mean very little; and certainly it is little short of blasphemous to call such a self-contradictory book the "Word of God."[13]

Apparently the able modernist journal, The Christian Century, agreed with Dr. Machen's interpretation. "One is not, then, required to affirm that there can be no other system of doctrine whose component parts

---

10   Ibid., 28.
11   "Stop, Look, Listen: Why the Plan of Organic Union Should be
       Opposed," 5.
12   Plan of Union, 13.
13   "Stop, Look, Listen:" 6-7.

are not also drawn from the teachings of the Bible. .... Professor Machen is, we think, right in so interpreting the new formula."[14]

Mr. John Murray of Westminster Theological Seminary also attacked the confessional statement, not only with respect to the authority of holy Scripture, but also its doctrine of creation, salvation, atonement, and of God the Father. His main thrust was aimed at the doctrine of the atonement which, he claimed, tended to teach universal atonement as opposed to the limited or definite atonement of the Westminster Confession of Faith, which means that the atonement is effectual only to those who are called of God.

Dr. Samuel G. Craig, editor of *Christianity Today*, and Dr. C. E. Macartney attacked the Plan of Union from a different point of view and warned the United Presbyterian Church that the Presbyterian Church in the USA was a doctrinally divided church. There were modernists, middle-of-the-roaders, and evangelicals, and as Dr. Craig pointed out, the modernist-indifferentist party was in control.[15] Dr. Macartney argued, "If the United Presbyterians wish to unite with our church, they should act in full knowledge of the lamentable doctrinal condition which now obtains within the Presbyterian Church."[16]

Dr. Gordon A. McLennan, pastor of the Shadyside United Presbyterian Church, Pittsburgh, writing in the *Christian Union Herald*, March 17, 1934, agreed with Dr. Craig and Dr. Macartney. "If anyone is in any doubt as to the division in the Presbyterian Church, surely the establishment of an independent Seminary, and now an independent Board of Foreign Missions is of a nature to remove such doubt."

From these criticisms it becomes clear that a very strange situation obtained. United Presbyterians were regarded as doctrinally sounder in membership than the Presbyterian Church in the USA, but at the same time as having a confessional statement much less orthodox than the Presbyterian Church in the USA.

The vast majority of the ministers of the Presbyterian Church in the USA favored this union. Dr. Robert E. Speer, senior secretary of the Board of Foreign Missions of the Presbyterian Church in the USA, in a semi-official article defending the new formula of creed subscription, stated that the words, "the system of doctrine taught in the Holy

---

14   *The Christian Century* 51 (March 14, 1934), 353-54.
15   *Christianity Today* 4 (April 1934), 2.
16   *Ibid.*, 19.

Scripture," is contained in the question asked of licentiates so that every candidate for ordination has already declared that he believes in only one system of doctrine as taught in the holy Scriptures.[17] Dr. Speer answered the criticism of the confessional statement by saying that the holy Scriptures are to be the final authority in matters of doctrine. He also mentioned that in 1928, in a Plan of Union between the Presbyterian Church in the US (southern) and the United Presbyterian Church of North America, the southern Presbyterian church accepted that confessional statement. This action on the part of the allegedly conservative southern church ought to warrant the Presbyterian Church in the USA in taking similar action.

The Plan of Union was vigorously defended by the Rev. W. J. Reid, D.D., chairman of the Committee on Presbyterian Unity of the United Presbyterian Church, and by the Rev. John McNaugher, D.D., President of Pittsburgh-Xenia Theological Seminary. Of the confessional statement Dr. McNaugher wrote, "However its clear recognition as having interpretative character scarcely lessens its influential value as an exponent of Reformed Theology."[18]

In appearing before the 1934 General Assembly of the Presbyterian Church in the USA as a guest to advocate the Plan of Union, Dr. McNaugher, in biting and sarcastic terms, ridiculed those who had found fault with the confessional statement. The objection to the phrase "spiritual truth," he said, warped it out of its context, "and in hermeneutics that is a damnable sin!" He remarked,

> Our critics are afflicted with astigmatism or abysmus, and, in addition, they need a heavy injection of First Corinthians thirteen! . . . Read this through [The Confessional Statement] with an open and unbiased eye before you retire, and it will compose you into an orthodox sleep—not that it is soporific, but it will make you happy, and when you roll over to sleep you will say, "Return unto thy rest, O my soul."[19]

When the general assembly of the Presbyterian Church in the USA met in 1934 to vote on the Plan of Union, the only real opposition to it

---

17   *Minutes of the General Assembly* 1934, Part 1, 290-91.
18   John McNaugher, "The Plan of Union: the Doctrinal Basic," *The United Presbyterian* 92 (January 11, 1934), 10.
19   *Christianity Today* 5 (July 1934), 41.

from the floor was voiced by the Rev. H. McAllister Griffiths, managing editor of *Christianity Today*, who objected to the union on the grounds of the confessional statement, the new formula of creed-subscription, and the unfairness to congregations who voted not to go into the union, since they could not retain their church property.[20] But an overture in favor of union and asking the presbyteries to express their approval was passed by a vast majority.[21]

On the other hand the United Presbyterian Church, by a vote of 123 to 113, turned down the Plan of Union so that any further attempts to unite with the United Presbyterian Church of North America would have to begin *de novo*.[22] But the defeat was due not so much to the doctrinal issues involved (although they were the real issues), as to the plea on the part of United Presbyterians that they would be overwhelmed, since their membership is only one-tenth that of the Presbyterian Church in the USA.

A second major attempt at union, still in progress, is that between the Protestant Episcopal Church in the USA and the Presbyterian Church in the USA. In 1888 the Protestant Episcopal Church approached the Presbyterian Church in the USA on the question of union, but the correspondence was terminated in 1896 because the Protestant Episcopal Church would not accept the doctrine of recognition and reciprocity "as a principle controlling negotiations."[23] But in 1937, the Rev. James De Wolfe Perry, presiding bishop of the Protestant Episcopal Church, addressed a communication to the secretary of the general council of the Presbyterian Church in the USA, informing him that the Protestant Episcopal Church urged the Presbyterian Church to consider the possibilities of organic union between the two bodies.[24]

Upon receipt of this letter, the general assembly of the Presbyterian Church in the USA adopted a resolution authorizing the moderator and stated clerk of the general assembly, together with the chairman of the Department of Church Cooperation and Union, to inform the presiding

---

20   *Ibid.*, 47. See also *Minutes of the General Assembly* 1934, Part 1, 272-73.
21   See Appendix, note 7.
22   See *United Presbyterian Minutes* 1934, 632.
23   *Presbyterian Digest*, Vol. 2 (1938), 199.
24   *Minutes of the General Assembly* 1938, Part 1, 219-20. See also Appendix, note 8.

bishop of the Protestant Episcopal Church that the Presbyterian Church "declares its earnest and prayerful purpose to cooperate with the Protestant Episcopal Church in the U.S.A. in the study and formation of such plans as may make possible the union contemplated."[25]

This concordat cannot be finally and definitely adopted until the general convention of the Protestant Episcopal Church meets in 1940. At the general assembly of the Presbyterian Church in the USA, June, 1939, no formal approval of the concordat was given, but the committee of the church was asked to continue negotiations.[26]

The proposed union has met strenuous objections among Presbyterians. Dr. C. E. Macartney set forth seven reasons why the union was not likely to succeed. First, it was undesired by the rank and file of both churches. Second, Presbyterians and Episcopalians would not seek ministers from each other. Third, the statement about the Bible is doctrinally latitudinarian. It recognizes the Scriptures as the supreme standard for faith and morals but also states, "in the assurance that with the Catholic fellowship there is room for diversity of interpretation." Fourth, with respect to ordination, the Presbyterians must make concessions by having bishops lay hands on Presbyterian ministers. Fifth, the Episcopal attitude toward social customs and amusements is different. Sixth, this union will drive a wedge between the Presbyterian Church in the USA and other Presbyterian bodies who are considering union. Seventh, these marked differences will really help to separate the two churches.[27]

Likewise, Episcopalians warned against undue haste in forming conclusions that the union will take place. Bishop Wilson, a member of the Protestant Episcopal Commission, wrote that the proposed concordat had not yet been approved by the Episcopal church. He also warned that the ordination element was very troublesome.

> For us to commission Presbyterian ministers without regard to ordination would involve us in endless difficulties. . . . Such a "commissioning" without ordination would do three things. (1) It would violate the whole spirit and intentions of the preface to the ordinal in our Prayer Book on which our own historic ministry is firmly founded. (2) It would run counter to the accepted

---

25   Ibid.
26   Minutes of the General Assembly 1939, Part 1, 58-61.
27   Clarence Edward Macartney, "Proposed Plan of Organic Union," The Presbyterian 109 (July 6, 1939), 3, 6.

standards of all other branches of the Anglican communion and might quite conceivably split us off from them. There is little to be said for that kind of unity achieved at the cost of still more disunion. (3) It directly contradicts our representation given to the Orthodox at the last Lambeth Conference on the subject of Holy Orders.[28]

Bishop William T. Manning, perhaps the most prominent bishop in the entire Protestant Episcopal Church, has very frankly cautioned against the proposed union as inimical to the good feeling between the two churches and as hindering the effective witness of the churches to the truth.[29]

In the meantime, four recommendations were made as "things that might be undertaken in common," namely, an exchange of preachers occasionally, an invitation to the members of each church to the Lord's table, an exchange of greetings from delegates of the churches, and an exchange of professors and students in the seminaries of both churches. None of these recommendations has been followed in either church to any appreciable extent.

The whole project is meeting with little enthusiasm and interest among Presbyterians and Episcopalians and the reasons seem to be quite obvious. The form of government of the Episcopal church with its conception of the ministry and its ritualism is considerably different from that of traditional Presbyterianism. The Episcopal church discipline is founded on the principle of rule by bishops with great concentration of power in their control, while Presbyterianism is a representative form of government, that is, a rule by teaching and ruling presbyters or elders. The parity of the clergy in Presbyterianism would make it difficult for ministers to accept the higher authority of the bishops in the Episcopal sense. Underlying this radically different view of the ministry is the scriptural interpretation of it. Most Presbyterians would surrender their form of government either completely or partially with great reluctance. Dr. Mark A. Matthews of the Presbyterian church expressed this view when he wrote, "The Presbyterian Church will never surrender its ordination by its presbyteries. . . . The Presbyterian Church will never surrender its form of government. . . ."[30]

---

28 Bishop Wilson, "Let's Know," *The Witness* (June 15, 1939).
29 William T. Manning, "Bishop Manning on Union," *The Presbyterian* 109 (October 12, 1939), 6-8.
30 Mark A. Matthews, "Keep the Record Straight," *The Presbyterian* 108 (December 8, 1938), 6.

The ritualism of the Episcopal church is another formidable barrier. Presbyterianism has followed a very simple form of worship with the sermon as the central part of the service, while the Episcopal church has a highly developed form of symbolism in worship, even in the low church congregations, with the sermon occupying a less prominent place than the ritualistic element in the service. The doctrinal statements of each church are fundamentally Calvinistic and so would not present such great difficulties.

But there is another phase to the whole enterprise which must give pause to many in the two churches, and that is the moral element. How can a Presbyterian in good conscience who believes that the Presbyterian form of government is that which is taught in the Bible give way, even by indirection, to episcopacy?[31] The whole tradition of the Presbyterian church is so fundamentally opposed to episcopacy that it is likely to be the deciding factor in the attempt to unite. There are indications that this factor will prevent the union at least for many years to come.

The attempt at organic union with the Presbyterian Church in the US (southern) is the most likely to succeed, because the two churches have the same confession of faith and much the same form of government. Two forces militate against such a union: the fear of the southern church that it will be submerged in the Presbyterian Church in the USA, which has four times as many members, and the suspicion and conviction of some that the so-called northern church is not true doctrinally to its constitution.

After the Civil War a committee was appointed by the general assembly of the Presbyterian Church in the USA to confer with the Presbyterian Church in the US to seek closer and more fraternal relations. In response the Presbyterian Church in the US from time to time appointed a similar committee on union but the movement advanced very little beyond this stage until 1917. At that time overtures were received from 195 presbyteries of the Presbyterian Church in the USA, urging the general assembly to unite with the Presbyterian Church in the US. The general assembly took action urging that organic union between the two churches be considered.[32]

The General Assembly of the Presbyterian Church in the US replied:

---

31   Ned B. Stonehouse, "The Road to Union in the Presbyterian Church in the U.S.A.,"*Presbyterian Guardian* 6 (February 1939), 23-25.
32   *Presbyterian Digest*, Vol. 2 (1938), 108. See also Appendix, note 9.

> While this Assembly does not regard organic union as practicable at this time, yet it hereby appoints the Committee of Conference on Union asked for by the Assembly of the Presbyterian Church in the U.S.A., and recommends to the proposed Conference the consideration of the federation of all the Presbyterian Churches of our country upon some practical and effective basis.[33]

A plan of reunion was presented to the Presbyterian Church in the US, and in reply the committee of the Presbyterian Church in the US drafted a Plan of Federal Union of all Presbyterian and Reformed Churches in the United States. This plan of federal union was presented not only to the Presbyterian Church in the USA, but also to the Reformed Church in the US, the United Presbyterian Church of North America, the Reformed Church in America, the Associate Reformed Presbyterian Synod, the Christian Reformed Church in North America, the Welsh Calvinistic Methodist or Presbyterian Church in the USA, the Synod of the Reformed Presbyterian Church of North America, the General Synod of the Reformed Presbyterian Church, the Cumberland Presbyterian Church, and the Cumberland Presbyterian Church, Colored.[34] In general the plan of federation was a loose one which called for a federal general assembly having very restricted powers.[35]

After much discussion it became evident that the Presbyterian Church in the US did not desire organic union, and that the Presbyterian Church in the USA saw no gain in entering into a union on the basis of the plan of federal union, because no closer association would be secured by it than already existed.

Committees from both churches have continued with conferences on the general subject of union but with little result. The Rev. Charles W. Welch, D.D., of the Presbytery of Louisville was elected moderator of the 1938 General Assembly of the Presbyterian Church in the USA, in the hope that a Southerner would appeal to the Presbyterian Church in the US. In fact, the individual who nominated him for this office made that the burden of his speech.

On the other hand, the Presbyterian Church in the US dismissed its Committee on Union at its general assembly in 1938. In 1939, by a

---

33 *Ibid.*
34 *Ibid.,* 111.
35 *Ibid.,* 112-13.

small margin, it voted to ask the presbyteries to express their attitude toward such a union.[36]

In other words, the enthusiasm and interest in the union are nearly all on the part of the Presbyterian Church in the USA. It seems almost certain that organic union between the two churches is very much in the future. If the Presbyterian Church in the USA continues along its present trend toward modernism, the union may never take place, unless there is a disruption in the Presbyterian Church in the US caused by modernism, in which case the liberal element of the church will be very much in favor of union.

The whole union enterprise in the Presbyterian Church in the USA in the past two decades has been motivated by the conviction that outward unity of organization is the great need and goal of Protestantism today. This spirit was expressed by John D. Rockefeller, Jr.:

> Only a united Christian world can stem the rising tide of materialism, of selfishness, of shaken traditions, of crumbling moral standards, and point the way out. How such a union might be brought about was once suggested by Dr. Stanley Jones, to whose stimulating address we have just listened. He proposed one Church, to be called the Church of Christ, or it might be called the Church of the Living God, with all sectarian churches as branches. Thus individual and non-essential differences would be preserved, while in the fundamentals of religion in God's love and Christ's loving spirit—all would be united.[37]

In fact, the whole Protestant world is under the spell of this conviction. A united Christian church may be a commendable goal, but the necessary doctrinal vagueness which must result from such a union would vitiate the whole enterprise. Any large union which may result in the future is most likely to be along doctrinal lines rather than denominational ones.

The time has come in each denomination for a separation between those who believe the Bible and those who do not; such a division would result in real Christian unity. But such vague and meager doctrinal bases which have been proposed so far as the foundation for a united Christendom would create a church which the historic Christian church would hardly be able to recognize, and which would certainly be ineffective for great spiritual work among individuals and the nations. What is needed, and needed badly, is a rebirth of genuine enthusiasm for, and belief in, the miraculous gospel of the Lord Jesus Christ, which

---

36   *Minutes of the General Assembly of the Presbyterian Church in the U.S.*, 1939, 56.

37   *Christianity Today* 7 (April 1937), 271.

proclaims that all men are lost in sin and separated from God and in need of redemption and reuniting with God, the Father. This should be the great message of the church; it should be the consuming desire of every minister in the Christian church. If that comes to pass, all ideas of a false and feeble outward church union will be forgotten, and the church will have returned to its true mission.

The spirit of unionism in the Presbyterian Church in the USA is strong, and will continue to grow as the doctrinal witness and consciousness of the church becomes weaker. It is safe to predict that, if modernism continues its present hold on the life of that church, union enterprises on a vague, meaningless doctrinal basis will be entered into and very likely consummated.

6
The Independent Board

THE CONTENTION and the belief that the boards and agencies of the Presbyterian Church in the USA were, and are, under the control and domination of those who do not hold to historic Christianity was a vital concern to the Board of Foreign Missions. For many years the conservatives of the church were critical and distrustful of the actions and missionary appointments of that board. While the other agencies were likewise under scrutiny, and in many cases considered even more liberal in their operation, it was the Board of Foreign Missions which received most of the attention. This may be explained on the ground that foreign missions have always been regarded as most intimately concerned with the real mission of the church in preaching the gospel of the Lord Jesus Christ. An examination of the other boards in a later chapter will reveal that what is stated here about the foreign board is equally true of the others.

In the fall of 1923, the Rev. Robert Dick Wilson, D.D., LL.D., professor of Hebrew and Old Testament literature at Princeton Seminary, wrote an article in which he criticized the board on two counts. He averred that the board had allowed itself to become entangled with bodies of missionaries differing in doctrine and polity from the Presbyterian Church in the USA, and that missionaries had been hindered from joining such a doctrinally sound organization in China as the Bible Union. He wrote,

> While believing that it is our duty to give adequate support to the missionaries already on the field who are loyal to the doctrine of the church, I cannot refrain from stating my conviction that the Board, and especially some of our secretaries, have erred grievously in some of their policies with regard to the work entrusted to them by the church.[1]

---

1   Robert Dick Wilson, "Friendly Advice to the Foreign Board," *The Presbyterian* 93 (October 25, 1923), 9.

In addition to the two causes which Dr. Wilson gave for lack of confidence in the board, others felt that the public repudiation by three members of the board of the doctrinal deliverances of the 1923 General Assembly, when they signed the Auburn Affirmation, made that board unworthy of the church's support.[2]

At the general assembly in May, 1924, the agitation against the Board of Foreign Missions found expression in the report of the Standing Committee on Foreign Missions. The following resolution of the committee was adopted:

> That while maintaining loyally the policy established by past General Assemblies in repeated enactments with regard to cooperation with other Evangelical bodies in our Foreign Missionary Work the Board be directed to exercise due care with regard to the Evangelical character of all such union and cooperative enterprises, and if there should arise in the work of these enterprises a situation in which teachings unsound or injurious to the Evangelical Faith are given, the Board, as it has declared to be its policy, should either secure the correction of such a situation or failing such withdraw from further participation.[3]

As far as is known, the board did not withdraw from any union enterprises, however questionable they were.

The discontent with the policy of the board increased in extent and intensity, and was brought to a climax in 1932 by the publication of a book entitled *Re-Thinking Missions*, which was issued as a report of the "Commission of Appraisal of the Laymen's Inquiry after One Hundred Years," the chairman of which was Dr. William E. Hocking, professor at Harvard University and a leader with strong liberal leanings. The minister representative of the Presbyterian Church in the USA was the Rev. William P. Merrill, D.D., a signer of the Auburn Affirmation. The work of the commission was largely financed by John D. Rockefeller, Jr., who had voiced his opposition to historic Christianity.[4]

Representatives of seven denominations—Congregational, Methodist, Episcopal, Northern Baptist, Protestant Episcopal, Presbyterian Church in the USA, Reformed Church in America, and the United Presbyterian Church—met unofficially in New York City in 1930 to consider the foreign missions enterprise. This group constituted the thirty-five direc-

2   *The Presbyterian* 93 (November 22, 1923), 4. See also chapter two.
3   *Minutes of the General Assembly* 1924, Part 1, 187.
4   John D. Rockefeller," The Christian Church, What of Its Future?" *The Saturday Evening Post* (February 9, 1918).

tors of the Foreign Missionary Inquiry, of which seven formed an executive committee. The inquiry resulting was independent of the denominational mission boards, but it received their cooperation in securing the facts. The inquiry was restricted to Burma, China, India, and Japan, and the work was divided into two parts; first, an accumulation of data, and secondly, "an appraisal of these facts in the light of the widest possible consideration of the meaning of the mission enterprises and of the world condition in which it is now, and is to be, carried out."[5]

The Institute of Social and Religious Research was engaged to gather the data and research workers were sent to the designated fields for this purpose. In September, 1931, this part of the report was completed and the facts were placed in the hands of the Commission of Appraisal of fifteen members. These commissioners made a visit to the several mission fields with the following purpose in mind:

> To aid laymen to determine their attitude toward Foreign Missions, by reconsidering the functions of such Missions in the world today. With this general aim,
>
> a. To make an objective appraisal of their activities in the fields visited;
>
> b. To observe the effect of Missions on the life of the peoples of the Orient;
>
> c. In the light of the existing conditions and profiting, though not bound, by missionary experience to work out a practical program for today, offering recommendations as to the extent to which missionary activities of every sort should be continued or changed.[6]

In September, 1932, seven volumes were issued by the commission containing the data gathered concerning the various aspects of the foreign missions enterprise and also the book, Re-Thinking Missions, which summarized the facts according to the foregoing expressed purpose. The last named book is of the most importance and contains three parts: I. General Principles, chapters 1-4; II. Aspects of Mission Work, chapters 5-12; III. Administration, chapters 12-14.

The parts of the book which have to do with personnel and methods are not so important to this study, but the recommendations of this commission with reference to the approach of Christianity to the other religions, and the message which missionaries should preach, are of the utmost concern in this study. The commission makes it plain that Christianity should unite with the other religions, Islam, Hinduism, or

---

5   Re-Thinking Missions (New York: Harper & Brothers, 1932).
6   Ibid., xi.

Buddhism, in a common front against materialism, naturalism, and immorality.

> It is no longer, which prophet? or which book? It is whether any prophet, book, revelation, rite, Church is to be trusted. All the old oracles are seeing a new sign: the scorn on the faces of students who know the experiments in anti-religion in Russia and non-religion in Turkey, and the actual religionlessness of much western life. . . . The case that must now be stated is the case for any religion at all.[7]
>
> . . . Thus it is that Christianity finds itself in point of fact aligned in this world-wide issue with the non-Christian faiths of Asia. . . . There are thus several factors conspiring to one end: namely, *the necessity that the modern mission make a positive effort, first of all to know and understand the religions around it, then to recognize and associate itself with whatever kindred elements there are in them.*[8]

There is no need to multiply these quotations because the whole attitude of the book is predicated upon the assumption that the germ of truth exists in all religions and that it is the duty of the missionary to recognize that germ of truth as the least common denominator and build thereupon.

In regard to the message of the missionary it is stated,

> The original objective of the mission might be stated as the conquest of the world by Christianity: it was a world benevolence conceived in terms of a world campaign. There was one way of salvation and one only, one name, one atonement: this plan with its particular historical center in the career of Jesus must become the point of regard for every human soul. The universal quality of Christianity lay not alone in its valid principles of truth and morals, but in an essential paradox, the universal claim of one historical fact: the work of Christ. . . . Hence, in respect to its central fact Christianity was necessarily dogmatic—it could only say *Ecce Homo*, Behold the Man; and it was committed to a certain intolerance, beneficent in purpose—in the interest of the soul it could allow no substitute for Christ.[9]

Concerning this point of view, the following hope was expressed, "In that case, the hope would be that Christianity, instead of tying itself to the sinking bulks, would hold itself clear and give a distinctive version of what religion, in its purity, may mean."[10]

It is very plain from these quotations that the modernist message of missions is entirely different from that of historic Christianity. According

---

7   *Ibid.*, 32-33.
8   *Ibid.*, 33.
9   *Ibid.*, 35-36.
10   *Ibid.*, 36.

to historic Christianity a missionary is not to make common cause with pagan religions, but to show these religionists the error of their ways and to point them to the one way of salvation through Jesus Christ. This was the method and the message of the apostles and has been for the Christian church these many centuries. In other words, the recommendations of the commission would mean a radical departure for the mission enterprise.

Since the commission and its report had received such wide newspaper comment, the publication of *Re-Thinking Missions* focused the attention of the Christian world upon foreign missions and demonstrated anew that drastic changes in missionary work and in the missionary message were taking place within the Protestant church. Ministers and organizations in practically every Protestant church made some mention of the report. In fact, it was the issuance of this book, as well as the presence of Pearl S. Buck on the foreign missionary roster of the Presbyterian Church in the USA, which crystallized the thoughts of Dr. Machen on foreign missions as they were related to the Presbyterian Church in the USA.

This Pearl S. Buck was no obscure missionary in a forgotten part of the world, but one of the most prominent and successful novelists of the day who lived in China and was associated with Nanking University. What makes the situation more reprehensible from the standpoint of the Board of Foreign Missions of the Presbyterian Church in the USA is the fact that Dr. Robert E. Speer, senior secretary of the board, was president of the board of founders of Nanking University. In fact, Dr. Speer's attitude was a source of amazement to Christian leaders.[11]

The manifest indifference of the board toward Pearl Buck's unbelief and the compromising attitude of the board toward *Re-Thinking Missions* produced the conviction that the time to take drastic action had come. Dr. Machen felt compelled to make public his opinion to the New Brunswick Presbytery of which he was a member. This he did in the form of an overture.

> I am presenting this Overture not because I desire to do so but because I am compelled to do so. I should be far happier if I did not know certain things about the Board of Foreign Missions of the Presbyterian Church in the U.S.

---

11   Editorial, *The Moody Monthly* (January 1934).

A.; but I do know those things, and the knowledge of them places upon me a duty which I cannot evade. My membership in a Presbytery seems to me to be a sacred trust, and it is in discharge of the obligations of that trust that I am presenting the proposed Overture and some of the reasons which have compelled me to advocate it.[12]

The overture was presented to the presbytery at its meeting on January 24, 1933, and made the order of the day for April 11, 1933. Dr. Robert E. Speer was invited to be present as the representative spokesman for the Board of Foreign Missions. The overture called for care on the part of the board to keep modernists from the board and the roll of missionaries, and to avoid doctrinally compromising union enterprises.[13]

Dr. Machen's argument in favor of the overture was printed in a 110-page pamphlet entitled, *Modernism and the Board of Foreign Missions of the Presbyterian Church in the U.S.A.*, and sent, before the meeting, to every minister and elder in the presbytery as well as to every member and secretary of the Board of Foreign Missions.

The drama and meaning of that day will remain long in the memory of those who were present to hear the debate. Before that large audience in the Fourth Presbyterian Church in Trenton, New Jersey, appeared two men, one the outstanding conservative theologian of America and the other the missionary leader of American Presbyterianism.

It was more than a conflict between two brilliant men set for an academic debate and verbal pyrotechnics for the entertainment and intellectual stimulation of the audience. It was even more than the clash of two opponents each ready to prove that his presentation of the case was right. In reality, it was a dramatic meeting in which two conceptions of Christianity were presented by two of the ablest men in the Christian world, one the historic orthodox point of view and the other the doctrinally indifferent attitude. One stood for a militant defense of the gospel and the other advocated a pacifistic view toward those ministers and missionaries of the church who were modernistic in their theology. The final outcome of the struggle in the church warrants the claim that this debate was one of real historic significance, and one that has had an

---

12   J. Gresham Machen, *Modernism and the Board of Foreign Missions of the Presbyterian Church in the U.S.A.* (Philadelphia: J. Gresham Machen, 1933), 4.

13   *Ibid.*, 1. See also Appendix, note 10.

influence on individuals and churches wherever the Presbyterian Church in the USA is represented both in America and abroad.

At the very outset Dr. Machen made it plain that his sole standard of judgment was the Word of God, and that every missionary, every institution, and every piece of literature supported and endorsed by the board must be tested and judged by adherence to the Bible. There are many standards of judgment, he said, but the Presbyterian Church in the USA has stated in its Confession of Faith, "The Supreme Judge, by whom all controversies of religion are to be determined, . . . and in whose sentence we are to rest, can be no other but the Holy Spirit speaking in the Scripture."[14]

With these preliminary remarks he plunged into the main stream of his argument and mentioned briefly the evidences of modernism in the Board of Foreign Missions contained in his pamphlet. Only one hour was allowed for the presentation of these facts, but the pamphlet had been sent to the presbyters well in advance of the meeting, so that the supporting evidence for his address was known to everyone present.

The moral earnestness, the dignity, and the tender appeal with which Dr. Machen closed his argument brought a hushed silence over the audience. He pled with them to return to the Word of God, to forsake the wisdom of man, to turn against the trend of the age, and to be faithful to the Christ of the Bible.

The main thesis of Dr. Machen's charges against the Board of Foreign Missions as stated in his pamphlet was that the board had become so entangled with modernism that the need for reform was imperative. He proceeded to prove this contention by making six charges against the board, all substantiated by evidence.

His first complaint had to do with the attitude of the Board of Foreign Missions toward the book *Re-Thinking Missions*. The board issued an official "Action of the Board of Foreign Missions," passed on November 21, 1932, and published in pamphlet form as well as in the *Presbyterian Magazine*, January, 1933. In this statement the board made no clearcut pronouncement against the appraisal commission's report, which had made "an attack against the very heart of the Christian religion."[15] Mr. James M. Speers and Mrs. John H. Finley were members of the Board

---

14   *The Confession of Faith*, chapter 1, section X.
15   Machen, *Modernism and the Board*, 6.

of Foreign Missions, and at the same time members of the Laymen's
Foreign Missions Inquiry. Dr. Machen asked the question,

> Did it [the Board] agree with its Vice-President, Mr. Speers, and another of its
> members, Mrs. Finley, in their action in issuing the Appraisal Commission's
> Report, or did it repudiate this action of these two of its members, and
> pronounce the Report of the Appraisal Commission as being, what it clearly
> is, hostile to the roots of the Christian religion?

Dr. Machen answered his own question: "It made no answer to these
inquiries. It dodged the issue."[16] The statement of the board relative to
the aim of missions reads,

> The supreme and controlling aim of Foreign Missions is to make the Lord
> Jesus Christ known to all men as their Divine Saviour and to persuade them
> to become His disciples; to gather these disciples into Christian Churches
> which shall be self-propagating, self-supporting, self-governing; to cooperate, so
> long as necessary, with these Churches in the evangelizing of their countrymen,
> and in bringing to bear on all human life the spirit and principles of Christ.[17]

In reply to this Dr. Machen said,

> Where is there any reference here to the things really distinctive of Christian
> missions, where is there, at least, any reference to such things in terms which
> are not often distorted by modern unbelief to mean something entirely different
> from what they used to mean?[18]

---

16   *Ibid.*, 7.
17   *Preliminary Reports of the Missionary and Benevolent Boards to the 145th
      General Assembly of the Presbyterian Church in the U.S.A.*, 16.
18   Machen, *Modernism and the Board*, 9. On March 20, 1933, the board
      took the following action which was not made public until after the
      meeting at New Brunswick Presbytery on April 11, 1933. "At the
      meeting of the Board on March 20, 1933, a unanimous vote declared,
      regarding the first four chapters of the Appraisal Report, that (1)
      These chapters do not conform to the fundamental aim of foreign
      missions as expressed in the manual of the Board, (2) The Board
      affirms its loyalty to the Standards of the Presbyterian Church and
      maintains the absolute finality, sufficiency and universality of the
      Gospel of Christ." *Report of Board to 145th General Assembly.*

The second charge of modernism against the board concerned its vacillating attitude toward Pearl S. Buck, the author of *The Good Earth*. Dr. Machen quoted largely from two articles by Mrs. Buck, "The Laymen's Mission Report," and "Is There a Case for Foreign Missions?" Dr. Machen's quotations from her articles very plainly show outspoken opposition to historic Christianity:

> The first three chapters [*Re-Thinking Missions*] are the finest exposition of religion I have ever read.[19]
>
> To some of us He is still the divine son of God, born of the virgin Mary, conceived by the Holy Spirit. But to many of us He has ceased to be that. . . . I do not believe in original sin. . . . I agree with the Chinese who feel their people should be protected from such superstition (Biblical teaching about salvation from sin).[20]

Such statements are so obviously opposed to historic Christianity that Dr. Machen hardly felt called upon to answer them.

When Dr. Machen first made these damaging charges against the board for allowing Mrs. Buck to remain as a missionary, the board had done nothing about it. At a later date, Mrs. Buck resigned as a missionary and the board accepted her resignation "with regret." The minute of the board reads,

> A letter was presented from Mrs. J. Lossing Buck, of the Kiangan Mission, requesting to be released from responsible relationship to the Board. The Board had hoped that this step might be avoided, but in view of all the considerations involved and with deep regret it voted to acquiesce in her request. The Board expressed to Mrs. Buck its sincere appreciation of the service which she has rendered during the past sixteen years and its earnest prayer that her unusual abilities may continue to be richly used in behalf of the people of China.

On May 31, 1934, Dr. Robert E. Speer in writing to the Rev. Carl McIntire stated,

> The Board did accept Mrs. Buck's resignation with regret. . . . Its regret in Mrs. Buck's case was because she was unable any longer to hold and proclaim the Christian faith as she had held it on her first appointment by the Southern

---

19   Pearl S. Buck, "The Laymen's Mission Report," *The Christian Century* 49 (November 23, 1932), 1434.

20   Pearl S. Buck, "Is There a Case for Foreign Missions?" *Harpers Magazine* (January 1933), 148-150; (these quotations appear in a different order in Mrs. Buck's article—editor).

Presbyterian Church as a missionary to China and her appointment as a missionary of our Church when she married Mr. Buck.[21]

Dr. Speer's answer seems rather strange, particularly when it is recalled that he had been president of the board of founders of Nanking University with which Mrs. Buck had been associated for many years, and must have known her attitude. Furthermore, on the face of the matter surely no one would possibly interpret the action as Dr. Speer interprets it.

Dr. Machen's third accusation concerned the board and its attitude toward the Auburn Affirmation. He made it clear that one of the most important officers of the board, the candidate secretary, Rev. Lindsay S. B. Hadley, was a signer of the Auburn Affirmation. Dr. Machen wrote,

> To the Candidate Secretary is entrusted the delicate task of interviewing candidates for the foreign field and of encouraging or discouraging them in their high ambition. Is there any agent of the Church who ought to be more completely clear as to what the Church's message is than the occupant of this position?[22]

In 1926, Dr. Machen had written to the board asking for an explanation of the presence of five signers of the Auburn Affirmation on the board. In reply Dr. Speer wrote, "We know of not one who does not accept the Constitution and Standards of the Church and who is not truly and loyally evangelical."[23] At the time that this letter was written there were five out of fifteen members of the board who were signers of the Auburn Affirmation. To such a state of affairs Dr. Machen made the reply, "It must be said very plainly that Bible-believing Christians can have no confidence in a Board whose standards of what is truly and loyally evangelical are such as that."[24]

The fourth count against the board concerned the modernist propaganda by the candidate department. This department recommended such books as *The Meaning of Faith*, by Harry Emerson Fosdick, *The Marks of a World Christian*, by D. J. Fleming, and *The Devotional Diary*, by J. H. Oldham. Dr. Machen examined these books and, judging by the standards of the Bible, he found them to be contrary to historic

---

21   Rev. Carl McIntire, *Dr. Robert E. Speer, the Board of Foreign Missions of the Presbyterian Church in the U.S.A. and Modernism* (n.p., April 11, 1935), 78.

22   Machen, *Modernism and the Board*, 25.

23   Ibid., 26.

24   Ibid.

Christianity. As a matter of fact, the Rev. Harry Emerson Fosdick, D.D., is regarded as one of the most outstanding modernist ministers in the bounds of the nominally Christian church. The other two authors are not as well-known, but their books which were there recommended are as offensive to the gospel of the Bible as the book of Dr. Fosdick.

Dr. Machen's fifth charge against the board was its commendation of such men as Sherwood Eddy and Kagawa. Dr. Machen made it clear that the teachings of Sherwood Eddy and Kagawa strike at the very heart of the Christian message as understood by the church for these many centuries.

The last indictment of the board was concerned with the fact that the board cooperates with modernist union enterprises in China. For evidence in this respect Dr. Machen depended upon communications from Dr. Albert B. Dodd of the North China Theological Seminary, a missionary of the church, and Chancellor Arie Kok of the Netherlands legation in Peiping. The citations of modernist propaganda and cooperation with modernist union enterprises in China of the board are overwhelming.

It is difficult to understand how one could read this pamphlet or have heard Dr. Machen and not come to the conclusion that the Board of Foreign Missions of the Presbyterian Church in the USA had been unfaithful to its trust.

Dr. Robert E. Speer spoke after Dr. Machen, but in no way was his address an answer to the charges in the pamphlet which had been sent to him well in advance of the meeting. In the main he said that the board was a servant of the church and, as such, it was up to the general assembly to take whatever actions were necessary to remedy a bad situation if that obtained. Dr. Speer defended the actions of the board and its missionaries and declared that these men were as faithful to the Bible as the men at home. This latter statement no one would deny, since the ministers of the church at home were probably less true to the Bible. Instead of replying to the charges in the pamphlet, Dr. Speer did attempt to answer the four parts of the overture which Dr. Machen had introduced. Concerning section one, he stated that it singled out the Board of Foreign Missions and so was discriminatory. Section two he declared was out of order because the board had no authority to sit in judgment upon a minister who was in good and regular standing. Dr. Speer could not deny that the candidate secretary was a signer of the Auburn Affirmation. Relative to section three, he stated that the question blanks which were sent by the board to prospective candidates in no way indicated that a tolerance for opposing views was essential to a missionary's attitude. The last paragraph of the overture refers to the dangers which lurk in union enterprises and the necessity for constant vigilance. This Dr. Speer admitted, but he also made it clear that there is danger in separation.

The Presbytery of New Brunswick voted overwhelmingly against Dr. Machen's overture, but this did not stop the questions and doubts which the pamphlet had created in the minds of Presbyterians everywhere. On May 1, 1933, the Presbytery of Philadelphia passed the identical overture so that the whole matter thus forced itself upon the attention of the general assembly.[25]

When the general assembly met in Columbus, Ohio, on May 25, 1933, the issue which overshadowed all other items on the docket was the overture from the Presbytery of Philadelphia, which was concurred in by the Presbytery of Aberdeen, and other overtures of a similar nature from Hudson, Chester, and Northumberland Presbyteries concerning the Board of Foreign Missions and its alleged unfaithfulness to the doctrinal standards of the church.[26] Since the boards of the church are the creation of the general assembly, this was the proper procedure for attempting to remedy a bad situation in any board.

The utter weakness of the Board of Foreign Missions' answer to the allegations in the overture was seen by the tactics of those who chose to "whitewash" the activities of the board, and so demonstrate their loyalty to it. Every conceivable parliamentary trick was used to stifle debate and to stir the emotions of the commissioners to loyalty to the boards of the church. In the midst of the majority report of the assembly's Committee on Foreign Missions, for example, the memorial roll of missionaries was read, a prayer was made, and then the whole assembly sang, "For All the Saints Who From Their Labors Rest," thus prejudicing the assembly in favor of the report. This show of bad taste in the midst of a controversial issue was evidently done to put the majority report in a good light. Another demonstration of prejudice and bad taste was the introduction which Dr. McDowell, the moderator, gave to Dr. Speer when he said, "Dr. Speer . . . of whom it could be said, as it was said of his Master, 'In him was life and the life was the light of men.'"[27]

25   Christianity Today 4 (May 1933), 31.
26   Minutes of the General Assembly 1933, Part 1, 27-29.
27   Christianity Today 4 (June 1933), 12-13.

The majority report of the assembly's Committee on Foreign Missions occupied practically all of the time allotted to the subject in extolling the virtues and accomplishments of the board.[28] Those who represented the minority on this committee, Peter Stam, Jr., an elder from Narberth, Pennsylvania, and the Rev. Robert S. Marsden, of Middletown, Pennsylvania, wished to speak in behalf of the overture, but were allotted a sum total of fifteen minutes. The usual courtesy of printing the minority report was denied. The minority made the following recommendations:

> Therefore, in answer to the overtures from the Presbyteries of Philadelphia and Aberdeen, and in reply to the other overtures, papers and memorials, the Committee recommends that the following resolution be adopted by this Assembly:
> "The 145th General Assembly has learned with sorrow of the acts and policies of its Board of Foreign Missions which have seriously impaired confidence in the minds of thousands of loyal and earnest Presbyterians. This Assembly proclaims anew its loyalty and love for the pure and everlasting gospel of the Lord Jesus Christ, declaring to men everywhere that there is only one way of salvation—through the substitutionary, atoning sacrifice of Christ upon the cross, where He shed His precious blood for the redemption of lost and sinful men. The Assembly pledges that the Presbyterian Church in the U.S.A. will, through its Board of Foreign Missions, preach this one, only gospel to the uttermost parts of the earth, to the exclusion of all other gospels or false paths to God."
> In order to take the first practical step to make this pledge effective and thus to reestablish confidence the Committee nominates the following persons to serve for three years as members of the Board of the Class of 1933-1936: . . .
> (Signed)
> Peter Stam, Jr.
> Robert S. Marsden

Dr. Machen appeared before the assembly's Standing Committee on Foreign Missions to defend his charges against the board, but the members of the committee were so obviously prejudiced that he made little impression upon them.

The majority report was overwhelmingly adopted, and the attempt to reform the Board of Foreign Missions in the most effective way according to Presbyterian procedure had failed completely. There was nothing left to do but to announce the formation of an independent organization operating outside the bounds of the church, and separate from the church, which would carry on truly biblical and truly Presbyterian foreign

---

28   *Minutes of the General Assembly 1933*, Part 1, 153-60.

missions. The conservatives who had attempted to bring about a reform in the Board of Foreign Missions were determined to have a foreign mission agency which would be true to the Bible. While still at Columbus, Ohio, Dr. Machen and the Rev. H. McAllister Griffiths, both of whom had been leaders in the reform movement, issued the following statement:

> In view of the action of the General Assembly of the Presbyterian Church in the U.S.A. resisting the movement for reform of the Board of Foreign Missions, a new Board will be organized by Bible-believing Christians to promote truly Biblical and truly Presbyterian mission work.[29]

On June 27, 1933, the Independent Board for Presbyterian Foreign Missions was formally organized and on October 17, 1933, the constitution was adopted and the following officers elected: the Rev. J. Gresham Machen, president, the Rev. Merrill T. MacPherson, vice-president, the Rev. H. McAllister Griffiths, secretary, and Murray Forst Thompson, treasurer. The board also issued an invitation to the Rev. Charles J. Woodbridge, a missionary of the church in the French Cameroun, West Africa, to serve as general secretary.[30]

The Rev. Charles J. Woodbridge returned to this country and began serving as general secretary in February, 1934. He accepted the responsibility because he was convinced that the old board was no longer faithful to its trust, and that an independent board which would be truly biblical and truly Presbyterian would have to be established.

With the coming of Mr. Woodbridge the Independent Board began to extend its influence and activities. Mr. Woodbridge, whose father had been for over forty years an honored missionary of the Presbyterian Church in the US in China, was no ordinary general secretary, but a man of exceptional personality and evangelistic appeal. As a result of his work, funds were contributed to the board with such liberality that within two months after his arrival, the Rev. and Mrs. Henry W. Coray were appointed in April, 1934, as the first missionaries of the board to be stationed in China.[31]

Dissatisfaction with the policy of the Board of Foreign Missions, however, was not confined to Philadelphia nor to Dr. Machen. The

---

29   *Christianity Today* 4 (June 1933), 13.
30   *Christianity Today* 4 (October 1933), 11-12.
31   *Christianity Today* 4 (April 1934), 23.

Presbytery of Chester sent a statement to the board on January 23, 1934, part of which is as follows:

> 1. ... Rightly or wrongly, the feeling prevails in many quarters that our Board has spoken feebly when the occasion demanded a thunder tone.
> 2. The Board's Candidate Department, so influential in determining the character of the reinforcements sent to the field, should be above suspicion in the matter of its loyalty to the doctrinal standards of our church. ...
> 3. We believe that there is an urgent need of improvement in mission study books recommended to our people. ...
> 4. The conviction prevails among many that the nature of some of the educational work in which our Board has a share is of questionable value. [32]

The board's reply to Chester Presbytery gave no new light on the accusations which had been levelled at it by Dr. Machen and others.

In April, 1935, the Rev. Carl McIntire, pastor of the Presbyterian Church in Collingswood, New Jersey, published a 96-page pamphlet entitled *Dr. Robert E. Speer, the Board of Foreign Missions of the Presbyterian Church in the U.S.A. and Modernism*, in which he gave additional proof of modernism in the Board of Foreign Missions along the same lines as Dr. Machen, that is, concerning the literature, missionaries, members of the board, and union enterprises of the board. Dr. Speer's reply to these charges was included in Mr. McIntire's booklet, but in most of the instances he denied the charges of modernism and "whitewashed" the board entirely.

Another indictment of the Board of Foreign Missions was made by the Rev. Donald G. Barnhouse, D.D., pastor of the Tenth Presbyterian Church in Philadelphia, who had made a sixteen months' tour of some of the mission fields of the church. In his report of this tour Dr. Barnhouse charged that modernism was to be found among some of the missionaries and in some of the missionary enterprises. [33] But his conclusions differed greatly from Dr. Machen's in that he advocated that the church give to the board, especially to its sound missionaries, and urged further that the church try to elect more members to the board who would be loyal to the standards of the church. Although Dr. Barnhouse's conclusions were weak and futile, nevertheless his testimony to modernism in the Board of Foreign Missions added to the weight of the evidence against the board.

---

32   *Christianity Today* 4 (February 1934), 22-23.
33   *The Presbyterian* 105 (October 31, 1935), 1, 5-10.

In addition to these rather formal protests against modernism in the Board of Foreign Missions, many articles continued to be written and overtures sent to the general assembly as late as 1935, two years after the Independent Board had been organized.

A strong indictment was delivered in an address by Dr. Charles G. Trumbull, editor of *The Sunday School Times*, at a mass meeting called by Presbyterian laymen in Philadelphia, February 28, 1935. Under the title, "Foreign Missionary Betrayals of the Faith," Dr. Trumbull asked the question, "What are the policies and practises of our Board of Foreign Missions that are undermining the work of the sound evangelical missionaries in the foreign field? They are *the policies and practises of Modernism.*" He then listed some of those policies and practises as evidenced by members of the board itself, by missionaries, by union enterprises, by the literature issued by the board, and concluded his address by saying, "How can *unfaithful Board members and unfaithful Board secretaries be expected to deal properly with unfaithful missionaries?*"[34]

Protests and communications relative to modernism were also sent to the Board of Foreign Missions so that the discontent with the board mounted higher and higher. In the meantime, the power and influence of the Independent Board grew as each month saw more converts to its cause. This alarming situation frightened the leaders of the ecclesiastical organization of the church to such an extent that unprecedented and drastic action was decided upon. The general assembly meeting in Cleveland, Ohio, May, 1934, was to witness the awful tragedy of the issuance of a deliverance which was to cause those who were most loyal to the Bible to resign, and so to deprive the church of a group who had been zealous in maintaining the truths of the gospel. The rulers of the church knew no bounds in their determination to rid the church of the so-called disturbers of the peace.

---

34   Charles G. Trumbull, "Foreign Missionary Betrayals of the Faith," *The Sunday School Times* 77 (March 23, 1935), 195-99.

7
The Deliverance of the
1934 General Assembly

IT BECAME increasingly evident that some official action against the organizers of the Independent Board would be taken at the 1934 General Assembly. Dr. John McDowell, moderator of the 1933 General Assembly, issued a statement in the fall of 1933 which hinted strongly that the formation of the Independent Board was, in his opinion, in violation of the provisions of the constitution of the Presbyterian Church in the USA.[1]

On May 3, 1934, Dr. Machen, the Rev. Paul Woolley, the Rev. H. McAllister Griffiths, and Mr. Murray Forst Thompson were called into a conference with representatives of the general council and told that it was the unanimous opinion of the general council that the Independent Board was contrary to the fundamental principles of the constitution of the church, and that the members of the Independent Board were violating their ordination and membership vows.[2] These men were also informed that a document was in the press setting forth the council's

---

1   Press release appearing in *The Presbyterian* 103 (November 16, 1933), 8. See Appendix, note 11.

2   *Statement of J. Gresham Machen to the Special Committee of the Presbytery of New Brunswick in the Presbyterian Church of the U. S. A. Which Was Appointed by the Presbytery at Its Meeting on Tuesday, September 25, 1934, to "Confer Further with Dr. Machen with Respect to his Relationship with The Independent Board for Presbyterian Foreign Missions, and to Make Recommendations to the Presbytery for the Disposition of the Matters Involving the Mandate of the General Assembly to the Presbytery and the Relation of Dr. Machen to The Independent Board of Presbyterian Foreign Missions"* (Philadelphia: J. Gresham Machen, 1934), 51, 54.

reasons for this opinion and that this document was to be sent to all the commissioners of the coming assembly.

Shortly before the convening of the 146th General Assembly at Cleveland, Ohio, on May 24, 1934, the general council of the general assembly sent out the above-mentioned document, a 43-page pamphlet, *Studies of the Constitution of the Presbyterian Church in the U.S.A.* These so-called *Studies* purported to lay the groundwork for the deliverance which was adopted by that assembly, and enunciated the principle that every member of the church is required by the constitution to support the missionary program of the church, in the same way that each member must take part in the Lord's Supper.[3]

The first question which arises is, Did the general council have the authority to issue such a document without direct orders from the general assembly, or was the general council presumptuous in this matter? The council defends its action by quoting chapter XXVI, section II, of the Form of Government which lists as one of the duties of the council, "to consider between annual meetings of the General Assembly cases of serious embarrassment or emergency concerning the benevolent and missionary work of the church, and to provide direct means of relief."

No one need be left in doubt as to the powers of the general council with reference to initiating action against members of the Independent Board. Chapter XXVI, section XII, of the Form of Government reads:

> General Councils shall handle and consider only such administrative business as may be referred to them by the electing judicatories as indicated in the succeeding sections, and shall have no power of initiation except as hereinafter provided. No judicial business shall be referred to a General Council.

The Rev. William B. Pugh, D.D., the alleged author of the *Studies* and now the stated clerk of the general assembly, claimed that this section refers only to general councils of presbyteries and synods and not to the general council of the general assembly as interpreted by the General Assembly of 1930.[4]

In answer to Dr. Pugh, it can be said that the interpretation of the general assembly is not a part of the constitution of the church, but simply an action of one assembly which has no binding effect upon the

3   *Minutes of the General Assembly* 1934, Part 1, 70-71, 110-11. See
      Appendix, note 12.
4   W. B. Pugh, "Presbyterians Are Awake," *The Presbyterian* 104
      (September 6 and 13, 1934), 6-9, 8-11; and *Minutes of the General*
      Assembly 1930, Part 1, 192.

succeeding assemblies. Even if this interpretation had binding effect upon the succeeding assemblies, the second part of that interpretation proves beyond doubt that the general council erred in initiating action against the Independent Board. It reads, "That business of a doctrinal or judicial character . . . shall not be originated by or referred to the General Council of the General Assembly." No one can deny that the business regarding the Independent Board was of a judicial or doctrinal character. As the Northumberland Presbytery stated, this action was practically "conviction before trial."[5]

Dr. Machen characterized the claims of the general council as follows:

> The whole notion that the General Council is a sort of ad interim Star Chamber court and supreme administrative agency combined is entirely abhorrent to the Constitution of the Church and entirely contrary to the sections of the Constitution in which the powers of the General Council are defined.[6]

It is also apparent that the organization of the Independent Board was not the cause for "serious embarrassment or emergency" in the missionary work of the church, but rather the result of a deplorable situation. The Board of Foreign Missions had refused to take a positive stand against the Laymen's Report and Pearl Buck's unbelief. It is very doubtful that the reductions in missionary giving would have been less even if the Independent Board had never been organized. Bible-believers had lost confidence in the board and its program and could not be induced to contribute unless a radical reform took place.

The *Studies* further argue that the general assembly "has all the power the Church would have if it were possible to convene the Church together in one place."[7] The only agency in the church which would have power even approaching this in degree is the general assembly plus two-thirds of the presbyteries, which combination can amend the Confession of Faith.[8] If the general assembly alone assumed such power it would simply nullify the constitution and place mere acts of the general assembly, which in themselves are only pious advice, on a par with constitutional provisions. The constitution has very wisely provided for protection of the individual, the session, and the presbytery against any tyranny of the

5   *Christianity Today* 5 (November 1934), 147.
6   Machen, *Modernism and the Board*, 50.
7   *Studies of the Constitution of the Presbyterian Church in the U.S.A.* (n.p., General Council of the General Assembly, 1934), II.
8   *Form of Government*, chapter XXIV, sections II-IV.

higher courts. As a matter of fact, the Presbytery of Northumberland exercised this right and repudiated the action of the general assembly with reference to the Independent Board when it adopted the report of its Ad Interim Committee on Bills and Overtures which stated that the action was unconstitutional.[9]

The entire pamphlet sent out by the general council and its argument that a serious emergency existed in the missionary work of the church is based upon the conviction that the Independent Board is within the church and so subject to the jurisdiction of the church courts. Such an argument is fallacious.

The Independent Board never made the claim that it was a missionary organization of the Presbyterian Church in the USA. The word "Independent" in its name implies that the board is not a part of the constituted mission agencies of the church. The first issue of the Independent Board's official magazine states, "Why is it called the 'Independent Board'? Because, according to its Charter, it is independent of ecclesiastical control. Its Charter expressly states that it is ecclesiastically independent."[10] In a statement adopted by the Executive Committee of the Independent Board on May 10, 1934, the independency of the board is clearly enunciated.[11]

As soon as the general secretary of the Independent Board took office in February, 1934, he sent out a pamphlet stating the program of the board. In this pamphlet no claim whatsoever is made that the board is within the church. Quite the contrary is stated. "It [the Independent Board] is independent in that it is not responsible, as an organization, to the General Assembly of the Presbyterian Church in the U.S.A., or to any other ecclesiastical body."[12] This is true of all the Independent Board literature, so that the statement of the general council that "certain ministers and laymen of the Presbyterian Church in organizing within

---

9   *Christianity Today* 5 (November 1934), 147.
10   *The Independent Board Bulletin* 1 (January 1935), 4.
11   *Christianity Today* 5 (May 1934), 27. See Appendix, note 13.
12   Charles J. Woodbridge, *The Independent Board for Presbyterian Foreign Missions: A Statement as to Its Organization and Program* (Philadelphia: n.p., [1934]), 1.

the denomination an 'Independent Board for Presbyterian Foreign Missions'" is without basis in fact. Furthermore, there were members of the Independent Board who were not ministers or members of the Presbyterian Church in the USA. One was a minister of the Presbyterian Church in the United States, and one was a member of another Protestant communion. How could an organization with such a mixed membership claim to be within the Presbyterian Church in the USA or be judged to be within the church?

The question then resolves itself to this: "Does the law of the church prohibit the formation of the Independent Board?" [13] Chapter XXIII of the Form of Government states that there may be organizations "for the conduct of a special work for missionary and other benevolent purposes, or for the purpose of instruction in religion and development in Christian nurture." Such agencies must be responsible to a session, presbytery, synod, or general assembly, depending upon the scope of their activities. But this chapter contemplates organizations within the church which have a relationship to its judicatories and in no way includes boards which operate outside of the jurisdiction of the church, even though members of such boards may also be ministers or members of the church. Individuals within the Presbyterian Church in the USA have a perfect right to associate themselves together along with others to form a charitable organization. In fact, many such agencies with the word Presbyterian in their title exist. As the editor of *Christianity Today* wrote,

> It is contrary to fact, we believe, to state that the Independent Board is an organization "within the Church" in the sense alleged by the General Council. If so, it would seem that the Presbyterian and Reformed Publishing Company, under whose auspices *Christianity Today* is published, is also an organization "within the Church" and subject to General Assembly control. It, too, is incorporated under the laws of the Commonwealth of Pennsylvania with a Constitution and ByLaws. All its officers and members are either ministers or elders of the Presbyterian Church in the U.S.A. Moreover, inasmuch as its editors are subject to its Board of Directors, it "assumes the direction of persons who are subject to the authority of church judicatories" and to that extent exercises what the General Council calls "ecclesiastical functions." It would seem also that without authority of the General Assembly it exercises what the general council calls "administrative functions" as it appeals to Presbyterians

---

13   See Murray Forst Thompson, "Have the Organizers of the Independent Board for Presbyterian Foreign Missions Violated the Law of the Presbyterian Church in the U.S.A?" *Christianity Today* 4 (December 1933), 4, 10-12.

to "provide the ways and means"—to make financial contributions in other words—by which the paper may continue to be published. What is true of the Presbyterian and Reformed Publishing Company is also true in all essential respects of the companies that publish *The Presbyterian*, *The Presbyterian Advance* and *The Presbyterian Banner*, not to mention a host of other educational and benevolent corporations. We submit that the Independent Board for Presbyterian Foreign Missions is no more an organization "within the Church" than are our religious newspapers or any educational or benevolent organization that employs Presbyterian ministers or that appeals to Presbyterians for financial support.[14]

It was further argued by those opposed to the Independent Board that the ministers and elders who had formed the Independent Board violated their ordination vows which promised, among other things, to study the peace, unity, and purity of the church.[15] It will be noticed that the vow pledges the minister "to be zealous and faithful in maintaining the truths of the gospel, and the purity and peace of the Church; whatever persecution or opposition may arise unto them on that account." It is plain from this pledge that peace is not to be gained at any price, but rather that the purity of the church and the truths of the gospel are to be maintained so that true peace will prevail. The minister is to accept "whatever persecution or opposition may arise . . . on that account," so that controversy is not to be avoided but rather borne for the sake of the gospel. Members of the Independent Board could rightfully claim that they were most faithful to their vows for they attempted with all their powers to warn the church of unbelief in its midst.

The argument of the council is based upon the false idea that the liberty of an individual ceases when he joins the Presbyterian Church in the USA. As Mr. Griffiths and Mr. Murray Forst Thompson so ably put it:

> The whole burden of the General Council's argument is that when one joins the Presbyterian Church he has exercised his one and only act of freedom, and henceforth must either be obedient to all that he is ordered to do, or withdraw from the Church. And this in a Church whose Standards declare, "All synods and councils since the Apostles' times, whether general or particular, may err, and have erred; therefore they are not to be made the rule of faith and practise

---

14   *Christianity Today* 5 (July 1934), 35.
15   *Form of Government*, chapter XV, section XII, and chapter XIII, section IV.

. . ." (Confession of Faith, chapter XXXI, section III). The General Council thus flouts the law of the Church, and requires of its members an obedience to "synods and councils" which the law itself does not require! Indeed the Confession of Faith in the preceding section distinctively repudiates this erroneous idea of the authority of Church courts, and says that their decrees are to be received only "if consonant to the Word of God."[16]

In other words, when the general council sent out the *Studies,* it was not only exceeding its power but interfering in an organization over which it had no jurisdiction and to which it had no relationship. It appeared then, and it appears even more clearly now, that the ecclesiastical organization of the church was determined to stifle the testimony of the Independent Board to the gospel and to keep the corporate testimony of the church in conformity with the liberal tendencies of the day.

The section of the *Studies* which deals with missionary giving strikes at the very heart of Protestantism and the Bible and so demands a full exposition and refutation. Dr. Machen's document is so able and states so clearly the great Christian principles which are involved in the controversy, that we can do no better than to consider its arguments.[17] The statements in this brief are practically a Christian manifesto of what the Bible teaches on missionary giving, and on the subject of obedience to the authority of the Word of God rather than to human authority.

Dr. Machen gives four reasons for refusing to obey the order of the general assembly to sever his connections with the Independent Board. First, "Obedience to the order in the way demanded by the General Assembly would involve support of a propaganda that is contrary to the gospel of Christ."[18] In chapter six it was pointed out plainly that the Board of Foreign Missions of the Presbyterian Church in the USA had been guilty of supporting and encouraging propaganda that is contrary to the Bible. Dr. Machen also rightly claimed that his charges against the policy of the board had never been refuted. After six years that claim is still valid. What is more, he argues, Pearl Buck's resignation was not asked for but was accepted "with regret" and "earnest prayer that her unusual abilities may continue to be richly used in behalf of the people of China."

---

16   H. McAllister Griffiths and Murray Forst Thompson, *Fallacies and Facts* (Philadelphia: The Independent Board for Presbyterian Foreign Missions, [1934]), 1-2.

17   *Statement of J. Gresham Machen.*

18   *Ibid.,* 16.

The Rev. Lindsay S. B. Hadley, a signer of the Auburn Affirmation, resigned as candidate secretary of the board, but the members of the board, so Dr. Machen continues, still regard him as capable and admirable for such a position so that the board continues to support a signer of the Auburn Affirmation in a responsible position. In other words, since the board condoned such modernism and allowed exponents of it to remain under its jurisdiction, Mr. Machen could not support the board and be true to the Bible.

In the second place, Dr. Machen states that he cannot obey the order of the general assembly because by so doing he would substitute human authority for the authority of the Word of God. This claim is substantiated by the fact that the general assembly has said that an individual who

> will not give to promote the officially authorized missionary program of the Presbyterian Church is in exactly the same position with reference to the Constitution of the Church as a church member or an individual that would refuse to take part in the celebration of the Lord's Supper or any other of the prescribed ordinances of the denomination as set forth in chapter VII of the Form of Government.[19]

This means that a member or minister of the church must support whatever missionary program may be established by successive general assemblies regardless of the program's faithfulness to the Bible. To prove that this is the true inference to be drawn from the above statement, Dr. Machen cites five examples.

First, the Presbytery of New Brunswick adopted a provision on September 26, 1933, stating that "all candidates seeking licensure or ordination shall be examined as to their willingness to support the regularly authorized Boards and agencies of the Presbyterian Church in the U.S.A., particularly the Board of Foreign Missions." As a second example, he says that some members of the Presbytery of Chester voted against the action of the presbytery in licensing certain candidates because these young men would not give a blanket promise to support the boards and agencies of the church. Thirdly, Dr. Machen maintains that the complainants of the Presbytery of Philadelphia were opposed to the reception of Dr. Machen from the Presbytery of New Brunswick, because they were not allowed to question him concerning his allegiance to the boards of the church. As a fourth example, he states that the Presbytery

---

19   *Studies*, 43.

of Baltimore refused to license Mr. Calvin K. Cummings on the same ground. As a fifth case, Dr. Machen argues that the stated clerk of the general assembly wrote to the stated clerk of the Presbytery of Baltimore,

> If and when any students from Westminster Seminary come before your Presbytery, they should be informed that the Presbytery will neither license nor ordain them until they have given a written pledge that they will support the official agencies of the church as a part of their pledge of loyalty to the government and discipline of the church.[20]

These examples are convincing evidence that Dr. Machen's interpretation of the assembly's action is correct.

In the third place, Dr. Machen could not obey the order of the general assembly because it advocates the principle that support of the church is "not a matter of free will giving but the payment of a tax enforced by penalties." The *Studies* seem to allow free will giving from the following quotation:

> On the contrary, it [the General Assembly] has always maintained that the right to control the property of the members of the Church, to assess the amount of their contributions, or to prescribe how they shall dispose of their money, is utterly foreign to the spirit of Presbyterianism. Every contribution on the part of an individual member must be purely voluntary.[21]

But the following quotation from the same report contradicts the first statement.

> In maintaining, however, this personal freedom of individual members, in their contributions to the Church, the General Assembly has never recognized any inconsistency in asserting with equal force, that there is a definite and sacred obligation on the part of every member of the Presbyterian Church to contribute to those objects designated by the authorized judicatory of the denomination.[22]

Dr. Machen paraphrases these conflicting assertions of the *Studies* as follows:

> Support of the Boards is voluntary; don't you dare say that it is not voluntary; but all the same, if you do not come right across with it we shall see that it will be the worse for you. . . . You may enter the Presbyterian Church in the U.S.A. or not as you please, . . . but if you do enter you must leave your Christian liberty behind. If you once enter you are slaves. Henceforth support of whatever missionary program successive General Assemblies may set up is obligatory

---

20   *Statement of J. Gresham Machen*, 22
21   *Minutes of the General Assembly* 1934, Part 1, 113.
22   *Ibid.*

upon you whether you think the program right or wrong. If you think that the missionary program of any General Assembly is so wrong that you cannot conscientiously support it, then the only thing for you to do is to leave the Church.[23]

In the fourth place, Dr. Machen claims that all of the three mentioned implications of obedience to the order of the general assembly are contrary to the Bible. The Bible requires that a Christian must preach the gospel of Christ and forbids him to preach any other gospel. "Though we, or an angel from heaven, preach any other gospel unto you than that which we have preached unto you, let him be accursed" (Gal 1:8). This statement, as Dr. Machen so clearly writes, is a summary of what runs throughout the entire Bible. Christianity is utterly exclusive.

The Bible forbids a man to substitute human authority for the Word of God. "Ye were bought with a price; be not ye the servants of men" (I Cor 7:23). As Dr. Machen claims,

> In demanding that I shall shift my message to suit the shifting votes of an Assembly that is elected every year, the General Assembly is attacking Christian liberty; but what should never be forgotten is that to attack Christian liberty is to attack the lordship of Jesus Christ.[24]

The Bible also upholds the principle of free will offerings as opposed to a tax enforced by penalties. "Every man according as he prospereth in his heart, so let him give; not grudgingly, or of necessity: for God loveth a cheerful giver" (II Cor 9:7).

Dr. Machen concludes his masterful brief on the subject by asserting, "Since the Action of the General Assembly was unconstitutional it should be ignored both by the individuals concerned and by the Presbyteries."[25] This advice the members of the Independent Board followed.

The *Studies of the Constitution* of the Presbyterian Church in the USA had been sent to the commissioners in advance of the 1934 General Assembly, but no one knew just what action the general assembly would recommend. On Friday (May 25th) at one o'clock, only a few minutes before adjournment for luncheon, and on the very afternoon set aside for consideration of this matter, the resolution of the general council was distributed to the commissioners. Most of the Commissioners hardly had time to read the proposed action, let alone prepare an answer to it.

---

23   *Statement of J. Gresham Machen*, 24.
24   *Ibid.*, 26.
25   *Ibid.*, 65.

Such a procedure failed to observe the ordinary rights of parliamentary justice and demonstrated the fear and unreasonableness which must have possessed the council.

The action which was read by the stated clerk of the assembly commanded the Independent Board to cease soliciting funds within the Presbyterian Church in the USA, and demanded that ministers of the church resign from the board or suffer discipline.[26]

As soon as the document was read, Dr. Mark A. Matthews, a member of the general council, arose and proceeded to deliver a long lecture on the theory of representative government and its divisions into executive, legislative, and judicial power. Most of his remarks were irrelevant to the issue, but his general discourse on Presbyterian law in a vague way tended to impress the commissioners that the Independent Board was illegal and that the members of it should be asked to resign from the board or suffer church discipline.

The Rev. H. McAllister Griffiths, managing editor of *Christianity Today* and a member of the Independent Board, obtained the floor and in a short but effective speech declared that the proposed action was unconstitutional and that the Independent Board was not within the jurisdiction of the Presbyterian Church in the USA. He used some of the arguments which have already been discussed. More speeches were made for and against the resolution, but after several hours of debate it was passed by a vote of approximately four to one.[27]

The issue raised by the deliverance of the 1934 General Assembly was not merely technical or legal, but of fundamental importance. Let no man maintain that the difference was only administrative or governmental or a question of interpreting the constitution of the church correctly. It placed in juxtaposition two authorities, the Bible on the one hand, and the decrees of a human council on the other. Allegiance to the Lord Jesus Christ is demanded in the Word of God, and when that conflicts with the commands of men, a Christian must follow Christ regardless of cost. Six years have elapsed since the deliverance was adopted, sufficient time to consider the controversy calmly and in the light of facts, but only one conclusion is possible: the general assembly erred and acted in a manner

---

26   *Minutes of the General Assembly 1934*, Part 1, 111-16. See also
      Appendix, note 14.
27   For further discussion of this matter see H. McAllister Griffiths,
      "Man Versus Machine: The 146th General Assembly," *Christianity
      Today* 5 (July 1934), 37-40.

contrary to the Word of God and contrary to its own constitution. And what is more tragic, it resulted in the resignation of ministers and laymen from the church, some of whom were among the most consistent and the most vigorous opponents of unbelief. It left the modernists and the doctrinal indifferentists in complete control of the church.

8
The Machen Trial

IMMEDIATELY AFTER the Deliverance of 1934 was issued, there were many in the church who did not and could not believe that the presbyteries would obey its orders and prosecute members of the Independent Board if they refused to resign from the board. The consensus among conservatives in the church seemed to be that no presbytery would discipline Presbyterians for joining any society whose object was to preach the gospel. This opinion went further in the belief that such action would only arouse members of the church to greater hostility toward the Board of Foreign Missions and the ecclesiastical organization.

In this opinion the conservatives were very wrong, for the relentlessness with which the hierarchy of the church began to function in enforcing the so-called mandate was not to be mistaken. While some presbyteries did nothing at first, the church was soon to witness real efficiency in court procedure.

On August 1, 1934, the administrative committee of the general council issued a letter defending the deliverance of the assembly, adding the information, "that excepting in relatively small areas of our Church, the significance of the action of the 1934 General Assembly with reference to the 'Independent Board for Presbyterian Foreign Missions' has been clearly understood and warmly approved."[1]

The Rev. A. L. Latham, D.D., minister of the Third Presbyterian Church, Chester, Pennsylvania, wrote an open letter in reply to the administrative committee. He said in part,

> I have no connection with the Independent Board, and never have had any. Nevertheless, I believe there is abundant ground for the formation of the same. The pity is this, that the Church Council and the General Assembly have done

---

1   *Christianity Today* 5 (September 1934), 97.

nothing to remove these grounds. . . . The Assembly has not sought to remove the disturbing cause; but rather, to coerce.[2]

The Rev. Clarence E. Macartney, D.D., issued a challenge to the action of the general assembly relative to the Independent Board under the title, "Presbyterians Awake!"[3] He challenged the action on six grounds: First, that the general assembly had no right to initiate such action; second, that it violated the right of private judgment; third, that it pronounced judgment without a hearing and trial; fourth, that it amended the constitution of the church by adding, to the subscription vows of candidates for licensure and ordination, a vow to support the boards and agencies; fifth, that it compelled every member of the church to contribute to the boards; sixth, that it was a usurpation of power and inaugurated an era of inquisition and persecution.

The Rev. William B. Pugh, D.D., the reputed author of the *Studies of the Constitution*, answered Dr. Macartney in an article entitled "Presbyterians Are Awake!,"[4] condemning Dr. Macartney's charges as "emphasized by the incorrect statements, the unsupported assumptions, the unwarranted inferences, the serious discrepancies, and the false interpretations which are inserted in the article in support of the various arguments or pleas for rebellion." Such abusive and intemperate language is rather indicative of the lack of judgment and objective attitude on the part of the one who wrote the *Studies*. After this tirade, Dr. Pugh attempted to answer each one of Dr. Macartney's points. Arguments similar to Dr. Pugh's have already been considered at length in the preceding chapter so no further discussion will be presented here.

A criticism of the action of the general assembly also came from the Rev. Henry S. Coffin, D.D., president of Union Theological Seminary, New York City, a well-known modernist institution. He regarded the founders of the Independent Board as bitter, intolerant, unfair, disloyal, and bigoted, and the officers of the general assembly and the Board of Foreign Missions as tried and true servants of the church. Nevertheless, he did write that the assembly "acted unwisely" and that he read the document with "mixed feelings."[5]

These protests by a liberal as well as by conservatives made little difference to the church machine. Shortly before the deliverance was

2   *Ibid.*, 88-89.
3   *The Presbyterian* 104 (July 19, 1934), 8-9.
4   *The Presbyterian* 104 (September 6 and 13, 1934), 6-9, 8-11.
5   *The Presbyterian Tribune* (November 1, 1934).

adopted, a foretaste of what was going to happen occurred in the Presbytery of Philadelphia when Dr. Machen transferred his membership from New Brunswick Presbytery to Philadelphia Presbytery in January, 1934.

Dr. Machen had been teaching at Westminster Theological Seminary for several years, so he considered it proper that he transfer his membership to the Presbytery of Philadelphia within whose bounds he then resided and labored. On January 23, 1934, he requested that he be granted a letter of dismissal from the Presbytery of New Brunswick to the Philadelphia Presbytery. The letter was granted and he was commended to the Presbytery of Philadelphia as a minister in good and regular standing. On March 5, 1934, the presbytery's Standing Committee on Candidates, Credentials, and Unemployed Ministers recommended that he be received upon the basis of his certificate of dismissal from New Brunswick. Certain members of the presbytery wished to ask Dr. Machen questions about his attitude toward the official agencies of the church. The moderator ruled that Dr. Machen was not required to answer these questions. By a vote of seventy-eight to forty-eight he was received into the presbytery and no appeal was taken to the moderator's ruling. Following this action, forty-four members of the presbytery filed a complaint with the Synod of Pennsylvania against the presbytery's action in receiving Dr. Machen. The synod voted to hold the complaint until the synod meeting in 1935.

In the meantime the general assembly issued its decree against the members of the Independent Board, and the stated clerk of the general assembly transmitted the action of the assembly to the clerk of New Brunswick Presbytery, instead of to the clerk of the Presbytery of Philadelphia, and added,

> The Stated Clerk of the General Assembly has on June 13, 1934 notified as therein provided the following named person who to the best of his information and belief is within the jurisdiction of your Presbytery, Rev. J. Gresham Machen, D.D., 206 South 13th Street, Philadelphia, Pennsylvania.

But the Presbytery of New Brunswick had anticipated the stated clerk of the general assembly in its zeal to obey the assembly's orders and on June 26, 1934, had passed the following motion,

> By motion, the Stated Clerk was authorized to ascertain from the Rev. J. Gresham Machen his answer in respect to the matter sent out by the Stated

Clerk of the General Assembly, entitled, 'The Independent Board for Presbyterian Foreign Missions.'[6]

A little later the Synod of Pennsylvania upheld the complaint and declared that Dr. Machen was a member of New Brunswick Presbytery.[7]

An excellent brief on the subject of jurisdiction was written by Dr. Machen's counsel, the Rev. H. McAllister Griffiths. Its arguments will be considered later on in this chapter. On the surface of the situation, however, it is evident that the stated clerk of the general assembly was presumptuous and, as Dr. Maitland Alexander, a former moderator of the general assembly remarked, "If we are to have a Pope give us one with the wisdom and conservatism of the Vatican."[8]

As a result of being reinstated in the Presbytery of New Brunswick, more or less by fiat, Dr. Machen was held to be subject to its jurisdiction, and the judicial process against him for membership on the Independent Board was begun by the Presbytery of New Brunswick. Action was started by other presbyteries against several members of the Independent Board, but since Dr. Machen was the president of the Independent Board, and since his trial formed the basis for all of the others, both in form and charges, his trial will serve as a basis for detailed study. On the other hand, mention might be made of other trials.

The other outstanding trials of Independent Board members were those of the Rev. Carl McIntire in West Jersey Presbytery; the Rev. J. Oliver Buswell, Jr., D.D., in the Presbytery of Chicago; five members of Philadelphia Presbytery: the Rev. H. McAllister Griffiths, the Rev. Merrill T. MacPherson, the Rev. Edwin H. Rian, the Rev. Charles J. Woodbridge, and the Rev. Paul Woolley; the Rev. Harold S. Laird, D.D., in New Castle Presbytery; and the Rev. Roy T. Brumbaugh, D.D., in Olympia Presbytery. Miss Mary W. Stewart and Mr. Murray Forst Thompson, members of the Holland Memorial Presbyterian Church in Philadelphia, were tried by the session of that congregation.

Ministers Griffiths, McIntire, MacPherson, Rian, Woodbridge, and Woolley were ordered suspended from the ministry.[9] Dr. Buswell was given the sentence of admonition.[10] Dr. Laird was rebuked by the

---

6   Machen, *Modernism and the Board*, 75.
7   *Minutes of the Synod of Pennsylvania*, 1936, 12.
8   Maitland Alexander, "The Hierarchy of the Presbyterian Church," *Christianity Today* 5 (July 1934), 34.
9   *Minutes of the General Assembly* 1936, Part 1, 83-95.
10   *Ibid.*, 142.

presbytery. Mr. Thompson and Miss Stewart were admonished. And Dr. Brumbaugh withdrew from the church before judgment could be pronounced. It is interesting to note that the Presbytery of Chester refused to take disciplinary action against the Rev. Wilbur M. Smith, D.D., pastor of the First Church, Coatesville, Pennsylvania, for his membership on the Independent Board when it adopted a minority report of its Judicial Committee.[11] Here was at least one presbytery which had the courage to stand by its constitutional rights.

Now for a detailed consideration of Dr. Machen's trial. In answer to the presbytery's request for information relative to his membership in the Independent Board, Dr. Machen replied on July 25, 1934,

> Without prejudicing the question whether I am or am not still under the jurisdiction of New Brunswick or whether, if I am still under the jurisdiction of that Presbytery, the Presbytery is warranted in addressing to me officially the inquiry contained in your letter, I desire to say, very respectfully, for the information of the Presbytery, that I have not severed my connection with the Independent Board for Presbyterian Foreign Missions; and that I regard the action of the General Assembly enjoining me to do so as being contrary to the Constitution of the Presbyterian Church in the U.S.A.[12]

When Dr. Machen's determination not to resign from the Independent Board was learned by the Presbytery of New Brunswick, the following action was taken by the presbytery on September, 1934:

> That a special Committee be appointed to confer further with Dr. Machen with respect to his relationship with the Independent Board for Presbyterian Foreign Missions and to make recommendations to presbytery for the disposition of the matter involving the mandate of the General Assembly to the presbytery and the relation of Dr. Machen to the Independent Board.[13]

A committee of five ministers and two elders was appointed, of which the Rev. D. Wilson Hollinger of Trenton, New Jersey, was the chairman. Dr. Machen never met with this committee because it refused to allow him the privilege of the presence of a stenographer. He wished this privilege for himself as well as for the committee if it desired, since every member of the committee was opposed to him. In fairness and for the sake of accuracy he believed that a written record was essential. After much correspondence, the committee finally allowed Dr. Machen to present his point of view concerning membership in the Independent

---

11   *Christianity Today* 5 (March 1935), 245.
12   Machen, *Modernism and the Board*, 76.
13   *Ibid.*, 78.

Board in written form. This statement has already been discussed in detail in the preceding chapter.

At a meeting of New Brunswick Presbytery on December 20, 1934, the following action was taken on recommendation of the special committee to confer with Dr. Machen.

> (1) That Presbytery prefer charges against the Rev. J. Gresham Machen, D.D., for offenses which are as follows: With the violation of his ordination vows; with his disapproval of the government and discipline of the Presbyterian Church in the U.S.A.; with renouncing and disobeying the rules and lawful authority of the Church; with advocating rebellious defiance against the lawful authority of the Church; with refusal to sever his connection with the Independent Board for Presbyterian Foreign Missions as directed by the General Assembly, with not being zealous and faithful in maintaining the peace of the Church; with contempt of and rebellion against his superiors in the Church in their lawful counsels, commands and corrections; with breach of his lawful promises; and with refusing subjection to his brethren in the Lord. (2) That a Prosecuting Committee be appointed by Presbytery, which committee shall conduct the prosecution in all its stages in whatever judicatory. (3) That the Presbytery transmit the case against Dr. Machen for hearing and decision to a special Judicial Commission to be duly elected by the Presbytery.[14]

Dr. Machen was cited to appear before the Special Judicial Commission on February 14, 1935, from which sessions the public was to be barred. The first session of the trial was held in the First Presbyterian Church, Trenton, New Jersey, in the presence of a large audience composed mostly of Dr. Machen's followers and a number of newspaper reporters. The protests of the defendant against a secret trial had compelled the commission to open the meetings of the trial to the public.

---

14   *Christianity Today* 5 (February 1935), 222.
      The following were elected to the Judicial Committee of the presbytery. Ministers: the Rev. Cordie J. Culp, Ph.D., pastor of the First Church, New Brunswick, N.J., the Rev. John E. Kuizenga, D.D., professor at Princeton Seminary, the Rev. Edward A. Morris, pastor of the First Church, Trenton, N.J., and the Rev. Parke Richards, First Church, Lawrenceville, N.J. Ruling Elders: John A. Hankinson, Pennington, N.J., William A. Cooley, Trenton, N.J., John G. Connor, Trenton, N.J. The Prosecuting Committee consisted of the Rev. D. Wilson Hollinger, D.D,, pastor of the Bethany Presbyterian Church, Trenton, N.J., the Rev. A. Kenneth Magner, Pennington, N.J., and ruling elder Henry Hardman, Trenton, N.J. The Rev. Parke Richards and ruling elder J. G. Connor resigned from the commission and the Rev. W. T. Magill and ruling elder Dr. Henry B. Kummel were elected in their places.

Every member of the commission was challenged by the defendant's counsel as to his right to sit on the commission. Dr. Culp was challenged because he had signed the Auburn Affirmation. Mr. Magill was challenged because he had been a member of the special committee to deal with Dr. Machen, and which committee had recommended that Dr. Machen be tried. Dr. Kuizenga was challenged because he occupied the chair of apologetics at Princeton Seminary, to which chair Dr. Machen had been appointed by the board of directors, and because there existed a doctrinal controversy between Princeton and Westminster Theological Seminary where Dr. Machen served as professor. Mr. Morris was challenged because his statements had already prejudiced the case, and because one of his elders was a member of the prosecuting committee. Mr. Morris had stated that if Dr. Machen could not keep step with the overwhelming majority of the general assembly he should get out of the church. Mr. Hankinson was challenged because his pastor, the Rev. A. Kenneth Magner, was a member of the prosecuting committee. Mr. Cooley was challenged because his pastor was a signer of the Auburn Affirmation. Dr. Kummel was challenged on the same ground, and further because he had been illegally elected to the commission.[15]

The charges and specifications against Dr. Machen, which were only an elaboration of those recommended by the special committee to confer with Dr. Machen, were also presented at the first session.[16] At the second meeting all the challenges against members of the commission were disallowed except those against Mr. Magill, so that six, instead of seven, continued to sit on the commission.

The attitude of the commission toward the central issue of the trial, that of doctrine, became evident when the defense objected to the presence of Dr. Kuizenga of Princeton Seminary on the commission. One of the prosecutors immediately arose and said, "We would like to object, Mr. Moderator, to the introduction of this, to anything that goes back to the Princeton Seminary, or the doctrinal phase of this case."[17]

The question of jurisdiction was the next matter argued. The defense maintained that New Brunswick Presbytery had no jurisdiction in the case for three reasons: first, Dr. Machen had been dismissed by the Presbytery of New Brunswick as a member in good and regular standing

---

15   *Transcription, Notes of Testimony in the case of the Presbyterian Church in the U.S.A. vs. J. Gresham Machen,* 14-25.

16   *Ibid.,* 32-37.

17   *Ibid.,* 67.

and received by the Presbytery of Philadelphia, March 5, 1934, on recommendation of the standing committee on Candidates, Credentials, and Unemployed Ministers by a vote of seventy-eight to forty-eight. That was an established fact which no one could refute. Second, the complaint which had been filed with the Synod of Pennsylvania by the forty-four members of Philadelphia Presbytery could not possibly stay the action of the presbytery in receiving Dr. Machen. The Book of Discipline, chapter XII, section 8, recognizes a complaint against a "particular delinquency, action or decision" of an inferior judicatory, but a "stay" or an arresting of the case until the decision is rendered by the next superior judicatory can only take place in the matter of a "decision." A "decision" involves contemplated action in the future, while in the case of Dr. Machen's reception an "action" had been taken which made it a *fait accompli*. Third, the required one-third had never properly signed the complaint. The Rev. W. K. Eubank, D.D., who had seconded the motion to receive Dr. Machen unanimously, had signed the complaint. There were 132 present at the meeting, so that with Dr. Eubank's name subtracted there lacked one for the required one-third to "stay" the action. What is more, the Rev. J. R. Jackson had withdrawn his name from the complaint, so that actually the complaint did not contain the required one-third.

With respect to this question it is worth noting that on April 1, 1935, by a vote of sixty-six to thirty-two, the Presbytery of Philadelphia adopted a memorial to the Synod of New Jersey stating that Dr. Machen was still under the jurisdiction of Philadelphia Presbytery.[18]

As a response to the arguments on jurisdiction, the prosecution set forth two grounds for believing that New Brunswick Presbytery did have jurisdiction over Dr. Machen. First, Dr. Machen had never presented a certificate of membership from Philadelphia Presbytery. Second, the stated clerk of the Philadelphia Presbytery had never returned the stub of Dr. Machen's certificate to the clerk of New Brunswick Presbytery. The defense immediately replied that the lack of receipt of the certificate stub by the clerk of New Brunswick Presbytery could not possibly change one's membership, and that the Book of Discipline recognized no degrees of reception as a member. No attempt was made by the prosecution to answer the three arguments of the defense. As was anticipated, the commission ruled in favor of the prosecution.

---

18   *Christianity Today* 5 (May 1935), 281. See Appendix, note 15.

Further objections by the defense relative to prejudgment of the case by New Brunswick Presbytery and to the fact that proper charges and specifications had never been presented by New Brunswick Presbytery to the commission were overruled, thus ending the second session of the trial.

On March 7, 1935, at the third session the dramatic and tragic point of the trial was reached. In order to appreciate this climax it is necessary to note the contrast between the defendant, Dr. Machen, and the personnel of the commission.

Without dispute it can be stated that before the commission of New Brunswick Presbytery stood one of the greatest theologians of his generation. His large and accurate fund of theological knowledge, his loyalty to the historic Christian position as held by the Presbyterian Church in the USA, his keen incisive mind, and his outstanding contributions to the defense of Christianity through his books and his teaching in the classroom for over twenty-five years, placed him above the members of the commission. Dr. Machen by common consent was regarded as a great defender of the faith. No one could accuse him of turning either to the left or to the right of sound doctrine. Yet, there he stood that day on trial for his ecclesiastical life because he had been willing to defend the truths of the gospel and accept whatever persecution would come to him on that account.

On the other hand, the members of the commission were not only inferior to him in theological knowledge, in brilliancy of mind, and in contribution to the defense of the faith, but at least one of these, the moderator of the commission, the Rev. Cordie J. Culp, Ph.D., had signed the Auburn Affirmation which attacked directly the full truthfulness of holy Scripture and declared that belief in the virgin birth of Christ, his bodily resurrection, his substitutionary atonement, and his miracles is nonessential to the Christian faith. Yet it was this very man as moderator of the commission who now asked Dr. Machen to stand, and in solemn stillness asked him the question, "It is now necessary for the court to inquire as to the plea. How does the defendant plead as to charge No. 1?" To each of the six charges Dr. Machen replied, "Not guilty!"

But the farcical and disgusting aspect of the entire proceedings followed immediately. The Book of Discipline states,

> Questions as to order or evidence, arising in the course of a trial, shall, *after* the parties have had an opportunity to be heard, be decided by the moderator,

subject to an appeal to the judiciary or judicial commission, to be determined without debate.[19]

Disregarding this rule and making the trial even more ridiculous, the commission issued the following ruling:

1. This court rules that it cannot accept and hear any further arguments or inferences based on the Auburn Affirmation, or on its signing by certain members of the Presbyterian Church in the U.S.A.

2. This court rules that it cannot accept and hear any further arguments or inferences against the Board of Foreign Missions of the Presbyterian Church in the U.S.A. It is not within the province of this Commission to hear either defence or attack of the Board of Foreign Missions of our Church, since both the General Assembly and the Presbytery of New Brunswick, from which this Commission derives its powers, have given the Board of Foreign Missions their vote of approval.

3. This court rules that it cannot accept and hear any further arguments or inferences based on the Princeton-Westminster Seminary controversy. We cannot entertain any arguments directed against any individuals, Boards, Agencies, Institutions, or Judicatories, against which no charges have been presented in the Presbytery of New Brunswick, and which are not on trial before this Judicial Commission.

4. This court rules that it cannot accept or regard any arguments questioning the legality or validity of the Mandate of the General Assembly in reference to the "Independent Board for Presbyterian Foreign Missions." It is one of the well established and fundamental principles of the Presbyterian system that a subordinate judicatory cannot sit in judgment upon the acts or deliverances of a superior judicatory, whether or not we think those acts or deliverances have been wise, equitable, and for the edification of the Church. So long as such acts and deliverances stand this Commission has no power but to obey.[20]

The defense asked for a short recess and then entered a protest.[21]

Another historic church trial comes to mind. Martin Luther, the German monk, was asked by the Diet of Worms to retract what he had written against the doctrines of the Roman church. He was asked two questions, "Do you acknowledge these books to have been written by you?" After the books were listed Luther replied, "As to the first, I acknowledge as mine the books which have just been named; I cannot deny them." A second question was put to him, "Are you prepared to

---

19   Chapter V, section 17.
20   *Transcription notes of testimony in the case of the Presbyterian Church in the U.S.A. vs. J. Gresham Machen*, 268.
21   Ibid., 272, 275-79. See Appendix, note 16.

retract these books, and their contents; or do you persist in the opinions you have advanced in them?" In reply to the second query, Luther asked for time to defend himself. "For this reason I entreat your imperial majesty, with all humility, to allow me time, that I may answer without offending against the Word of God."[22] Luther's request was granted and the next day was set as the time for a defense. On the next day he gave his defense and ended with the historic words, "And I neither can nor will revoke anything, seeing that it is not safe or right to act against conscience. God help me. Amen."[23]

In other words, even in those dark days when justice was supposed to be dead and when alleged heretics were burned at the stake, Martin Luther had an opportunity to defend his accusations against the church and to show that his doctrines were in accord with the truth of the Word of God. But Dr. Machen, in the twentieth century of enlightenment, was denied the very basis of justice and fairness and practically condemned without a hearing.

As a result of this unexpected and unfair move by the commission, the rest of the proceedings became more or less meaningless. The opening speech by the prosecution was given by the Rev. D. Wilson Hollinger, in which he reiterated that the case was not doctrinal but administrative and that the Presbytery of New Brunswick and the church were perfectly orthodox.[24] After this the prosecution offered various documents, mostly pamphlets issued by the Independent Board, as evidence to prove their case against Dr. Machen. The whole procedure was little short of ridiculous, especially since the defendant was not allowed to prove that his charges against the Board of Foreign Missions were true.

As a formality, the defense moved for a verdict for the defense which was overruled by the commission. The defense then expressed the willingness to prove that Dr. Machen's charges against the Board of Foreign Missions were true.[25] When the court refused to hear this evidence, the counsel for the defense stated:

---

22   J. H. Merle d'Aubigne, *History of the Reformation*, trans. H. White (Edinburgh: Oliver & Boyd, 1846), 2:254-55, 265.
23   James Mackinnon, *Luther and the Reformation* (London: Longmans, Green, and Co., 1928), 2:302.
24   *Transcription notes*, 280-89.
25   *Ibid.*, 302-304.

Mr. Moderator, the rulings of this court relating to argument and evidence have deprived this defendant of the right to introduce facts and arguments essential to his defense against these charges, and to be heard concerning the same. Since this defendant is thus precluded from offering the defense to which he is entitled by the constitution of the Church, the exercise of which right has been denied by this commission, he does not find himself able to present a so-called "case" which would not include these essential facts and arguments, for such a "case" would not be the case which, by the law of the Church, he is entitled to present.

Therefore, Mr. Moderator, under these circumstances the defense has nothing further to say.[26]

At the final session of the trial held on March 29, 1935, the commission declared Dr. Machen guilty, suspended him from the ministry of the Presbyterian Church in the USA, but recommended that the sentence take effect only after appeal to the higher courts had been heard.[27] Dr. Machen stated afterwards,

The Special Judicial Commission of the Presbytery of New Brunswick has simply condemned me without giving me a hearing. I am condemned for failing to obey a lawful order; but when my counsel, the Rev. H. McAllister Griffiths, offered to prove that the order that I had disobeyed was not lawful but unlawful the court refused to him a word of argument. I am condemned for making false assertions about the Modernism of the official Board of Foreign Missions but when my counsel offered to prove that those assertions were not false but true, the court would not hear a word of the evidence that we were perfectly ready to produce. It is not too much to say that a trial conducted in that fashion is nothing but a farce. . . . The customary attempt is being made to obscure the issue, by representing it as merely administrative and not doctrinal, but I think real Christian people and even the general public are being less and less deceived by such evasion.[28]

The Rev. Daniel Russell, D.D., moderator of the Presbytery of New York, said in an interview published in *The New York Times* of March 31, 1935,

Most Presbyterians hold no brief for the Independent Board for Presbyterian Foreign Missions. Many regret what has seemed at times an intolerant attitude on the part of Dr. Machen toward his brethren.

Nevertheless, there must be a widespread feeling of sorrow together with something of sympathy for the accused in that, after thirty years of distinguished service to religion, this famed scholar, whether through his own fault or otherwise, has been condemned by his Presbytery . . . and that his denomina-

---

26   *Ibid.*, 306.
27   *Transcription notes*, 404-12.
28   *Christianity Today* 5 (May 1935), 294.

tion, if the condemnation is sustained, can find no place in which his brilliant gifts may be utilized. . . .

Was Dr. Machen's trial a fair one? Ecclesiastical lawyers maintain that no question of doctrine is involved. In the more adequate view there are doctrinal differences which run into the heart of the entire problem. These the accused was not permitted to discuss in his defense.

The Rev. A. Z. Conrad, D.D., pastor of the Park Street Congregational Church, Boston, Massachusetts, described the trial as follows:

> Not for a generation has anything so high-handed, so unjust, so utterly un-christian been witnessed as the trial of Dr. Gresham Machen in the New Brunswick Presbytery. . . . It will be a sorry day for Presbyterians if such a travesty as the pretended trial of Dr. Machen is permitted to stand as the judgment of the majority.[29]

Dr. Clarence E. Macartney commented,

> Sad, lamentable, tragic, unthinkable that the Church Dr. Machen has served for thirty years, and more than twenty of them at our oldest and most famous seminary, and to which he has brought renown by his great talent, should now repay him by casting him out of its fellowship.[30]

Thus ended the trial of the Rev. J. Gresham Machen, D.D., Litt.D., before the Special Judicial Commission of the Presbytery of New Brunswick. Dr. Machen appealed the decision to the Permanent Judicial Commission of the general assembly, but he lost the appeal and was suspended from the ministry of the church.[31] The years that have intervened only make the decision all the more unfair and sad. This travesty of justice remains as a blot on the history of the Presbyterian Church in the USA, and as an illustration that history repeats itself. The church is once more in a state of apostasy and spiritual decay, for how else could it "excommunicate" one of its greatest and most valiant soldiers of the truth?

In 1893 the church suspended Dr. Charles A. Briggs of New York from the ministry because he did not believe in the infallibility of the Bible, and in 1936 the same church suspended Dr. Machen from the ministry because he was determined to follow the teachings of the infallible Word of God. Do not these two actions indicate the tremendous transformation in the Presbyterian church from orthodoxy to modernism?

---

29 *Christianity Today* 6 (June 1935), 13-14.
30 *The Presbyterian* 105 (April 4, 1935), 16.
31 *Minutes of the General Assembly* 1936, Part 1, 95-101.

9
The 1935 General Assembly

THE 1935 General Assembly met in Cincinnati, Ohio, in an atmosphere tense with feeling for and against the deliverance concerning the Independent Board and its members. The conviction of Dr. Machen by New Brunswick Presbytery had created more antagonism against the hierarchy of the church, as well as a feeling of futility in the hearts of the conservatives, while the vast majority of the church was more determined than ever to rid the church of the "trouble makers." It was manifest that the church would witness a pitched battle between the two forces.

Shortly before the convening of the general assembly, a very significant "Testimony" against the 1934 deliverance, under the auspices of a nationwide committee of ruling elders, was addressed to the entire eldership of the Presbyterian Church in the USA. It is important to note that these elders of the committee, none of whom was connected with the Independent Board, stated deliberately,

> We believe that doctrinal differences lie at the heart of and furnish the motivating cause for the present discord in our Church, and that issues having the aspect of administrative and governmental matters are only collateral manifestations and outgrowths of fundamental and irreconcilable differences in belief.[1]

The Rev. Burleigh Cruickshank, D.D., not associated with the Independent Board, also wrote, "The real issue is between two theological points of view which have become, during the last years, mutually exclusive."[2]

The Rev. William C. Robinson, D.D., a professor in Columbia Theological Seminary, Decatur, Georgia, and a minister of the Pres-

---

1   *Christianity Today* 6 (June 1935), 10.
2   Burleigh Cruickshank, "The Present Crisis in the Presbyterian Church in the U.S.A.," *The Presbyterian* 105 (April 18, 1935), 9.

byterian Church in the US (southern Presbyterian), made the accusation, "Theoretically, your church stands upon the Word of God as the rule of faith and practise. I regret to state, however, that practically she seems to be making the voice of the Church her rule of faith and manners."[3] Such testimony is in direct contradiction to the opinion of the Special Judicial Commission of New Brunswick Presbytery, which claimed that the issue was administrative and not doctrinal.

Thirteen presbyteries had sent overtures or resolutions relative to the Independent Board. Six urged the general assembly to take care that the foreign missionary program of the church be in full accord with the Bible, and that only those who are fully aware of the danger in which the church stands and who are faithful to the Word of God be elected to membership on the Board of Foreign Missions. Five overtures and four resolutions asked the general assembly to rescind the action against the members of the Independent Board or drop the process against them.[4]

But the opposition to and agreement with the action against the Independent Board which had been generated since the 1934 General Assembly found even more vehement and drastic expression in the general assembly. The assembly was hardly officially constituted when the Rev. George E. Barnes, D.D., a signer of the Auburn Affirmation and a minister in Philadelphia, arose and read a petition signed by other ministers, protesting the enrollment of the Rev. H. McAllister Griffiths, the Rev. Merrill T. MacPherson of Philadelphia Presbytery, and the Rev. Carl McIntire of West Jersey Presbytery on the ground of their refusal to resign from the Independent Board. The petition was given to the Standing Committee on Polity, and the three ministers were granted full membership in the assembly pending the report of the committee.[5]

On Monday, May 27, the general assembly adopted the committee's report, recommending "That the Rev. H. McAllister Griffiths and the Rev. Merrill T. MacPherson, of the Presbytery of Philadelphia, and the Rev. Carl McIntire of the Presbytery of West Jersey, be not enrolled in this General Assembly."[6] The three unseated commissioners were

---

3   William Childs Robinson "Which is the Rule of Faith and Life: The Word of God or the Voice of the Church?" *Christianity Today* 6 (June 1935), 4.
4   *Minutes of the General Assembly 1935*, Part 1, 27-38.
5   *Minutes of the General Assembly 1935*, Part 1, 8.
6   *Ibid.*, 70.

allowed to speak a few words of protest and later in the assembly a formal protest against this action was filed by certain members of the assembly.[7]

This action not only demonstrated the temper of the general assembly and its control by those who were set against the Independent Board, but it also showed little regard for the constitutional rights of the three commissioners. These men were members in good and regular standing in their presbyteries and had been duly elected as commissioners to the general assembly. They were not under the condemnation of their presbyteries, nor had they been cited to appear before their presbyteries because they had failed to obey the "mandate" of the general assembly relative to the Independent Board. The General Assembly of 1934 had instructed the presbyteries "to institute, or cause to be instituted, promptly such disciplinary action as is set forth in the Book of Discipline,"[8] if the members of the Independent Board within their jurisdiction did not resign from the Independent Board. Until a minister or member of the Independent Board had been brought to trial and some disciplinary action pronounced upon him by his presbytery, he remained a member of the presbytery in good and regular standing. In other words, the general assembly had no constitutional right to deprive him of membership in the assembly. When the assembly ousted these three ministers by a majority vote it exhibited the worst kind of tyranny.

This action also made it plain that the general assembly failed to distinguish between administrative and judicial actions. When the general assembly delivered its "mandate" against the Independent Board, it was acting in its administrative capacity. The special commission of 1925 made an observation which has always been accepted and agreed to by the Presbyterian Church in the USA:

> The General Assembly sits sometimes in an executive and administrative capacity, again it may act as a legislative body; and yet again as a judicial tribunal, but always with restricted powers. . . . The failure to distinguish among these functions performed by the Assembly, as they have been distinguished in our American civil government, is the cause of the confusion which has crept into our minds regarding this matter.[9]

The late Francis L. Patton called administrative acts of the general assembly "pious advice." The very essence of Presbyterianism is that the liberties of the individual minister or member are protected because those

---

7   *Ibid.*, 95-96.
8   *Minutes of the General Assembly 1934*, 116.
9   *Minutes of the General Assembly 1926, Part 1, 82.*

rights can only be abrogated by judicial process, which begins ordinarily in a presbytery and proceeds through the synod and general assembly. The general assembly is just as bound by the constitution in its acts as the humblest member of the church. In other words, the members of the Independent Board had not disobeyed an order of the supreme court of the church simply because no case in connection with membership on the Independent Board had as yet come before the general assembly sitting in its judicial capacity as a court of Jesus Christ. In the meantime, the so-called mandate of the 1934 General Assembly only had the force of an administrative action which presbyteries or individuals are not compelled to follow.

The irony of the whole situation was seen in the fact that the one who had raised the protest against the three members of the assembly was a signer of the Auburn Affirmation. As such, he had himself defied the action of the 1923 General Assembly which declared that certain doctrines are essential to the Word of God. His right to disregard an administrative act of the general assembly had been conceded—although while doing so he revealed heretical tendencies, since the five doctrines mentioned in the Affirmation are at the very heart and core of Christianity. And yet Dr. Barnes, who had denied the very essence of historic Christianity as taught by the Presbyterian Church in the USA, now stood up and urged that the assembly deprive men of their constitutional rights because they had disregarded a declaration of the assembly pertaining to the administration of the church. The shift of the church from the conservative to the liberal doctrinal position and also a drift toward tyranny can be seen quite clearly from this procedure. Such action would have been incredible twenty-five years earlier.

The cleavage in the 1935 General Assembly was also plain in the election of the moderator. Dr. Stewart M. Robinson, editor of *The Presbyterian*, was nominated by the Rev. Burleigh Cruickshank, D.D. of Philadelphia, on the platform of loyalty to the Bible and the need for reform within the church. The Rev. Joseph A. Vance, D.D., of Detroit, was placed before the general assembly as president of the Board of National Missions, and staunch defender of the status quo in the church. He was a typical "machine" man. Several others were nominated but these men typified the two doctrinal factions within the church, although Dr. Robinson had never been associated with the Independent Board movement nor had he been actively aligned with the group in the church which had made a consistent fight for the faith. Dr. Vance was elected by an overwhelming majority, making it evident again that the church was controlled by those who were liberals and who were content with the drift of the church toward unbelief.

A surprise came when the Permanent Judicial Commission of the general assembly presented its decision in the Blackstone-Kauffroth case. These two young men, James H. Blackstone and John A. Kauffroth, had presented themselves for licensure to the Presbytery of Chester on June 12, 1934.[10] In addition to the regular constitutional questions, several relative to the foreign missions situation, occasioned by the "mandate" against the Independent Board, were asked the candidates. Then each one read a prepared statement, saying that at present the Board of Foreign Missions, in his opinion, was not entirely loyal to the constitution of the church; however, they said that they held themselves open to receive new facts.[11]

After these statements the presbytery, by a vote of forty-five to twenty-two, proceeded to license the two candidates in the regular constitutional manner. Against this action seventeen members of the presbytery complained to the Synod of Pennsylvania.[12] The Judicial Commission of the Synod of Pennsylvania sustained the complainants. In turn, the action of the synod was complained against which brought the case before the Permanent Judicial Commission of the general assembly. The Permanent Judicial Commission reversed the decision of the synod, and found that the presbytery had acted properly in licensing the two candidates.[13]

This decision implied what members of the Independent Board and conservatives had been saying, namely, that the mandate of 1934 adds to the constitution of the church when it requires blind allegiance to the boards of the church and makes it the duty of each member to support the authorized missionary program of the church, whether or not he regards it as in accord with the Bible. In other words, the decision of the Permanent Judicial Commission, which became the decision of the general assembly in the Blackstone-Kauffroth case, repudiated the central principle upon which the action of the 1934 General Assembly was based, that of blind allegiance to the boards.

---

10   *Minutes of the General Assembly 1935*, Part 1, 81.
11   Ibid., 82-83. See also Appendix, note 17.
12   Ibid., 83.
13   Ibid., 86.

Immediately, modernists in the assembly interpreted the decision as favoring them, because each presbytery was left free to do as it pleased. A careful reading of the decision, however, reveals that presbyteries must proceed strictly according to the constitution. While this decision practically reversed the action of the 1934 Assembly, it became clear almost immediately that those in control of the machinery of the church would not be bound by it.

What took place in New Brunswick Presbytery on April 6, 1936, established this statement. Nine candidates for licensure appeared before the presbytery and each one was asked questions to this effect: "Are you willing to support the authorized boards and agencies of the Presbyterian Church in the USA and particularly the Board of Foreign Missions?" The presbytery asked this question on the basis of its rule passed on September 26, 1933,

> All candidates seeking licensure or ordination shall be examined as to their willingness to support the regularly authorized Boards and Agencies of the Presbyterian Church in the U.S.A., particularly the Board of Foreign Missions. A record of this examination shall be made in the Minutes of Presbytery.

Six candidates answered the above question in the affirmative, while the other three expressed their unwillingness to make a blanket pledge for the future, but they finally satisfied the presbytery that they could support the boards as then constituted, and would withdraw from the church if there came a time when they could not give unquestioned loyalty to the boards.[14]

Another instance of the same nature, proving that the rulers of the church refused to be bound by a general assembly decision even though it was in a judicial case, and therefore final, occurred in Kalamazoo Presbytery with respect to the reception of the Rev. G. H. Snell from the Presbytery of Cincinnati. Mr. Snell had been called as pastor of the Presbyterian Church at Allegan, Michigan, but the presbytery refused to receive him because he would not give a blanket pledge of loyalty to the boards. However, it allowed him to remain as stated supply of the church.[15] Such were the reactions of the ecclesiastical rulers to the

---

14   Bruce F. Hunt, "New Brunswick Presbytery meets; Requests Candidates Pledge 'Loyalty' to Official Boards," *Presbyterian Guardian* 2 (April 20, 1936), 37.

15   *The Presbyterian Guardian* 1 (November 18, 1935), 67, *Record of Special Judicial Commission of the Presbyterian Church in the U.S.A.*

decision of the Permanent Judicial Commission in the Blackstone-Kauf-froth case.

The overtures and resolutions urging the general assembly to rescind the action against the Independent Board were voted down with dispatch, and to show the temper of the 1935 Assembly more pointedly, it concurred in the resolution of the Presbytery of Niobrara, reaffirming the action of the 1934 General Assembly relating to the Independent Board.[16]

The Presbyteries of Chester and Philadelphia had always been regarded as outstanding conservative strongholds which the modernist element had found it difficult, if not impossible, to control. It was the Presbytery of Philadelphia under the leadership of the Rev. Clarence E. Macartney, D.D., which had initiated the action against Dr. Harry E. Fosdick. In fact, Philadelphia Presbytery had led the fight to keep the church true to the Bible and the Westminster Confession of Faith. This fact had troubled the leaders of the church very much, but the action which was adopted at the 1935 General Assembly eventually solved that problem and placed the modernists and the ecclesiastical "machine" group in complete domination of these presbyteries. Two memorials, identical in form, one from a group of eighteen ministers and twenty-nine elders in Chester Presbytery, and the other signed by fifteen ministers and ninety-eight elders in Philadelphia Presbytery, petitioned the general assembly to investigate conditions in those presbyteries.[17]

It is significant that of the five ministers designated by the self-appointed group in Philadelphia Presbytery to argue their case before the standing committee of the general assembly, four were signers of the Auburn Affirmation. The Committee on Bills and Overtures recommended that a commission be appointed for the investigation and report to the next assembly.[18]

The ecclesiastical organization was determined to crush the evangelical majorities in these presbyteries and compel them to do their bidding. In the next chapter the complete success of this determination will be considered.

In conclusion, it is well to recognize one rather amusing incident in the 1935 Assembly which illustrates further the true condition of the

---

16   *Minutes of the General Assembly* 1935, Part 1, 110.
17   *Ibid.,* 110-112.
18   *Ibid.,* 113.

church, as well as the complete doctrinal indifference and insincerity of some members. After the three members of the general assembly were unseated, considerable comment resulted in the newspapers, over the radio, and among laymen visiting in Cincinnati. To answer this unfavorable publicity, the Rev. W. C. Covert, D.D., moderator of the 1934 General Assembly, asked for the floor and, after making threatening remarks to the offenders, called upon the assembly to recite the Apostles' Creed in order to demonstrate the doctrinal soundness of the church. After the assembly had recited the creed, one member arose and asked naively if the assembly would not go on record as showing that it really believed the creed. The moderator answered that of course the assembly believed the creed. But it was apparent to everyone that such a request showed definitely that the integrity of the church's own pronouncements of doctrinal soundness was questioned. And well might that suspicion be, when it is realized that signers of the Auburn Affirmation, who had denied certain dogmas of the creed as essential to Christianity, repeated the creed with the rest.[19]

The 1935 Assembly gave modernism another victory. The church in its corporate witness was nearer the goal of complete capitulation to unbelief. Anyone who could not see that the struggle in the church was between two different conceptions of religion must have been blind.

---

19   *Christianity Today* 6 (July 1935), 41.

10
Philadelphia and Chester Presbyteries

THE PRESBYTERIES of Philadelphia and Chester were particularly obnoxious to those in control of the Presbyterian Church in the USA because in these two bodies the modernists, the doctrinal indifferentists, and the supporters of the ecclesiastical organization were in a decided minority. For many years these two presbyteries could be counted upon to oppose any move in the church at large which would tend to weaken its testimony to the full truthfulness of the Bible and to compromise the church's attitude toward unbelief.

The minority report which the General Assembly of 1923 adopted, and which declared that five central verities of Christianity are essential doctrines of the Word of God, was made by the Rev. A. Gordon McLennan, D.D., then pastor of the Bethany Presbyterian Church, Philadelphia. It was in Philadelphia that Westminster Theological Seminary had been launched to carry on the scholarly and Presbyterian traditions of Princeton Theological Seminary before its reorganization in 1929 so as to be complacent toward modernism. It was by Philadelphia Presbytery that the overture asking for drastic reform within the Board of Foreign Missions had been adopted in 1933. In a very consistent fashion the conservatives in this presbytery had elected their men as moderators and as members of the various important committees. All of these actions were accomplished according to the rules of the presbytery and the constitution of the church, simply because the Bible-believers vastly outnumbered the modernists. This fact irked the Auburn Affirmationist members of the presbytery, of whom there were eleven, and when they discovered that their case was hopeless in the presbytery, they decided to appeal to the general assembly which was overwhelmingly sympathetic with their point of view.

The Presbytery of Chester had taken less spectacular actions and had not been the storm center of the church in the controversy between Bible-believers and modernists; nevertheless, the men in the presbytery had stood firmly for historic Christianity. It had dared to challenge the orthodoxy of the Board of Foreign Missions by its criticism of it. It had licensed Blackstone and Kauffroth after the 1934 "mandate," even though both of the young men refused to pledge blind allegiance to the boards and agencies of the church, which licensures were upheld by the 1935 General Assembly. It also had refused to bring the Rev. Wilbur M. Smith, D.D., a member of the Independent Board, to trial for his failure to obey the "mandate." In these and other ways the majority in the presbytery revealed their steadfast determination to be faithful to the Bible and the Westminster Confession of Faith despite the general assembly and the ecclesiastical overlords.

The minority in the Presbytery of Chester was made up mostly of followers of the Rev. W. B. Pugh, D.D., an assistant in the office of the stated clerk of the general assembly and the heir-apparent to that position. In fact, he was elected to that office by the 1938 General Assembly. During the struggle within the church between the two forces, Dr. Pugh did everything in his power to thwart the actions of the conservatives. But in spite of his ingenuity and persistence, he, like the minority in Philadelphia Presbytery, was unable to sway the presbytery to his viewpoint. Consequently, he and his satellites also petitioned the general assembly for aid.

The memorial to the general assembly from the minority in the Presbytery of Philadelphia, signed by fifteen ministers and ninety-eight elders, listed their grievances under two headings, (1) direct violations of the constitution, and (2) violations of the general rules for judicatories. Under the first caption the licensure of several candidates for the ministry was criticized on the ground the presbytery refused to compel the candidates to be subjected to questions concerning their loyalty to the boards and agencies of the church. The presbytery did this on the ground that such questions were extra-constitutional. As has been already stated, the Permanent Judicial Commission of the general assembly, approved by the general assembly, upheld the Presbytery of Chester on this point.

They also objected to the presbytery's delay in bringing to trial the members of the Independent Board. The other so-called violations under the second heading were largely due to the fact that the majority voted for its men as committee members and officers, leaving the minority without the representation which it desired, a situation which happens in a deliberative body where the majority rules. The other objections were mostly trivial, such as an inaccurate roll call, unseemly interruptions, and visitors mingling with members of presbytery. Grievances of a similar nature were also filed by the minority in Chester Presbytery.[1]

A commission of nine was appointed by the general assembly with instructions to dissolve the differences in the presbyteries.[2] In October and November, 1935, this committee held executive meetings in Philadelphia with groups and individuals representing various shades of opinion in both Philadelphia and Chester Presbyteries. The public and the press were barred from these investigations. Because each one was pledged to secrecy, most of the conservative leaders of Philadelphia refused to appear, so that a printed statement was issued on their behalf by the Rev. H. McAllister Griffiths, in which the conflict between modernism and Christianity in the world and in the Presbytery of Philadelphia was enunciated, and a strong plea for the elimination of modernism was entered.[3]

After hearing members of both presbyteries and after deciding on a plan of action, the commission submitted a program of twelve points to each presbytery, which was adopted with only the militant members of each presbytery dissenting. It urged the members of the presbyteries to love one another, to respect minorities, to create a general council, to establish a Vacancy and Supply Committee, to adopt a rule of retirement of ministers at age seventy, and to establish a metropolitan presbytery composed of several surrounding presbyteries.[4]

In this twelve-point program no mention whatsoever is made of the profound doctrinal differences which existed in the two presbyteries and which were the real cause of the trouble. This is studiously avoided and instead the groundwork is laid for streamlining the organization of the presbyteries so that it would be in harmony with the trend of the whole church. Strong committees on vacancy and supply were recommended, which committees could control the supplying of vacant pulpits with men who would fit in with the doctrine of those on the committees. The

---

1   *Minutes of the General Assembly* 1935, Part 1, 110-114.
2   *Ibid.*
3   H. McAllister Griffiths, "The Doctrinal Issue in Philadelphia," *Presbyterian Guardian* 1 (November 4, 1935), 57-58.
4   *Minutes of the General Assembly* 1936, Part 1, 121-23. See also Appendix, note 18.

Auburn Affirmationist members of Philadelphia Presbytery got exactly what they wanted, because when the Independent Board members left the presbytery, the modernists and those conservatives whom they had cowed into submission actually held the majority. In fact, shortly before the Independent Board members resigned from the presbytery, that situation obtained.

Two particular recommendations of the committee calling for constitutional changes were aimed at those associated with Westminster Theological Seminary and the Independent Board, and the graduates of Westminster Seminary, because they had been called "centers of dissension" and "disturbers of the peace." The committee urged that only pastors and elders be allowed to vote and that candidates for the ministry from seminaries not under the control of the general assembly be referred to the synod's Committee on Licensure and Ordination.[5]

An overture which would accomplish this and tend to eliminate graduates of Westminster Theological Seminary and other institutions not under the jurisdiction of the general assembly from the ministry of the Presbyterian Church in the USA was presented to the 1937 General Assembly, but the Standing Committee on Polity's recommendation of no action was adopted.[6]

The commission of nine also recommended that a large metropolitan presbytery be formed in Philadelphia, which would eventually include Philadelphia Presbytery and portions of Philadelphia North and Chester Presbyteries. In 1937, the commission recommended that this matter be referred to the Synod of Pennsylvania for further study. Up to this writing no changes have been made in the boundaries of those presbyteries.

The commission reported to the 1937 General Assembly that the Presbyteries of Philadelphia and Chester were reorganizing along the lines suggested. Having concluded their work, the commission said that it, "Having now helped these Presbyteries to set their feet upon the paths of peace, and confident that the good work which has begun in them will be perfected by the Holy Spirit, respectfully asks to be discharged."[7]

The prediction of the conservative leaders that the complexion of these presbyteries would be changed by the recommendations of the commission, from one of militant defense of the faith and loyalty to the

---

5   *Ibid.*, 126-27. See also Appendix, note 19.
6   *Minutes of the General Assembly 1937*, Part 1, 157.
7   *Ibid.*, 154.

Confession of Faith to one of docility toward the leaders of the church and compromise with modernism, was evident immediately. The Rev. George E. Barnes, a signer of the Auburn Affirmation, was elected moderator of Philadelphia Presbytery for two successive terms, a procedure almost without precedent, and this honor was bestowed upon one who had flouted the doctrines of the church. When the founders of the Orthodox Presbyterian Church left the Presbyterian Church in the USA, the Auburn Affirmationists and their friends were in the saddle in the Presbytery of Philadelphia.

The Presbytery of Chester was also reorganized and from then on controlled by the Rev. W. B. Pugh, D.D., and his followers according to the dictates of the leaders of the church. The voice of protest against modernism and modernists in the church, which had been so loud and clear in these two presbyteries, became strangely silent. Philadelphia and Chester Presbyteries, which had been the real bulwarks of the faith, which had carried the brunt of the battle to keep the church true to its Confession of Faith and the Bible, and which had attempted to warn the church of the encroachments of modernism, were now mere instruments in the hands of the rulers of the church. The demise of a noble testimony had taken place, and the church was deprived of the witness of two presbyteries where some real constructive action in favor of the Bible might have been taken.

11
"We Must Obey God"

IN ORDER to appreciate the full significance of what took place at the general assembly of the Presbyterian Church in the USA, which was held at Syracuse, New York, in May, 1936, a brief resumé of the issues involved is necessary.

The central point raised in the matter of the Independent Board and the deliverance of the 1934 General Assembly concerned the ultimate source of authority in religion. Should a Christian obey the voice of the church speaking through its councils and general assemblies, or the voice of God speaking in the Bible? When all bitterness, strife, name-calling, and hatred are brushed aside, there remains this paramount question and no amount of verbiage can make it otherwise. This issue was brought to a focus in two aspects: first, with respect to the authority of the courts of the church and second, with respect to the support of the established and official program of the boards and agencies of the church.

Those in control of the Presbyterian Church in the USA argued that the church is under a constitution, and under this constitution the general assembly is the highest court, and when it delivers a mandate, an order, or a decision, it must be obeyed by the members of the church. Presbyterianism recognizes the right of protest and free discussion, these men said, but if these protests are not allowed by the church, a member must obey or leave the church.[1] The general assembly "has all the power the church would have if it were possible to convene the church together in one place."[2] The general assembly, in other words, is the official interpreter of the constitution and the Bible, and all members of the church must abide by its decisions regardless of what those decisions may be.

---

1   *Minutes of the General Assembly* 1934, 73-78.
2   *Ibid.*, 80.

On the other hand, those opposed stated that the Bible itself is the final arbiter for doctrine and life and that the constitution of the church makes that abundantly clear.[3] The general assembly and its decrees are to be received *only if consonant* with the Word of God. The general assembly and all the courts of the church are as subject to this important and essential principle of the constitution of the church as the humblest member. The Confession of Faith states emphatically that "they [synods and councils] are not to be made the rule of faith or practice, but to be used as a help in both."[4] The holy Scriptures are "the *only* rule of faith and manners." "The Supreme Judge, by whom all controversies of religion are to be determined, and all decrees of councils, opinions of ancient writers, doctrines of men and private spirits, are to be examined, and in whose sentence we are to rest, can be no other but the Holy Spirit speaking in the Scripture."[5]

In this difference between the two parties lies the fundamental difference between Protestantism and Roman Catholicism. Roman Catholicism believes in an infallible Bible, but it adds to this an infallible church as the final interpreter and arbiter in doctrine and in life. The Roman Catholic must obey the voice of the church speaking through its Pope and councils. On the other hand, the Protestant holds that the Bible alone is the supreme judge in faith and practice, and that all decrees and commands of the church are to be tested by their adherence to the Bible. The Protestant must obey the voice of God in the Bible rather than the voice of the church speaking through its councils.

When the Permanent Judicial Commission of the general assembly sat at Syracuse to decide the cases involving members of the Independent Board, this was the question. But the personnel of the Judicial Commission made it inevitable that its decision would favor the position that a member must obey the voice of the church. Three of the seven ministerial members of the commission, Herbert K. England, Robert Hastings Nichols, and Archibald Cardle, were signers of the Auburn Affirmation, which document attacked directly the inerrancy of the holy Scriptures. The question of the final authority of the Bible is at the very heart of Protestantism. When men no longer believe in this dogma, it is only

---

3   *Form of Government*, chapter 1, section VII; and *Confession of Faith*, chapter XXXI, section II and III.
4   *Confession of Faith*, chapter XXXI, section III.
5   *Confession of Faith*, chapter I, section X.

logical that they should place the seat of authority in religion in some word or experience of man, which is exactly what the commission did.

The second aspect of the question concerned support of the official missionary agency of the church. The deliverance of the General Assembly of 1934 had stated,

> A Church member or an individual church that will not give to promote the officially authorized missionary program of the Presbyterian Church is in exactly the same position with reference to the Constitution of the Church as a church member or an individual church that would refuse to take part in the celebration of the Lord's Supper.[6]

Such a statement makes it plain that the general council, which issued the *Studies of the Constitution*, and the general assembly which adopted this document, elevated the decrees of a human council to equal position with the command of the Lord Jesus Christ. When it is realized that evidence had been presented, and not refuted to this day, showing that at least some of the program of the Board of Foreign Missions was unfaithful to the teachings of the Bible as defined by the Westminster Confession of Faith, the full import of this position is plain.

Dr. Machen and the other members of the Independent Board who had appealed their cases to the Permanent Judicial Commission of the general assembly had said in effect that neither the New Testament nor the constitution of the church made support of the church and its agencies a compulsory matter. On the other hand, the New Testament stresses free-will contributions. To say that a member must support the agencies of the church regardless of their loyalty to the Bible is like putting the minutes of the general assembly on top of the pulpit Bible.

In these two aspects of the same question is found the recurring theme and question which divided the founders of the Independent Board and the rulers of the church, and which is really the fundamental difference between Bible-believers and modernists. When once the sufficiency and infallibility of the Bible and its final authority in faith and practice are denied, the authority that is substituted must be something human and fallible even though it is a church council. In accordance with this principle, the members of the Independent Board were expelled from the Presbyterian Church in the USA, and another denomination now known as the Orthodox Presbyterian Church was organized.

---

6   *Minutes of the General Assembly* 1934, 110.

The same question arose in the 1936 General Assembly with reference to other cases than those concerning members of the Independent Board. The Rev. Arthur F. Perkins, Merrill, Wisconsin, had helped to organize an interdenominational summer camp for young people known as the Crescent Lake Bible Fellowship. Members of the Presbytery of Winnebago objected to this camp because two similar camps under the jurisdiction of the presbytery were already in existence, so that competition and rivalry resulted. The Presbytery of Winnebago further alleged that Mr. Perkins refused to support the Board of Foreign Missions of the church. Because of these so-called evidences of insubordination and disobedience, Mr. Perkins was tried by a special judicial commission of the presbytery and suspended from the ministry for two years. He appealed the decision to the synod, which changed the suspension to one year, and then he appealed further to the Permanent Judicial Commission of the general assembly, which confirmed the suspension until such time as Mr. Perkins would give evidence of repentance and reformation.[7]

Mr. Perkins, according to his testimony, had established a summer camp for young people because the speakers and programs of the two camps of the presbytery were not wholly true to the Bible. Any number of such independent camps conducted by ministers of the Presbyterian Church in the USA are carried on each year, but because Mr. Perkins had dared to challenge the Board of Foreign Missions, and because he had dared to criticize certain aspects of the denomination's work, he was not allowed to organize an independent camp but was suspended from the ministry. This is simply another testimony to the fact that every minister and every member must support the full program of the church, or leave. In other words, the courts of the church are the final arbiter of faith and practice.

Still another case, that of the Rev. John J. DeWaard, Cedar Grove, Wisconsin, came before the Permanent Judicial Commission of the general assembly in 1936. Mr. DeWaard had criticized not only the Board of Foreign Missions but also the Board of Christian Education of the church for unfaithfulness to the Bible. The Presbytery of Milwaukee had ordered Mr. DeWaard to do three things: (1) cease his attacks upon the boards of the church, (2) bring all his charges against the church, its

---

7   *Minutes of the General Assembly* 1936, Part 1, 105.

boards, and its judicatories to presbytery, and (3) encourage the session in the distribution of undesignated benevolence funds according to quotas assigned.[8]

Mr. DeWaard expressed his willingness to obey the second command, but refused to cease his attacks on the boards or to encourage his session to support the boards of the church. The presbytery then voted to dissolve the pastoral relationship and to continue Mr. DeWaard as stated supply for a period of six months. The Permanent Judicial Commission of the general assembly sustained this decision.[9]

The hierarchy of the church was determined to stamp out all forms of alleged insubordination and refusal to follow their dicta and program. It is significant in this respect to note that the one presbytery, namely Chester, which refused to try the Rev. Wilbur M. Smith, D.D., because he would not obey the mandate of the 1934 General Assembly, was also ordered by the 1936 General Assembly to try Dr. Smith.[10]

It is impossible to discuss the 1936 General Assembly of the Presbyterian Church in the USA without considering the tremendous drama that was enacted there. Here was not one minister but *eight*, all of whom were well-known for their loyalty to the Bible as the Word of God and their unequivocal devotion to the Westminster Confession of Faith, suspended from the ministry of that church because they had the courage and the grace to obey the God of the Bible rather than the voice of the church. The ecclesiastical leaders of that church will never admit that it was a case of the Bible versus the church, but men not associated with the Presbyterian Church in the USA, and some, not even Christians, saw the real issue and did not hesitate to make it plain.

The Presbyterian Church in the USA is what is known as a creedal church because each minister and each office-bearer must pledge loyalty to the Westminster Confession of Faith as the system of doctrine taught in the holy Scriptures. The church had been known as an intellectual defender of the historic Westminster Confession of Faith, even though that defense had depended largely in the last decade upon a minority. But by the 1936 decisions the Lord Jesus Christ was dethroned as Head and King of his church, and the authority of human councils was placed above the Word of God. A missionary program which was contrary to

---

8   *Minutes of the General Assembly* 1936, Part 1, 106.
9   *Ibid.,* 107.
10   *Ibid.,* 39.

the teachings of the Bible was forced upon the church and its members, and the penalty for lack of support and for effective criticism was suspension from the ministry. The Confession of Faith of the church was not altered, but it was so interpreted by the highest court of the church sitting as a court of Jesus Christ that for all practical purposes the Confession of Faith was changed. From that time forth each informed member of the Presbyterian Church in the USA was fully aware of the meaning of the Confession of Faith and the constitution for him. He must obey men.

The decision of the Presbyterian Church in the USA in the case of Dr. Machen and the others is almost identical with that in the case of Martin Luther. Luther declared that his teachings were in accord with the Bible and he tried to prove it. The Roman Catholic Church, on the other hand, said that it must decide what teaching is true to the Bible. When Luther refused to recant he was excommunicated. The one great difference between the two trials and decisions is that for the Roman Catholic, the church is the supreme judge in all matters of doctrine; it is the official and final arbiter for Roman Catholics in spiritual matters. But in the case of Dr. Machen, the constitution of the Presbyterian Church in the USA states emphatically that "the Supreme Judge, by whom all controversies of religion are to be determined . . . can be no other but the Holy Spirit speaking in the Scriptures."[11] In other words, the Roman church was wrong in Luther's case in its lack of faithfulness to the Bible but right in loyalty to its constitution, while the Presbyterian Church in the USA was not only untrue to the Bible in its decisions but was also unfaithful to its own constitution.

At least one of the eight suspended from the ministry of the Presbyterian Church in the USA was a world-famous theologian who was honored by the world for his sound learning and cogent reasoning in defense of the Bible. Dr. Machen was by far the most distinguished minister of the Presbyterian Church in the USA in his generation. The Rev. Caspar Wistar Hodge, Ph.D., professor of systematic theology at Princeton Theological Seminary and a member of the famous Hodge family, wrote, "I regarded him as the greatest theologian in the English-speaking world."[12]

---

11   *Confession of Faith*, chapter 1, section X.
12   *Presbyterian Guardian* 3 (February 13, 1937), 189.

This blow to Dr. Machen by the church which he had served with distinction for over thirty years, together with the disloyalty of certain Independent Board members to Presbyterianism, filled his cup of sorrow. Six months later, on January 1, 1937, on a trip to Bismarck, North Dakota, to speak against unbelief in the church and the world, he contracted pneumonia and died. When he had passed to his reward a flood of tributes came from men and women of all shades of opinion, confirming not only his greatness but also the truth of his contentions in the conflict with the Presbyterian Church in the USA.

H. L. Mencken, who by no means can be designated a believer in historic Christianity, wrote,

> He saw clearly that the only effects that could follow diluting and polluting Christianity in the modernist manner would be its complete abandonment and ruin. Either it was true or it was not true. If, as he believed, it was true, then there could be no compromise with persons who sought to whittle away its essential postulates, however respectable their motives.
>
> Thus he fell out with the reformers who have been trying, in late years, to convert the Presbyterian Church into a kind of literary and social club, devoted vaguely to good works. . . .
>
> His one and only purpose was to hold it resolutely to what he conceived to be the true faith. When that enterprise met with opposition he fought vigorously, and though he lost in the end and was forced out of Princeton it must be manifest that he marched off to Philadelphia with all the honors of war.[13]

Albert C. Dieffenbach, religious editor of *The Boston Evening Transcript*, and a Unitarian minister, said,

> Out of the historic issue of fundamentalism, which began about 1920 in the Northern Baptist churches but has continued unabated among a minority in the Presbyterian Church in the USA, that is, the Northern Presbyterian church, he [Dr. Machen] emerges in death as the theologian and crusader, as learned and valiant a spiritual warrior as the Protestant church has produced in modern times. . . .
>
> Now all that Machen ever did was hold fast to the faith and insist that those of his denomination who had taken their vows should do likewise. He was unwilling to yield an inch to the trend of modern thought.[14]

Pearl S. Buck, noted author and former missionary of the Presbyterian Church in the USA, whom Dr. Machen had opposed because of her

---

13   *Baltimore Evening Sun*, 18 January 1937.
14   *The Boston Evening Transcript*, 9 January 1937.

unbelief, eulogized Dr. Machen's efforts to combat the rulers of the church even though she disagreed violently with his theological position.

> We have lost a man whom our times can ill spare, a man who had convictions which were real to him and who fought for those convictions and held to them through every change in time and human thought. There was power in him which was positive in its very negations. He was worth a hundred of his fellows who, as princes of the church, occupy easy places and play their church politics and trim their sails to every wind, who in their smug observance of the convictions of life and religion offend all honest and searching spirits. No forthright mind can live among them, neither the honest skeptic nor the honest dogmatist. I wish Dr. Machen had lived to go on fighting them.[15]

Many other glowing tributes were paid Dr. Machen by leaders in other denominations and by outstanding Presbyterians, but these persons are quoted to demonstrate that the convictions and contentions of the minority in the Presbyterian Church in the USA that the issue was doctrinal, and that the authority of the Bible was at stake, were upheld even by men and women who declared themselves avowedly against historic Christianity. Individuals like Mencken, Dieffenbach, and Pearl Buck surely had no personal interest in the matter nor any axe to grind. They were spectators and, if anything, more in agreement theologically with modernists. No, the princes of the church may fool some of the people, and even a majority of the Presbyterians, by crying that the issue was "administrative," but they cannot stampede outsiders and they cannot keep down the truth forever.

Dr. Machen is gone, the supporters of the Independent Board have left the Presbyterian Church in the USA, and, sad to state, the consistent and clear testimony against unbelief that once made that church a bulwark of the faith is silent. Occasionally an individual voice is raised through a sermon or an article in a theological journal, but the corporate witness of the church through its boards and agencies is no longer on the side of historic Christianity. The church is large in membership, it is rich in endowments and buildings, it is praised and recognized by the world, but its great Calvinistic heritage, its adherence to the Bible as the Word of God, has been cast aside and "Ichabod" is written over its door. As each year passes the church becomes less doctrinally conscious and more in tune with the modernism of the day!

---

15   Pearl S. Buck, "Tribute to Dr. Machen," *The New Republic* 89 (January 20, 1937), 355.

12
The Orthodox Presbyterian Church

THE SPIRIT and the decisions of the 1935 General Assembly made it clear that the conservatives of the church would have to organize and unite on a definite program of reform and preparation for what seemed like the inevitable—a split in the church. Accordingly, a letter was written by two elders and a layman and addressed to 100 or more conservative leaders in the East, inviting them to be present at a meeting in Philadelphia on June 27, 1935, for the purpose of considering a plan of united action.

Approximately 100 attended the meeting at which time the Presbyterian Constitutional Covenant Union was organized, officers elected, an executive committee formed, and a constitution adopted. A campaign was launched to obtain signers of the covenant, to form chapters, and to promote the program of the Covenant Union. The covenant read as follows:

> We, the members of this Covenant Union, are resolved, in accordance with God's Word, and in humble reliance upon His grace, to maintain the Constitution of the Presbyterian Church in the U.S.A., (1) making every effort to bring about a reform of the existing church organization, and to restore the church's clear and glorious Christian testimony, which modernism and indifferentism have now so grievously silenced, but (2) if such efforts fail and in particular if the tyrannical policy of the present majority triumphs, holding ourselves ready to perpetuate the true Presbyterian Church in the U.S.A., regardless of cost.

It became obvious that the officers and executive committee of the Covenant Union were determined not only to expose modernism in the boards of the church and to attempt a reform, but also to prepare for the probable division in the church if the members of the Independent Board were ousted. This was certain from the second part of the pledge.

Immediately, the Covenant Union was attacked not only by the church machine but also by the Rev. Samuel G. Craig, D.D., a former member of the board of trustees of Westminster Theological Seminary and a former member of the Independent Board, because the Covenant Union by its pledge committed men to withdraw from the church if members of the Independent Board were expelled from the church.

> While in our opinion one of the planks of that platform should commit its supporters to the defense of the members of the Independent Board against the unchristian and unconstitutional mandate of the 1934 Assembly, we are persuaded that it must be broad enough to provide seats for many who think that the formation of the Independent Board was unwise or premature, and even for some who think its formation of questionable constitutionality. It is high time, it seems to us, for a conference of representative conservatives or evangelicals or fundamentalists—call them what you will—to discover whether it is not possible to agree on such a platform and in such leadership.[1]

Such outspoken criticism and opposition on the part of one who was editor of *Christianity Today*, the paper which had been launched in 1930 to carry on the fight against modernism in the church, and to which the conservatives in the church looked for leadership, called for an important decision. If the Covenant Union could not express its views and promote its program through the pages of *Christianity Today*, then another journal had to be started which would further the aims of the Covenant Union and those who were carrying the main burden of the conflict.

Prior to this Dr. Machen, as well as other members of the Independent Board, had carried on an extensive correspondence with Dr. Craig because of his indirect attacks on the Independent Board. Dr. Machen contended that in 1933, *Christianity Today* and the editorials in the paper had defended the Independent Board.[2] An editorial in the paper, June, 1933, stated, "As matters now stand, they [Bible-believers] must either make their contributions to Foreign Missions through non-Presbyterian channels or they must establish a new agency." In the September, 1935, issue of *Christianity Today*, Dr. Craig assumed an entirely different attitude. He then defended a third alternative, namely, the designation of gifts to sound missionaries under the Board of Foreign Missions of the Presbyterian Church in the USA.

---

1   *Christianity Today* 6 (September 1935), 74.
2   See November 1, 1935 letter to Edwin H. Rian from J. Gresham Machen.

In answer to this allegation, Dr. Craig argued that the first editorial was written by Mr. Griffiths, then managing editor of *Christianity Today*, and so the opinion expressed was not his own, yet now Dr. Craig claimed, "Whatever of praise or blame is due its editorial policy should be placed wholly to the account of its editor."[3]

Dr. Machen made further criticisms of Dr. Craig's policy, among them the lack of attention given to trials of members of the Independent Board, particularly in the September, 1935 issue, when all of the Independent Board trials which were the center of controversy in the church were dismissed with a third of a column in the paper.

This "drift" in the policy of the journal which left the conservatives in the church without an adequate organ of expression, and this open attack on the newly organized Covenant Union, brought the resignation of the Rev. H. McAllister Griffiths as managing editor of *Christianity Today*, and the establishment of the *Presbyterian Guardian* as a paper directly under the sponsorship of the Covenant Union and edited by Mr. Griffiths, with Thomas R. Birch as assistant editor. Mr. Griffiths was also made general secretary of the Covenant Union and offices were opened in Philadelphia.

This division in the ranks of the conservatives was a great blow to their cause and a source of satisfaction to the leaders of the church. It was founded upon a fundamental difference of approach to the whole problem of reform and the battle for the faith, which will be considered in detail in another chapter under the title, "Reform From Within."

In the very first issue of the *Presbyterian Guardian*, Dr. Machen set the standard for the movement when he wrote,

> We cannot trust the world; we cannot trust that elusive something known as "civilization!" We cannot, alas, trust the visible church. But when God speaks we can trust Him. He has spoken in the Bible. We can find our way through all the mists if we will make that blessed Book our guide.

Another article in the same issue stated, "By the grace of God we will contend against all forms of unbelief. We shall not cease to maintain and defend the inspired Word of God and the Constitution of the Presbyterian Church in the U.S.A. 'regardless of cost.'"

The Covenant Union began immediately an intensive campaign to interest individuals in the support of its program and to form chapters throughout the nation. Public rallies were held in support of the new

---

3   *Christianity Today* 6 (September 1935), 76.

organization and in opposition to the tyranny of the church in its apparent determination to force the members of the Independent Board from the church. Not only did the Covenant Union add members to its cause, but in line with the pledge to bring about a reform in the existing church organization, a full exposé of modernism in the other boards and organizations was begun. Even in the Board of Foreign Missions more evidence was produced of its unfaithfulness to the Bible and the doctrinal standards of the church.

Nine articles by different men were written concerning unbelief in the Board of Christian Education. What was exposed in that agency corresponded largely with the facts discovered in the Foreign Mission Board. Signers of the Auburn Affirmation were found in places of authority in the educational program of the church,

> (1) Two, as members of the Board; (2) One, as an officer of the Staff of the Board, in charge of the Department of Colleges, Theological Seminaries and Training Schools; (3) Five as Field Representatives who are responsible at headquarters to the Secretary of the Board, who work under the supervision of synodical or presbyterial committees on Christian Education in order to make the Board's program effective; and (4) Ten among the university pastors . . . . [4]

The literature issued by the board was found to be not only silent concerning the great and central doctrines of Christianity, but in some instances opposed to them. The books recommended included three written by outstanding modernists of the day, among them, *The Meaning of Prayer*, by H. E. Fosdick, and *The Life of Prayer in a World of Science*, by William Adams Brown. The various departments under the sponsorship of the board were found to be anything but faithful to the central message of Christianity. For example, the direction of the board's program in higher education was under the leadership of Dr. W. L. Young, a signer of the Auburn Affirmation.[5]

---

4   Ned B. Stonehouse, "Modernism and the Board of Christian Education of the Presbyterian Church in the U.S.A.," *Presbyterian Guardian* 1 (January 6, 1936), 109.

5   Ned B. Stonehouse, et al., "Modernism and the Board of Christian Education of the Presbyterian Church in the U.S.A.," *Presbyterian Guardian* 1 (January 6, 1936), 108-109; (February 3, 1936), 140-42, 155; (February 17, 1936), 161-62; (March 2, 1936), 179-80; (March 16, 1936), 198-99; 2 (April 6, 1936), 6-7, 19; (May 4, 1936), 50-52; (May 18, 1936), 72-72.

In order to implement these charges against the Board of Christian Education in the way provided by the constitution of the church, an overture was introduced in the Presbytery of Philadelphia asking that the board exercise care in electing members, secretaries, in issuing literature, and in cooperating with union movements, in order to keep modernism from the board's program.[6] Dr. George E. Barnes, newly elected Auburn Affirmation moderator of the presbytery, ruled this overture out of order.

Strangely enough, this overture was worded in the accustomed way. In fact, it followed the wording of the overture concerning the Board of Foreign Missions which had been passed by the Presbytery of Philadelphia in 1933. The difference was that in 1933 the conservatives controlled the presbytery, but in 1936 the Auburn Affirmationists were in the saddle.

An overture from the Presbytery of Philadelphia North was presented to the 1936 General Assembly, asking that the Board of Christian Education see to it that its literature be in accord with the standards of the church.[7] This overture was referred to the Board of Christian Education and more or less forgotten.

A similar overture was presented by the Presbytery of Milwaukee and referred to the Board of Christian Education by the 1936 General Assembly for due consideration.[8] An exposé was also begun with respect to the Board of National Missions and the same results obtained—modernism held the upper hand.[9]

Of the seventeen minister members of the Board of Christian Education, seven were signers of the Auburn Affirmation and of these seven at least one, the Rev. Henry Sloane Coffin, D.D., president of Union Theological Seminary, New York City, is one of the leading modernists in America. Not only did he sign the Auburn Affirmation, but his books reveal clearly what his opinions are concerning the great

---

6   *Presbyterian Guardian* 2 (May 4, 1936), 60. See also Appendix, note 20.

7   *Minutes of the General Assembly* 1936, Part 1, 25, 28, 74.

8   *Ibid.*, 74.

9   Edwin H. Rian, "Modernism and the Board of National Missions of the Presbyterian Church in the U.S.A.," *Presbyterian Guardian* 1 (March 2, 1936), 176-77.

doctrines of the church. In his book *Some Christian Convictions*, he writes as follows about the canon of holy Scripture:

> He [a Protestant] is not bound by the opinion of others, however many and venerable; and unless a book commends itself to his own spiritual judgment, he is under no obligation to receive it as the Word of God to him. As a matter of fact every Christian does make such a Bible of his own; the particular passages which "grip" him and reproduce their experience in him, they, and they alone, are his Bible.[10]

Nothing could more flatly contradict the Westminster Confession of Faith on the canon of holy Scripture and the authority of all Scripture. Chapter I, section II, after naming the sixty-six books of the Bible, states, "All which are given by inspiration of God, to be the rule of faith and life."

The Rev. W. H. Boddy, D.D., pastor of the large and influential Westminster Presbyterian Church, Minneapolis, Minnesota, not only signed the Auburn Affirmation, but also was a member of the National Committee of the Modern Missions Movement, whose avowed purpose was

> . . . to foster the further consideration of the possible world service of Christianity as indicated by the Laymen's Foreign Missions Inquiry; to serve as a medium of information; and to cooperate with any Board, Church or other agency which is making effective the principles and recommendations of the Report [*ReThinking Missions*] and of the Regional Reports by the Commission of Appraisal.[11]

The anti-Christian religion of *Re-Thinking Missions* has already been considered.

Not only were some members of the board aligned against biblical Christianity, but also the general secretary, the Rev. E. Graham Wilson, D.D., was a signer of the Auburn Affirmation. The literature issued by the board was also examined and found to be wanting in its adherence to the Confession of Faith.[12] And so another board of the church was proven to be untrue to the Confession of Faith.

---

10   Henry Sloane Coffin, *Some Christian Convictions* (New Haven: Yale University Press, 1915), 64.

11   *Modern Missions Movement—An Announcement*, 9.

12   Murray Forst Thompson, "Modernism and the Board of National Missions of the Presbyterian Church in the U.S.A.," *Presbyterian Guardian* 2 (May 18, 1936), 75-76.

While the Covenant Union was continuing its attempt to reform the existing church organization by bringing the true situation to the attention of the members of the church, the prosecution of the Independent Board members went on unabated, and the goal toward which the rulers of the church were working came closer with each month. Philadelphia and Chester Presbyteries were reorganized so as to be controlled by those in sympathy with the princes of the church. The Rev. Roy T. Brumbaugh, D.D., pastor of the First Church, Tacoma, Washington, and a member of the Independent Board, was forced to leave his church building and with over five hundred members formed the First Independent Church of Tacoma. Kalamazoo Presbytery refused to receive the Rev. G. H. Snell from the Presbytery of Cincinnati because of his unwillingness to pledge support of the Board of Foreign Missions without qualification. The Permanent Judicial Commission of the general assembly upheld the action of Lackawanna Presbytery in erasing the name of the Rev. Henry W. Coray from its roll because he had become a missionary of the Independent Board, and in interpreting his action as making him "independent" even though he did not declare himself "independent."

The Judicial Commission of the Synod of Wisconsin upheld the Presbytery of Milwaukee in dissolving the pastoral relationship of the Rev. J. J. DeWaard because he refused to cease his criticism of the boards of the church, and it sustained Winnebago Presbytery in suspending the Rev. Arthur F. Perkins from the ministry because he had established an independent Bible camp and had criticized the boards. All of these actions made the *terminus ad quem* of the whole conflict certain. The members of the Independent Board would be suspended from the ministry and a new church organization would be launched as a result. The "machine" of the church was rolling along, crushing all opposition in its path and making the victory at the end a hollow one.

The inevitable took place, for in Syracuse, New York, in June, 1936, certain members of the Independent Board were suspended from the ministry of the Presbyterian Church in the USA. This action had been foreseen by the Covenant Union so that its first annual convention had been called for June 11-14, 1936, in Philadelphia. To this gathering came delegates from thirteen states who realized what the meeting meant and were prepared for action. The Covenant Union was dissolved and on the afternoon of June 11, 1936, thirty-four ministers, seventeen ruling elders, and seventy-nine laymen signed an act of association and doctrinal statement.[13]

The ministers and elders then constituted themselves the general assembly of the Presbyterian Church of America. The Rev. J. Gresham Machen, D.D., who had led the conflict against unbelief, was elected moderator without a dissenting vote, and the long-awaited, long-prophesied parting of the ways between Bible-believers and the Presbyterian Church in the USA became a reality.

The First General Assembly of the Presbyterian Church of America was concerned largely with the election of committees which would prepare the necessary organization of the church in readiness for the next assembly, which was called for November 12–15, 1936. On the other hand, several important and far-reaching decisions were made which stamped the Presbyterian Church of America as thoroughly Calvinistic in its doctrine and fair in its recognition of the rights of congregations to retain their local properties.

A Committee on the Constitution was elected with the power to recommend the adoption of the Westminster Confession of Faith, the Larger and Shorter Catechisms, and the elimination from these standards of the 1903 amendments and the Declaratory Statement.[14] The changes in the Confession of Faith of the Presbyterian Church in the USA which were made in 1903 and which were discussed in chapter one, impaired the church's testimony to the Bible and the Reformed faith.

A resolution with reference to church property grew out of the unfair practice of the Presbyterian Church in the USA in claiming all church property for the denomination, even though the church building had been erected and paid for by the local congregation. Each local church under this provision is allowed to retain its property, which shall only revert to the Presbyterian Church of America if the congregation becomes extinct.[15] Committees on home missions and Christian education were also elected.

---

13   *Minutes of the First General Assembly of The Presbyterian Church of America*, 3-4. See also Appendix, note 21.

14   *Ibid.*, 7. See also Appendix, note 22.

15   *Ibid.*, 19-20. See also Appendix, note 23.

Another action was taken making the decisions of the general assembly of the Presbyterian Church in the USA regarding the members of the Independent Board invalid. In part, it read,

> all censures inflicted by courts of the Presbyterian Church in the U.S.A., upon any of the defendants in Judicial Cases 1–5 mentioned above who are now connected with this church, are by the action of this Assembly, as the supreme judicatory of this church, terminated, lifted, and declared at an end.[16]

One outstanding characteristic marked the First General Assembly of the Presbyterian Church of America. It was a truly deliberative body where every commissioner had an equal opportunity to express his opinion and where lively debate preceded each action. There was no attempt to shut off discussion, to call for the previous question, and to use all sorts of parliamentary tricks to force motions to a vote. When a matter had been thoroughly considered, each man voted according to his convictions, unafraid of any recriminatory measures later by a coterie of office-holders and office-seekers.

Immediately following the First General Assembly of the Presbyterian Church of America, congregations and ministers began to leave the Presbyterian Church in the USA, the Knox Presbyterian Church, Philadelphia, being the first to unite with the new body. Within two months after the new body had been formed, seventy-five ministers were under its jurisdiction, nine presbyteries had been erected (California, the Dakotas, Iowa, the Northwest, New Jersey, New York, and New England, Ohio, Philadelphia, and Wisconsin), and there were congregations or groups of the Presbyterian Church of America meeting for worship in California, Connecticut, Delaware, Illinois, Indiana, Iowa, Maine, Maryland, Massachusetts, New Hampshire, New Jersey, New York, North Dakota, Ohio, Oregon, Pennsylvania, South Dakota, Washington, Wisconsin, and the District of Columbia.[17]

Even before the Presbyterian Church of America was formed, it was certain that the Presbyterian Church in the USA intended to continue its persecution of the Independent Board members even though they were in another church body. The Christ Reformed Episcopal Church, 43rd and Chestnut Streets, Philadelphia, had extended the courtesy of the use of its building to the Covenant Union for its evening meetings

---

16   *Ibid.*, 13.
17   Edwin H. Rian, "The Presbyterian Church of America," *Presbyterian Guardian* 2 (August 17, 1936), 213.

during the convention of June 11-14. To prevent this and to persuade
the Reformed Episcopal Church to cancel the contract with the Covenant
Union, the Rev. Lewis S. Mudge, D.D., stated clerk of the general
assembly, and the Rev. George Emerson Barnes, D.D., moderator of
Philadelphia Presbytery of the Presbyterian Church in the USA, appeared
before the vestry and actually convinced it that to allow the former
ministers of the Presbyterian Church in the USA to use the Reformed
Episcopal Church building would be to violate comity relations between
the Reformed Episcopal Church and the Presbyterian Church in the
USA.[18] However, the Reformed Episcopal Church of the Atonement in
Germantown offered its auditorium to the Presbyterian Church of
America, and a telegram of greeting was read to the general assembly of
the Presbyterian Church of America from the Rev. Robert Westly Peach,
presiding bishop of the Reformed Episcopal Church.

In an almost ludicrous session of the Philadelphia Presbytery of the
Presbyterian Church in the USA, the five minister members of the
Independent Board, who had been ordered suspended from the ministry
of that church by the general assembly, were formally ordered suspended,
even though these men had already renounced the jurisdiction of the
Presbyterian Church in the USA and so were no longer members of it.
The same procedure was reenacted by the Presbytery of New Brunswick
in the case of Dr. Machen. And to make the whole proceeding even more
ridiculous, five ministers, the Rev. A. A. MacRae, the Rev. Ned B.
Stonehouse, the Rev. Robert Moody Holmes, the Rev. Albert B. Dodd,
D.D., and the Rev. David Freeman, all of whom had renounced the
jurisdiction of the Presbyterian Church in the USA and had joined the
Presbyterian Church of America, were ordered to face trial before the
Presbytery of Philadelphia.[19]

The full force of vindictiveness against the Presbyterian Church of
America on the part of the Presbyterian Church in the USA was yet to
come. On August 13, 1936, just two months after the formation of the
Presbyterian Church of America, a bill of complaint in equity was filed
in the Court of Common Pleas No. 5 in Philadelphia by Henry B. Master,
moderator of the general assembly, Lewis S. Mudge, stated clerk of the
general assembly, et al., claiming to represent the Presbyterian Church

18   *Presbyterian Guardian* 2 (June 22, 1936), 143.
19   *Presbyterian Guardian* 2 (July 6, 1936), 160.

in the USA *versus* J. Gresham Machen, Paul Woolley, et al., and all officers and members of the Presbyterian Church of America, asking the court to enjoin the defendant church from using the name on the ground of its similarity to that of the Presbyterian Church in the USA.[20]

On April 28, 1937, the hearing began in the Court of Common Pleas No. 5 before the Honorable Frank Smith. The plaintiff's arguments fell under three heads. First, the Presbyterian Church in the USA was by general consent the largest and most representative Presbyterian Church in the United States. It had invested millions and millions of dollars in buildings and organizations, and these had to be protected. Secondly, in a proposed union between the Presbyterian Church in the USA and the United Presbyterian Church of North America, the name "The Presbyterian Church of America" had been mentioned as the one for the united church. Thirdly, the Presbyterian Church in the USA had carried on happy comity relations with many churches, and it would be unfortunate if the Presbyterian Church of America should enter these areas with a competitive spirit and by a misleading name confuse its identity in the minds of the public.

To prove that the Presbyterian Church of America had been confused with the Presbyterian Church in the USA in the mind of the general public, one letter and one telegram were produced which had been mailed by a newspaper office to the Presbyterian Church of America and incorrectly addressed to the office of the stated clerk of the general assembly of the Presbyterian Church in the USA.[21]

In answer to these arguments, the defendants stated: First, while the Presbyterian Church in the USA is the largest Presbyterian body in the United States, it is not *the* Presbyterian Church and has no more right to the name "Presbyterian" than any of the other ten or more churches in America using that descriptive title. "Presbyterian" designates a certain form of doctrine and church government developed by John Calvin and others, so that any body conforming to this well-accepted historical type of church is qualified to use the word "Presbyterian" in its title. Furthermore, there is no such thing as property rights in the future contributions of members of any church. It is a totalitarian conception of the church

---

20   *Presbyterian Guardian* 2 (September 12, 1936), 235. See Appendix, note 24.

21   *Notes of Testimony in the case of Henry B. Master, Moderator of the General Assembly et. al. versus J. Gresham Machen, Moderator, et al.,* Common Pleas Court No. 5, June Term, 1936, 50-51.

that members of evangelical churches must support the official agencies of the church to the utmost of their ability.

In the second place, the proposed union between the Presbyterian Church in the USA and the United Presbyterian Church of North America, which was to use the name, was voted down by the United Presbyterian Church years ago and any attempt to revive this movement would have to be started *de novo*. Certainly, it was misleading to create the impression that a proposed union which was defeated warranted the Presbyterian Church in the USA in preempting the name Presbyterian Church of America. In fact, such an implication was absurd.

In the third place, the argument against proselytizing struck at the very heart of religious freedom in the United States. Even Dr. Mudge had to admit on the witness stand that he would urge the Presbyterian Church in the USA to proselytize among Unitarians.[22] Every church has a right under the constitution of the United States to proselytize. At this point it is well to note that the judge in the case refused to allow the introduction of evidence by expert theologians to prove that a fundamental difference in doctrinal belief caused the members of the defendant church to withdraw from the plaintiff body. Therefore, argued the defendants, since the great doctrinal conflict which separated the two churches could not be introduced, only one valid issue remained, namely, the question of confusion of the names in the minds of the general public. This hearing took place nearly a year after the defendant church had been organized, and yet the plaintiffs could only produce two pieces of evidence of mistaken identity. This was no positive proof that any state of confusion existed. On the other hand, the defendants cited many secular and religious papers to demonstrate that no obscurity or confusion whatsoever obtained in the minds of the writers.[23]

The court handed down a decision on June 27, 1938, in favor of the plaintiff church.[24] The defendants gave notice of appeal to the State Supreme Court of Pennsylvania, but the appeal was not taken. On February 9, 1939, at a specially called Fifth General Assembly, the Presbyterian Church of America adopted the name "The Orthodox Presbyterian Church," and the suit was terminated.[25]

---

22   *Ibid.*, 138.
23   *Ibid.*, 269-73.
24   *Presbyterian Guardian* 5 (August 1938), 160. See Appendix, note 25.
25   *Minutes of the General Assembly of The Orthodox Presbyterian Church* 1939, 11

The Second General Assembly of the Presbyterian Church of America in November, 1936, only five months after the formation of the church, was held in order to adopt a Confession of Faith and so provide an adequate doctrinal basis for the new body. It claimed to be the "spiritual succession" of the Presbyterian Church in the USA, so that the Westminster Confession of Faith would logically be its doctrinal confession. However, in 1903 certain changes and additions had been made to the Westminster Confession of Faith by the Presbyterian Church in the USA, which changes toned down the biblical and Calvinistic witness of the Confession, and these had to be eliminated if the Presbyterian Church of America were to continue in the true tradition of the Reformed faith.[26] Therefore the Committee on the Constitution was given power "to recommend the elimination, from that form of these Standards [The Westminster Confession of Faith], of the changes made in the year of our Lord 1903." The committee did recommend the adoption of the Westminster Confession of Faith with the elimination of most of the 1903 amendments, but with the retention of two small changes in chapter XXII concerning oaths, and chapter XXV, section VI, which designates the pope as the antichrist.[27] By an overwhelming majority the recommendation of the committee was adopted.[28]

Another subject already discussed in chapter four developed into the central issue of that assembly, namely, the question of modern dispensationalism and premillennialism. As has been stated, professor R. B. Kuiper of Westminster Theological Seminary had written an article, "Why Separation was Necessary," which first appeared in *The Banner* (Christian Reformed), and was reprinted in the *Presbyterian Guardian* of September 12, 1936. The section which received the most attention read,

> It would have warmed the cockles of the heart of any Christian Reformed minister to hear how closely they [candidates for ordination at General Assembly] were questioned about the two errors which are so extremely prevalent among American fundamentalists, Arminianism and the Dispensationalism of the Scofield Bible. The Assembly wanted to make sure that these prospective ministers were not tainted with such anti-reformed heresies.

---

26 See chapter one.
27 *Minutes of Second General Assembly of the Presbyterian Church of America*, November, 1936, 13.
28 *Ibid.*, 18.

Prior to this, professor John Murray of Westminster Theological Seminary had been discussing "The Reformed Faith and Modern Substitutes" in a series of articles appearing in the *Presbyterian Guardian* on the general themes of Arminianism and modern dispensationalism. One article in particular was given over to this latter subject.

> In entering upon an exposition of what we called "Modern Dispensationalism," and the establishment of our thesis that it contradicts the teaching of the standards of the Reformed Faith, in particular those of the Presbyterian Church in the U.S.A., it is necessary to remind our readers that we have no objection to the word "dispensation," nor to the idea of designating the various periods that may and must be distinguished in the divine economy of the history of the world as distinct "dispensations." What we are intent upon showing is that the system of interpretation widely prevalent in this country, and set forth, for example, in the Scofield Reference Bible and in the books of various Bible teachers of prominence, is palpably inconsistent with the system of truth embodied in our Presbyterian standards.[29]

It is well to take cognizance of the fact that the word "premillennial," or reference to premillennialism, does not occur in either professor Kuiper's or professor Murray's articles. Mr. Murray made it clear that

> The "Dispensationalism" of which we speak as heterodox from the standpoint of the Reformed Faith is that form of interpretation, widely popular at the present time, which discovers in the several dispensations of God's redemptive revelation distinct and even contrary principles of divine procedure and thus destroys the unity of God's dealings with fallen mankind.[30]

Furthermore, Dr. Machen emphasized that as such the premillennial view of the return of Christ, namely, that Jesus Christ "will return before a thousand-year period held to be mentioned in the Book of Revelation, that during that period He will reign upon this earth, and that after that period will come the final judgment," was not being attacked. In fact, he pointed out definitely,

> Can a person who holds the premillennial view be a true Calvinist; can he, in other words, hold truly to the Calvinistic or Reformed system of doctrine which is set forth in the Westminster Standards? We think that he can; and for that reason we think that Premillennialists as well as those who hold the opposing

---

29   John Murray, "The Reformed Faith and Modern Substitutes," Part VI: "Modern Dispensationalism," *Presbyterian Guardian* 2 (May 18, 1936), 77.

30   John Murray, "The Reformed Faith and Modern Substitutes," *Presbyterian Guardian* 1 (February 3, 1936), 143.

view may become ministers or elders or deacons in The Presbyterian Church of America.[31]

In spite of all these precautions and carefully worded statements safeguarding the liberty of view of the individual minister and congregation with respect to the return of our Lord, the *Christian Beacon*, edited by the Rev. Carl McIntire, pastor of the then Independent Presbyterian Church, Collingswood, New Jersey, and a minister of the Presbyterian Church of America, carried an editorial on October 1, 1936, claiming that attacks were being made upon premillennialists, as especially manifested in professor Kuiper's article, "Why Separation was Necessary." Mr. McIntire insisted that "The remark in regard to the 'Dispensationalism of the Scofield Bible' is an attack upon the premillennialists, as heretics." Professor Kuiper replied to the editorial, but Mr. McIntire refused to publish it. Among other things professor Kuiper stated in his reply,

> It is a matter of common knowledge that there is ever so much more to the dispensationalism of the Scofield Bible than the mere teaching of Premillennialism. Nor do the two stand and fall together. There are premillennarians who have never heard of Scofield's dispensations. More important than that, there are serious students of God's Word who hold to the premillennial return of Christ and emphatically reject Scofield's system of dispensations as fraught with grave error.[32]

The Presbyteries of California and New Jersey overtured the general assembly, asking that some declaratory statement be adopted setting forth "eschatological liberty" in the church.[33] The assembly did not adopt such a declaration, nor write such a statement into its constitution, as the Presbytery of California demanded, because members of the assembly believed that such liberty already existed within the constitution of the church.

But another question began to absorb the attention of the Presbyterian Church of America, namely, that of Christian liberty. In numerous private and public utterances, Westminster Seminary and its faculty were attacked as an institution and a faculty which encouraged its students to drink fermented beverages. The source of such baseless attacks appeared to be those who were followers of the Rev. Carl McIntire and supporters of the *Christian Beacon*.

---

31   *Presbyterian Guardian* 3 (October 24, 1936), 21.
32   *Presbyterian Guardian* 3 (November 14, 1936), 54.
33   *Minutes of the Second General Assembly*, 16-17.

Dr. J. Oliver Buswell published several volumes at this time, one of which, *The Christian Life*, dealt with the subject of Christian liberty and worldliness. The thesis that moderate drinking inevitably leads to drunkenness is defended rather strongly, and total abstinence is upheld as the requirement in this matter for Christians.

In order to answer these charges, an editorial appeared in the *Presbyterian Guardian* stating the historic Presbyterian position concerning the subject of Christian liberty.[34] The Bible was set forth as the only rule of faith and morals and as the only guide to right conduct. There must be no appeal to the rules of men unless they agree with the Word of God. Certain things are expressly forbidden in the Bible, while other calls to duty are by "good and necessary consequence" deduced from the Scriptures. Every Christian must obey these injunctions and if he does not, he is engaging in sinful practice. On the other hand, certain things either expressly or through silence are regarded by the Bible as indifferent in themselves. Engaging in these practices is a matter of the individual's Christian liberty. He must be guided by the circumstances in expressing his Christian liberty, always keeping in mind the weaker brother and the high standard of holiness set by the Word of God. The editorial then continued to deal with the particular problem of the use of wine.

The principle enunciated was that, according to the Bible, it is not wrong at any and all times to partake temperately of wine. The Bible condemns intemperance, but clearly it allows the moderate use of wine under certain conditions. The editorial concluded with the warning, "In every instance we must keep before us the goal of the salvation and the edification of men's souls through our testimony to Christ. And let us take care that our testimony to Christ be to the Christ of the Bible. Jesus said, 'Blessed is he, whosoever shall find no occasion of stumbling in me!'"

This issue came to a climax in the Presbyterian Church of America at the Third General Assembly. Three overtures to the assembly recommended total abstinence as the principle to maintain, while a fourth warned the assembly against man-made rules and urged the church to re-study the subordinate standards of the church, particularly the Larger and Shorter Catechisms, as containing the principles of holy Scripture

---

34   *Presbyterian Guardian* 3 (February 27, 1937), 201-204.

which is the guide to godly living. The three overtures relative to total abstinence were defeated, and the fourth overture was adopted directing the attention of the church to the Westminster Standards as containing sufficient and adequate instruction on this subject.[35]

The question of independency in church government also became a live issue in the third assembly as it related to support of the Independent Board. The church had organized a committee on foreign missions, but because most of its missionary volunteers had been sent out to the foreign field under the Independent Board, the foreign committee had always recommended the support of the Independent Board.

In the fall of 1936, however, a disruption had taken place in the Independent Board over the question of church government. The pledge of the Independent Board requires approval of the charter of the board, which charter in section III demands a belief in the "fundamental principles of Presbyterian church government." After the 1936 General Assembly of the Presbyterian Church in the USA, there began to develop a pronounced tendency toward independency in church government on the part of some members. The November, 1936 meeting of the Independent Board produced a clash over this issue.

Dr. Machen had been president of the board since its founding, but now certain members of the board had grown discontented with his policy of preserving the board's Presbyterian character and doctrine. These members had met before the meeting of the board and had decided to attempt to remove Dr. Machen from the presidency. The discontented members placed an ecclesiastically independent member in nomination for president, and he was elected. Thus a non-Presbyterian point of view had gained control of the board and its original purpose to support "truly Biblical and truly Presbyterian" foreign missions was abandoned.

Another example of this spirit of independency among board members was the Rev. Merrill T. MacPherson, vice-president of the Independent Board, who formed an independent church known as The Church of the Open Door of Philadelphia in June, 1936. Its constitution, article VII, section I, forbids any relationship with a denomination.

> This Church acknowledges only the Lord Jesus Christ as its Head; the Holy Scriptures as the only infallible guide on matters of faith, discipline and order; the Holy Spirit as its Teacher; and is not and never shall be amenable to or

---

35   *Minutes of the Third General Assembly,* June, 1937, 22. See Appendix, note 26.

under the jurisdiction or supervision of any other ecclesiastical body of any
kind or nature whatever.

Mr. MacPherson has since frequently stated that he has no desire or
intention of uniting with any denomination. This spirit of independency
was not manifest when he first became a member of the board and while
he was pastor of the Central-North Broad Street Presbyterian Church.
There were others on the Independent Board who also showed tendencies in the same direction.

Certain members of the board attempted to remedy this situation and
to compel the board to remain true to its charter, but they failed and
resigned from the board.[36] This left the Independent Board in opposition to the great Presbyterian purpose for which it had been founded.
These resignations from the Independent Board caused the Third
General Assembly to adopt a resolution urging the church not to support
it.[37] A minority report was also presented in which the allegation of
independency in church government was denied, and a plea for support
of the Independent Board by the Presbyterian Church of America was
entered.

As a result of these differences concerning dispensationalism, Christian liberty, and church government, fourteen ministers and three elders
withdrew from the Presbyterian Church of America and formed the Bible
Presbyterian Synod. The synod immediately announced its intention to
revise the three hundred-year-old Westminster Confession of Faith "in
any particulars in which the premillennial teaching of the Scriptures may
be held to be obscured."[38]

The First General Synod of the Bible Presbyterian Synod took definite
steps to alter the Westminster Confession of Faith so that it would
express the premillennial view. Changes were made in chapters VIII,
XXXII, XXXIII, and XXXIV in the Confession of Faith, and in questions
eighty-two, and eighty-four through ninety of the Larger Catechism, in
order to make them conform to premillennialism.[39] Thus, in a few
months the three hundred-year-old Westminster Confession of Faith,

---

36   *Presbyterian Guardian* 4 (June 12, 1937), 80. See Appendix, note 27.
37   *Minutes of the Third General Assembly*, June, 1937, 16-17. See
     Appendix, note 28.
38   *Presbyterian Guardian* 4 (June 26, 1937), 99.
39   *Changes in the Westminster Confession of Faith, adopted at the First
     General Synod, September 6–8, 1938, held in the Bible Presbyterian
     Church of Collingswood, N.J.*, 21-23.

which had been in harmony with the whole Presbyterian and Reformed tradition concerning the second coming of Jesus Christ, was hastily changed to conform exclusively to premillennialism.

The Fourth General Assembly of the Presbyterian Church of America was concerned largely with the adoption of a form of government. The form of government finally adopted is essentially that which has been used by the Presbyterian Church in the USA for over one hundred years. In several instances, however, changes were made in order to guard against the strong tendency of centralization which had dominated the Presbyterian Church in the USA during the last decade. The powers of the presbyteries over the congregations and the powers of the general assembly over the church were limited. The general assembly's powers which had been so abused in the Presbyterian Church in the USA were restricted in this way:

> whenever such deliverances, resolutions, overtures and other actions are additional to the specific provisions of the Constitution, they shall not be regarded as binding unless they have been approved by the general assembly and presbyteries in the manner provided in this Form of Government for the amendment of the Constitution.[40]

Several other minor changes were made, providing that baptized infants should be placed on the membership roll of the church;[41] that only communicant members of the church may vote in congregational meetings;[42] and that amendments to the form of subscription required of ministers, licentiates, ruling elders, and deacons must go through the same procedure as changes in the Confession of Faith and Catechisms.[43] The other amendments are of a very minor nature.

The Fifth General Assembly of the Presbyterian Church of America voted not to continue the suit concerning the name of the church and adopted the name, "the Orthodox Presbyterian Church."

The Directory for the Public Worship of God was adopted by the Orthodox Presbyterian Church at the Sixth General Assembly in May, 1939. It contains the same principles as the one in use by the Presbyterian

---

40   *Form of Government of the Orthodox Presbyterian Church*, chapter XI, section VI.
41   *Ibid.*, chapter IX, section IX.
42   *Ibid.*, chapter XXIII, section II.
43   *Ibid.*, chapter XXIV, section II. See Ned B. Stonehouse, "Some Distinctive Features of the Proposed Form of Government," *Presbyterian Guardian* 3 (November 14, 1936), 48-49.

Church in the USA but yet differs from that directory in several important features. First, it only includes forms for the public worship of God and so no burial service, or form for the visitation of the sick is found. Second, an entire new chapter was added on the principles of public worship, and suggested forms which are not part of the directory were proposed for the celebration of the Lord's Supper, public profession of faith, ordinations, and installations. Third, a few changes which are minor but nevertheless significant concern the pronouncement of the apostolic benediction only at regular services of worship, the use of hymns which are in agreement with the Word of God, the celebration of the sacrament only in the church building except in rare cases approved by the session, and the public profession of faith before the congregation.[44] A Book of Discipline has been provisionally adopted and is likely to be adopted finally in the next general assembly of the Orthodox Presbyterian Church in June, 1940.

In the formation of the Orthodox Presbyterian Church, Calvinism was given a new impetus in America. The spiritual heritage of Reformed teaching which had been stifled in the Presbyterian Church in the USA received a welcome in this church body, and the great doctrines of the Reformation, such as the sovereignty of God and salvation by grace alone, came to life again. Upon this high biblical ground the Orthodox Presbyterian Church stands, convinced that God will be pleased to use her to his glory and to the advancement of his kingdom. The original purpose and determination to make the church a truly biblical and truly Presbyterian body which would carry on the spiritual succession of the Presbyterian Church in the USA was insured.

The Orthodox Presbyterian Church is what its name implies, truly Presbyterian. Its doctrinal standards, the Westminster Confession of Faith, and the Larger and Shorter Catechisms are in practically the same form as they were when written by the Westminster divines nearly three hundred years ago. All compromise with modernism has been eliminated and strict adherence to the Presbyterian and Reformed traditions characterizes the testimony of the church. It is a church devoted to the Bible as the final authority for faith and practice and convinced that only through the sacrificial death of Christ upon the cross can men be saved.

---

44   See editorial in the *Presbyterian Guardian* 6 (October 1939), 188, for
        further discussion of this subject.

It is too early to evaluate the importance of the Orthodox Presbyterian Church in the religious life of America, but it is safe to state emphatically that this church is true to the Word of God and is true to the great Presbyterian heritage handed down by the church fathers of American Presbyterianism. While many of the Protestant churches in America are floundering in the quagmire of modernism and its ministers are preaching man-made philosophies and moral essays based upon naturalism, here is one church which relies not upon itself and man's wisdom but trusts emphatically in the Bible as God's revelation to man and as containing God's plan of salvation for man. The Orthodox Presbyterian Church's ministers do not say, thus says so and so, or even, so says the church, but they speak above the clamor of men, "Thus saith the Lord, hear ye Him !"

13
Church Property Rights

A S SOON AS the Orthodox Presbyterian Church was formed, ministers and congregations of the Presbyterian Church in the USA began renouncing the jurisdiction of the church and uniting with the new body. This involved the question of the ownership of church property. Did it belong to the denomination as a whole or to the individual congregations which built it and paid for it?

A Special Committee on Legal Procedure was appointed by the 1936 General Assembly of the Presbyterian Church in the USA,

> to take such measures as may be adequate to maintain the full constitutional authority of the Presbyterian Church in the U.S.A., guard all its interests and protect all its property rights, and associate with them, in the above responsibilities, such ministers and ruling elders, not exceeding seven in number, as they may deem wise counsellors, and to make full report to the next General Assembly.[1]

Two of the six ministerial members of this committee, the Rev. George E. Barnes, D.D., and the Rev. Robert B. Whyte, D.D., were signers of the Auburn Affirmation.[2]

In practically every instance, with the exception of two congregations, one in North Dakota and the other in Wilmington, Delaware, those congregations which voted to withdraw from the Presbyterian Church in the USA were divided in their allegiance. In most cases only a few desired to remain in the Presbyterian Church in the USA, but these individuals, apparently, expressed no desire to prevent the vast majority of the congregation from using the building as a place of worship under their new relationship with another denomination. Yet in every case, whether the minority desired it or not, and even where the congregation voted unanimously to leave the Presbyterian Church in the USA, the Committee on Legal Procedure of that church entered a suit in the civil

---

1   *Minutes of the General Assembly* 1936, Part 1, 114-15.
2   *Minutes of the General Assembly* 1937, Part 1, 67.

173

courts to restrain the congregation from using the property as a place of worship under any other denomination than the Presbyterian Church in the USA. Suits involving property valued at more than two million dollars were begun in the civil courts in the Synods of New England, New Jersey, Baltimore, Pennsylvania, Iowa, North Dakota, South Dakota, and Wisconsin.[3]

This committee used as its guide the principles of Presbyterian church property laid down by the Supreme Court of the United States in the case of Barkley vs. Hayes, which states that a local congregation is an integral part of the church as a whole, and as such its property is owned ultimately by the denomination.[4]

The most outstanding case involving church property was that of the Presbyterian Church in the USA vs. The Presbyterian Church of Collingswood, New Jersey, of which the Rev. Carl McIntire was pastor. Mr. McIntire, a member of the Independent Board for Presbyterian Foreign Missions, had been suspended from the ministry of the Presbyterian Church in the USA and had subsequently renounced the jurisdiction of that church and had united with the Presbyterian Church of America. The congregation then voted on June 15, 1936, to withdraw from the Presbyterian Church in the USA and to remain independent ecclesiastically, but continued to use the church building and Sunday School rooms, valued at some $200,000.[5] On June 26, 1936, the Presbyterian Church in the USA, through five members of the Collingswood Presbyterian Church who were opposed to Mr. McIntire, applied for an injunction to restrain the congregation from the use of the buildings. The congregation filed an answer within ten days, and as a result the Rev. Carl McIntire and congregation were allowed to worship in the church until the case had been heard and a decision had been rendered.

On March 3, 1937, the case of J. Earnest Kelly *versus* Carl McIntire, et al., was heard before vice chancellor Francis B. Davis in Camden, New Jersey. The plaintiffs in the case argued that an individual Presbyterian church is an integral part of the whole denomination so that its property belongs to the denomination and cannot be used for any purpose not sanctioned by the judicatories of the church. Mr. McIntire had been

---

3   *Minutes of the General Assembly* 1937, 70.
4   Ibid., 68-69.
5   *Christian Beacon* 3 (March 24, 1938), 1.

suspended from the ministry of the church and, being under this censure, he had no right to preach in the church until his censures had been removed and his right to minister fully restored. The congregation had withdrawn from the denomination and so should not be allowed to use the building for worship but must seek other premises for such purposes.

The defendants, on the other hand, maintained

> that the agencies and judicatories of the Presbyterian Church in the U.S.A. have so departed from the fundamental principles, faith and constitution of the denomination, that these denominational agencies and those avowing loyalty to them, are not entitled to the property of the Collingswood Presbyterian Church as against the members thereof who have steadfastly remained loyal to the principles as set forth in the Constitution of the Presbyterian Church in the U.S.A. under which title was acquired and under which the congregation of the local church was formed.[6]

With reference to the Rev. Carl McIntire, the defendants claimed,

> The express violation of the Constitution of the Presbyterian Church in the trial and suspension of defendant, Carl McIntire, is evident in four particulars; first, the mandate forming the basis of the charges against him was an improper basis for the procedure; second, the presbytery failed to stay the proceedings after a complaint was filed with the Synod; third, there was a variance in the charges and specifications which were presented and those upon which the actual trial was held; and fourth, the synod violated the constitution in affirming the judgment of the lower court although many specifications of error were sustained.[7]

These matters mentioned above were express violations of the constitution of the Presbyterian Church in the USA, and the censures placed upon the Rev. Carl McIntire had no legal effect. In view of this situation, the defendants said no other action was possible than for Mr. McIntire to renounce the jurisdiction of the Presbyterian Church in the USA and for the congregation to do likewise. The congregation had not seceded from the denomination but had simply announced that it could not "accept the jurisdiction of a body which openly and avowedly defies this Constitution."[8]

The judge ruled in favor of the Presbyterian Church in the USA on the principle that a local congregation is subject to the church as a whole,

---

6   *The Defendants' Brief.*
7   *Ibid.*
8   *Ibid.*

and cannot use the property contrary to the wishes of the denomination.[9] The judge refused to rule on the doctrinal controversy as immaterial to the case. Therefore the congregation was restrained from using the property and Mr. McIntire from preaching and conducting services in the building "until his censures are removed and his right to minister has been restored by due proceedings according to the constitution and practices of the Presbyterian Church in the U.S.A."[10] Mr. McIntire and the congregation which left with him did not appeal the decision to a higher court but left the building to worship in a newly constructed tabernacle.[11]

The principles by which the Special Committee on Legal Procedure of the Presbyterian Church in the USA was guided in this case, and which were upheld by the civil courts in most of the property cases, were as follows:

> 1. An individual Presbyterian Church is an integral part of the whole Presbyterian denomination, and is subject to the Constitution of the Presbyterian Church in the U.S.A. Its entire property belongs to the denomination itself, and cannot be used for any purposes which are not sanctioned by the judicatories of the Church.
> 2. The members of an individual Presbyterian Church cannot by solemn resolution repudiate the authority of the Presbyterian Church in the United States of America, then by subsequent resolution attempt to take their church property out of the denomination, even if their effort in so doing is unanimous.
> 3. In the event of secession, the property remains for the use of the loyal members of the congregation recognized by the judicatories of the Presbyterian Church in the United States of America.
> 4. The orders and decisions of the judicatories of the Presbyterian Church in the U.S.A. are final and binding upon its members and every part of the Church, and must be accepted in litigation before the civil courts as conclusive.
> 5. Civil courts consider themselves incompetent judges in matters of faith, doctrine, and ecclesiastical law, and consequently will not inquire into such matters, particularly when the religious denomination has its own system of courts to determine cases of that character.[12]

Every case to date involving church property between the Presbyterian Church in the USA and those who renounced its jurisdiction since 1936,

---

9   *Conclusions of Vice Chancellor, Francis B. Davis, Chancery Court,*
       Camden, N.J., in case of J. Earnest Kelly vs. Carl McIntire, et al.
10   *Ibid.*
11   *Christian Beacon* 3 (March 31, 1938), 1.
12   *Minutes of the General Assembly* 1938, Part 1, 45.

has been awarded to the Presbyterian Church in the USA upon these principles, with the exception of one case.

The First Presbyterian Church in Leith, North Dakota, voted unanimously on August 2, 1936, to renounce the judicatories of the Presbyterian Church in the USA. The Rev. Samuel J. Allen, the pastor, had already done so and had become affiliated with the then Presbyterian Church of America, later known as the Orthodox Presbyterian Church. Immediately, the Presbyterian Church in the USA, through its Presbytery of Bismarck, brought suit in the civil courts against the officers and members of the First Presbyterian Church of Leith, attempting to secure possession of and title to the church property. The same arguments in substance were presented by both parties in this case as in the case involving the Collingswood Presbyterian Church. However, the First Presbyterian Church of Leith had voted unanimously to renounce the jurisdiction of the Presbyterian Church in the USA. On June 17, 1939, the courts handed down a decision in favor of the defendant church. In the mind of the court the case hinged upon the unanimous vote of the congregation.

> It seems clear that a minority, or even one member of a congregation, may prevent the use of the church property for purposes other than the trust for which it was created. . . .
>
> If there isn't even one to object, then can the general organization of the denomination (plaintiff in this case) which is no part of the Congregation, prevent the unanimous congregation from using the property as it sees fit?
>
> The Church at Leith, North Dakota, is a North Dakota corporation under the control of trustees. The cestuis que trust are the members of the Congregation. The Presbyterian Church in the U.S.A. is in no way a party to this trusteeship. . . .
>
> If the trustees act within the scope of their authority which they received from the Congregation with respect to the property, it seems the plaintiff in this case would be interfering with the powers and duties of the trustees in attempting to take the property away from them. . . .
>
> . . . The Trustees represent the Congregation, and the trustees may do with the property whatever the cestuis que trust unanimously consent to their doing.
>
> There was no schism. There was no disagreement whatever in the congregation, or with the trustees, and the court can find no operation of the law, or under the Constitution of the plaintiff which makes it the equitable owner of the property.[13]

---

13   Opinion of the Court, Minot, North Dakota, June 17, 1939, as recorded in the *Presbyterian Guardian* 6 (August 1939), 159-60.

The court in this case directly contradicted the principle laid down by the Special Committee on Legal Procedure of the Presbyterian Church in the USA, that "the members of the individual Presbyterian Churches cannot by solemn resolution repudiate the authority of the Presbyterian Church in the U.S.A., then by subsequent resolution attempt to take their church property out of the denomination, even if their effort in so doing is unanimous."

A similar case is now pending before the courts of Delaware, that of the Presbyterian Church in the USA *versus* the members and officers of the Eastlake Presbyterian Church of Wilmington, Delaware, which voted unanimously on June 24, 1936, to renounce the jurisdiction of that denomination.

Another case involving church property is now before the courts in Portland, Maine, but this suit is somewhat different. The Second Parish Presbyterian Church in Portland and its pastor, the Rev. John H. Skilton, voted on June 30, 1936, to withdraw from the Presbyterian Church in the USA and to unite with the then Presbyterian Church of America. The Presbyterian Church in the USA applied for an injunction asking the court to restrain the congregation from using the property for worship. This the court refused to grant. The case proper is now being heard before the civil courts.

The Second Parish Presbyterian Church building is owned by a corporation known as the Second Parish in the Town of Portland, which leases the property rent free to the Second Parish Presbyterian Church. Members and contributors to the church can become members of the Second Parish in the Town of Portland only by election which is conducted by the corporation as an organization separate from the church. This means that the church building is held by the corporation entirely separate from the congregation. Since this difference in owner-ship obtains, the decision of the court is awaited with much interest.

Certain individuals of the Presbyterian Church in the USA look upon this legal action against members who have left the denomination as "highly discreditable to the Presbyterian Church in the U.S.A.,"[14] because in most instances the church buildings were purchased by the local congregations without financial aid from the denomination as a whole. The entire proceedings have not advanced the cause of the Presbyterian Church in the USA in the estimation of the public. As was

---

14   *Christianity Today* 9 (Spring 1939), 102.

pointed out in chapter twelve, the Orthodox Presbyterian Church has made such legal action impossible and thereby has avoided a potentially great wrong.

In practically every case the withdrawing congregations have built new edifices and their work has gone on unabated. The technical legalities have compelled the courts to yield to the demands of the Presbyterian Church in the USA, while the underlying doctrinal differences have been brushed aside. Yet the decisions in favor of the Presbyterian Church in the USA have in no way destroyed the basic conflict of theology which really caused hundreds of members to leave that communion.

The ministers and the members of the Orthodox Presbyterian Church have demonstrated their allegiance to the Bible rather than to bricks and mortar, and have tried to live out the words of Martin Luther's hymn,

> Let goods and kindred go,
> This mortal life also;
> The body they may kill;
> God's truth abideth still,
> His Kingdom is forever.

14
Reform from Within

THE "reform from within" movement in the Presbyterian Church in the USA is based upon the belief that the church has a sound Confession of Faith, and although the courts, boards, and agencies of the church have been disloyal to the standards in many instances and are controlled by those who are out of agreement with the Confession, nevertheless, it is the duty of each minister and member to contend for the faith and to lead the church back to a place of faithfulness to the Bible. This is the position of men like the Rev. Samuel G. Craig, D.D., editor of *Christianity Today*, who wrote, "Reform is imperatively needed and every true Presbyterian should give himself for the task."[1]

When the members of the Independent Board were suspended from the ministry of the church and the Orthodox Presbyterian Church was formed, Dr. C. E. Macartney and others urged the ministers and members of the Presbyterian Church in the USA not to leave the church. But at the same time they deplored the "severe treatment" meted out to men like Dr. Machen and the other members of the Independent Board and admitted that we "are convinced that doctrines not in accord with her [Presbyterian Church in the USA] standards are being tolerated and even fostered by boards and agencies of the church."[2]

They have maintained this position quite consistently, for they resigned from membership on the board of trustees of Westminster Theological Seminary and refused to support the Independent Board when it became evident that these two organizations would eventually lead to a separation from the Presbyterian Church in the USA. They have always been of the opinion that the church could be saved from modernism and that their duty was to fight from within.

---

1   *Christianity Today* 7 (October 1936), 126.
2   *Presbyterian Guardian* 2 (July 6, 1936), 161.

On the other hand, some of those who renounced the jurisdiction of the Presbyterian Church in the USA and formed the Orthodox Presbyterian Church argue that, although the doctrinal standards of the church, with the exception of the 1903 amendments, are sound, the decision of the 1936 General Assembly sitting in its highest capacity as a court of Jesus Christ so interpreted the constitution in favor of modernism that the church is now apostate, at least until that decision is reversed. In addition, these men reason that the boards, agencies, and courts of the church are completely dominated by those who are out of accord with the doctrines of the church. And finally, says this group, the theological seminaries of the church, which are the source of ministerial supply, are not teaching the gospel of the Lord Jesus Christ, but employ professors who deny the very essentials of the Christian faith. What is more, the barriers against ministerial candidates from seminaries outside of the Presbyterian Church in the USA are mounting each year. With such a deplorable situation facing the church, what possible chance is there of effecting any real reform?

The question arises, "What are these advocates of 'reform from within' doing to alter the serious doctrinal defection in the church and to return it to the control of those who believe that the Bible is the Word of God?" The attempt to reform the Presbyterian Church in the USA from within became an organized movement when the Presbyterian League of Faith was launched in April, 1931.[3] The Rev. Walter D. Buchanan, D.D., had been accustomed to invite well-known conservative leaders of the church to New York City once every month or two for the purpose of discussing the present situation in the church and of laying plans for combating the advance of modernism. It was from this group that the launching of Westminster Theological Seminary received great impetus and support. The ministerial members of the board of trustees of the seminary were drawn largely from these men, and the churches represented became the largest contributors to the institution. The men who gathered in New York City at the invitation of Dr. Buchanan were the recognized leaders and contenders for the faith. Besides Dr. Buchanan, there were Dr. Machen, Dr. Frank H. Stevenson, Dr. C. E. Macartney, Dr. S. G. Craig, Dr. O. T. Allis, Dr. David Burrell, and many others, who later assumed a conspicuous place in the conflict.

---

3   *Christianity Today* 2 (May 1931), 19.

The proposed union between the larger Presbyterian and Reformed bodies in the United States, which did not proceed further than a plan, revived the discussion of the Auburn Affirmation as evidence of theological impurity. It was at this time that the Rev. E. T. Thompson, D.D., professor of church history at Union Theological Seminary, Richmond, Virginia, felt compelled to discuss the subject, "Is the Northern Church Theologically Sound?"[4] in order to allay suspicions in the southern church. He pronounced the northern church sound and the suspicions of his brethren in the South as groundless. But his declaration fell on deaf ears because discussions continued, and the three leading papers in the southern church, *The Presbyterian Standard*, *The Presbyterian of the South*, and *The Christian Observer*, reprinted the Auburn Affirmation in substance, all of which helped to focus attention on the Auburn Affirmation.

Dr. Buchanan and the men meeting in New York City decided that they had too long neglected to organize an attack on the Auburn Affirmation, and that the need for united action on the part of the conservatives was urgent. Accordingly, the organization known as The League of Faith was launched in April, 1931, and a constitution adopted and signed by 150 ministers, many of whom were among the best known in the church, and sent to every minister in the church. Eventually about twelve hundred ministers joined the league, a number approximately equivalent to the number of those who had signed the Auburn Affirmation.

The constitution states the objects of the league to be a maintenance of loyalty to the Bible and insistence, in opposition to the Affirmation, that the full truth of the Bible, the virgin birth of Christ, the substitutionary atonement, the bodily resurrection, and the miracles of Christ are essential doctrines of the Word of God.[5]

Meetings of the league were held several times each year, usually in New York City at the Broadway Presbyterian Church, of which Dr. Buchanan was pastor, for the purpose of Christian fellowship and discussions. But no real program of reform was ever adopted or executed. The outstanding struggle with modernism on the Board of Foreign Missions was carried on by individuals who were members of the league

---

4   Ernest Trice Thompson, "Is the Northern Church Theologically Sound?" *Union Seminary Review* 42 (January 1931), 109-134.

5   *Christianity Today* 2 (May 1931), 19. See Appendix, note 29.

but in their capacity as individuals. Many of the league members helped in the conflict, but at no time did the league as an organization enter the struggle concerning foreign missions. In fact, most of the members of the league regarded it as a protest against the Auburn Affirmation and very little beyond that.

When the members of the Independent Board were suspended from the ministry of the Presbyterian Church in the USA and the Presbyterian Church of America was organized in 1936, the league was reorganized and continued by a group of ministers led by Dr. C. E. Macartney, who were imbued with the idea that the Presbyterian Church in the USA was still fundamentally sound.

At the invitation of Dr. Macartney a group of ministers and elders met in Pittsburgh on June 16, 1936, and adopted resolutions expressing their loyalty to the standards of the church, deploring the severe treatment meted out to members of the Independent Board, and designating *Christianity Today* and *The Presbyterian* as "channels for this militant testimony."[6]

On June 26, 1936, the Presbyterian League of Faith convened in the Broadway Presbyterian Church, New York City, elected Dr. Macartney as its president, and expressed a determination to fight from within the church for loyalty to the doctrinal standards.

The league met in Columbus, Ohio, on May 25th and 26th, 1937, at the time of the assembly of the Presbyterian Church in the USA, and decided to wage a strong fight against a proposed revision of chapter XXIII of the Confession of Faith, which revision was being advocated by pacifists in the church in order to condemn war.[7] A testimony in general terms extolling the importance of remaining true to the Word of God was adopted and also the following paragraph opposing the proposed change in chapter XXIII of the Confession of Faith with reference to war:

> Therefore, we deplore, and pledge ourselves to oppose the adoption by our Church of any measure or measures which would leave our nation defenceless in the midst of its foes, or which would give encouragement to those anti-Christian and anti-social movements and organizations who plot for the downfall of all that the Church of Christ holds sacred.[8]

---

6   *Presbyterian Guardian* 2 (July 6, 1936), 161.
7   *Christianity Today* 8 (July 1937), 50.
8   *Ibid.*

This expressed determination to oppose any change in the Westminster Confession of Faith, which change would outlaw all wars as un-Christian and sinful, became the first specific project of the reorganized League of Faith to keep the Confession of Faith pure, and began the movement to reform the church from within.

The 1938 General Assembly of the Presbyterian Church in the USA had adopted the report of its special committee recommending that chapter XXIII, part of which reads,

> It is lawful for Christians to accept and execute the offices of a magistrate, when called thereunto: in the managing hereof, as they ought especially to maintain piety, justice, and peace, according to the wholesome laws of each commonwealth; so, for that end, they may lawfully now under the New Testament, wage war upon just and necessary occasions,

be changed to read in part,

> War wherever it appears, is a manifestation of the power of sin in the world. It defies the righteousness of God, disrupts His worldwide family, and outrages the human personality which Christ Jesus came to redeem. Even when war is waged with sincere purpose to restrain evil, it tends to produce greater evils than those against which it is directed. The Church, which is the body of Christ, set in the world to preach the Gospel of Peace, must ever bear witness to this character of war.[9]

In fact, a revision of the entire chapter was proposed.

In pursuance of the endeavor to resist this change in chapter XXIII of the Confession of Faith, an outstanding article entitled "The Christian Attitude Toward War," by Dr. Loraine Boettner, a layman, appeared in *Christianity Today*.[10] Dr. Boettner contended that the Bible does not condemn wars which are waged upon just and necessary grounds, and on certain occasions God actually commanded the Israelites to go into battle against the enemy. He included many other arguments against the proposed changes and concluded, "The proposed new amendment is unScriptural and treasonable."

Members of the Presbyterian League of Faith wrote articles and made speeches against the proposed amendment. But the opponents of the amendment were not confined to the members of the league nor to

---

9   *Minutes of the General Assembly* 1938, Part 1, 47-48.
10   Loraine Boettner, "The Christian Attitude toward War," *Christianity Today* 9 (Winter 1939), 57-71.

so-called conservatives. Outstanding modernists like the Rev. John A. MacCallum, D.D., a signer of the Auburn Affirmation, fought so strenuously against the amendment and against pacifism in general that he was asked to resign as editor of *The Presbyterian Tribune*, whose board of directors were committed to the amendment.[11] The Presbytery of Philadelphia, which is controlled by Auburn Affirmationists, voted against the amendment, while the supposedly conservative Presbytery of Northumberland voted for it.[12]

The amendment failed to receive the required vote of two-thirds of the presbyteries and so was lost, but in no sense of the word can the issue be regarded as a doctrinal one, since modernists and Bible-believers fought on the same side. The Confession of Faith was not altered, but the battle was not in this instance between Christianity and modernism.

Since the reorganization of the league in 1936, only one struggle has been fought, which was an out-and-out conflict between Christianity and modernism. It concerned the election of the Rev. E. G. Homrighausen as professor of religious education at Princeton Seminary, as well as the presence of Dr. Emil Brunner of Zurich, Switzerland, as guest professor at Princeton Theological Seminary. Dr. Homrighausen had been appointed a professor by the board of trustees of Princeton Seminary, but his appointment required the confirmation of the general assembly of the Presbyterian Church in the USA since Princeton is under its jurisdiction. Dr. Brunner had accepted the invitation of the board of trustees to occupy the chair of systematic theology made famous by the three Hodges—Charles, Archibald Alexander, and Casper Wistar.

Members of the League of Faith opposed most strenuously the election of Dr. Homrighausen and the presence of Dr. Brunner on the faculty at Princeton Seminary. Others, not members of the Presbyterian Church in the USA, also called attention to these two professors and their liberalism, indicating that Princeton Theological Seminary was no longer the citadel of orthodoxy, and that its reorganization in 1929 and the establishment of Westminster Theological Seminary the same year marked clearly the beginning of a trend toward modernism.

An issue of *Christianity Today* devoted considerable space to the reprinting of several articles by theologians outside of the Presbyterian

---

11   J. A. MacCallum, "Valediction," *The Presbyterian Tribune* 54 (April 13, 1939), 3-4.
12   *Minutes of the General Assembly* 1939, Part 1, 173-74.

Church in the USA, attacking the theological beliefs of these two professors.[13] One article was by Clarence Bouma of Calvin Seminary, and one by Cornelius Van Til of Westminster Theological Seminary, both of whom contended that Barthianism, which Dr. Brunner advocates, is directly contrary to the historic position of Calvinism and Christianity.

Professor Van Til pointed out that Dr. Brunner does not believe in the infallibility of the Bible nor even in the Scriptures as a trustworthy record of history. The view of history in the plain sense of the term is denied by Dr. Brunner and in its place he substitutes a new conception of history known as "supra history." Events like the bodily resurrection do not belong to history but to eternity. There must be a distinction between the dimension of becoming and that of history, according to Brunner. Such a distinction, said Dr. Van Til, destroys the real historical basis of Christianity.

In 1929 when Princeton Seminary was reorganized there were those who maintained that the conflict was administrative and personal, but Dr. Craig declared that with the coming of Dr. Homrighausen and Dr. Brunner no one could hold that the issue at Princeton was not one of doctrine.

> Since that event, however, a number of things have happened that would seem to indicate that the founders of Westminster Seminary were not far wrong when they maintained that a new Seminary was needed to carry on and perpetuate the policies and traditions of Princeton Theological Seminary as that institution existed prior to its reorganization by the general assembly.[14]

Dr. Craig expressed the "hope that the Board of Trustees of Princeton Seminary would reconsider this whole matter."[15]

In subsequent issues of *Christianity Today*, Dr. Craig assailed the appointment of Dr. Brunner not only on the grounds established by Dr. Van Til and others, but because Dr. Brunner rejected infant baptism, the virgin birth, the Pauline authorship of the pastoral epistles, and because he maintained a wrong view of church and state. Dr. Brunner later denied these allegations, but Dr. Craig claimed that his contentions were corroborated by books and articles of Dr. Brunner's.[16]

13   *Christianity Today* 9 (October 1938), 34-41.
14   *Christianity Today* 9 (October 1938), 2.
15   *Ibid.*, 3.
16   *Christianity Today* 9 (Spring 1939), 105-110.

In a letter to Dr. Craig professor Brunner stated, "I think it is no news that President MacKay whilst differing in some points from me has the intention of leading Princeton Seminary back to the real Reformation theology, the real Biblical theology of which Warfield's theology is a decided deviation."[17] Of this statement Dr. Craig made much, to indicate that the president of Princeton was intent on changing Princeton's historic position. The fight against Dr. Brunner's appointment as a professor never came to a conclusion because Dr. Brunner decided to return to Switzerland in 1939.

Dr. E. G. Homrighausen, who was appointed to the chair of Christian education, received considerable attention from Dr. Craig and others because he was regarded as an American exponent of Barthianism, and more expressly because of his view of the Bible as expressed in his book, *Christianity in America*. In this volume Dr. Homrighausen repudiated a belief in the full truthfulness of the Bible (p. 121) and contended that the gospel must be expressed in modern thought forms (p. 49).

With these facts in mind, Dr. Macartney and Dr. Craig appeared before the Standing Committee on Theological Seminaries of the 1938 General Assembly and argued against the confirmation of Dr. Homrighausen's appointment as professor of Christian education at Princeton Seminary. After hearing both sides the committee decided to take no action, so that the general assembly had no opportunity to vote on the appointment.[18]

Between the time of the 1938 and 1939 General Assemblies of the Presbyterian Church in the USA, Dr. Homrighausen issued a declaration of his faith which seemed to prove that he had changed from a Barthian to a staunch believer in the Bible and Calvinism.[19] This declaration apparently satisfied Dr. Craig and members of the League of Faith that Dr. Homrighausen was orthodox. The objections to his professorship were dropped so that his appointment was confirmed at the 1939 General Assembly.[20]

However, Dr. Van Til contended that the many changes in professor Homrighausen's theology from an out-and-out modernism to Barthianism and finally to a mild evangelicalism, all within the space of a

17   *Ibid.*
18   *Christianity Today* 9 (October 1938), 14.
19   E. G. Homrighausen, "Convictions!" *The Presbyterian* 109 (May 11, 1939), 8-9.
20   *Minutes of the General Assembly* 1939, 104.

few years, was no guarantee of his Calvinism or of his fitness as professor at an institution which was committed to the Westminster Confession of Faith.

> Thus the latest pronouncements of Dr. Homrighausen are at best hopelessly confusing. His trumpet gives forth an uncertain sound. It is difficult to see how anyone so confused on the fundamental issues of theological thought can with clarity and conviction present the Reformed Faith to his students. . . .
>
> But granted we could overlook his Barthianism—which is absolutely destructive of the notion of an infallible Bible—where is the evidence that Dr. Homrighausen has now adopted the Reformed Faith? It is not to be found in the Article on "Convictions," which the editor of *The Presbyterian* commended to the commissioners of the Assembly as evidence on the basis of which they might judge whether Dr. Homrighausen was a fit candidate for a professorship at Princeton Seminary. . . . It has not been customary in the past to appoint professors at Princeton who are merely "on the way" to becoming Reformed; of Dr. Homrighausen it cannot even be shown that he is "on the way."[21]

The struggle against Professor Homrighausen thus came to an end and he was officially installed in the chair of Christian education at Princeton Theological Seminary, October 10, 1939, giving further evidence of the lack of strict adherence to the Westminster Confession of Faith which the seminary is pledged to defend.

Up to the present time no other definite projects for reform have been undertaken by the "reform from within" group, except that of opposing the proposed union between the Presbyterian Church in the USA and the Protestant Episcopal Church.[22] The National Committee of the Ruling Elders Testimony issued its initial blast against the unfaithfulness of the boards and agencies of the church, but since then the organization has remained more or less inarticulate. With respect to the whole movement to reform the Presbyterian Church in the USA from within, the question might well be asked, What are the chances for success?

The answer to this question can be given quite positively: the chances for success are very poor indeed! This unequivocal reply is based upon two considerations: First, the "reform from within" group has no thorough-going plan to reform the church, nor is any program being actively promulgated. Secondly, the facts of church history are arrayed against the successful reform of an individual communion when once

---

21   Cornelius Van Til, "Homrighausen Approved," *Presbyterian Guardian* 6 (July 1939), 136-37.

22   See chapter five for a discussion of this subject.

the ecclesiastical organization has come under the control and influence of modernists.

In the first place, there is no program of reform being pursued. The members of the League of Faith admit that the decision of the 1936 General Assembly in suspending members of the Independent Board from the ministry of the Presbyterian Church in the USA was a wrong decision and a discredit to the church. Dr. Craig wrote,

> More might be said, but surely we have said enough to justify our characterization of the fifth anniversary of the 1934 mandate and accompanying "Studies of the Constitution" as an inglorious anniversary. It is not necessary to approve the organization of the Independent Board in order to maintain that for the good of the Church they ought to be rescinded or at least very considerably modified.[23]

Dr. Macartney likewise stated, "Indeed, in some instances, such as the tragic expulsion of that great theologian, Dr. J. Gresham Machen, our church has seemed to witness against its creed rather than for it."

Aside from these and other statements and articles, the league is doing nothing to have that decision rescinded. The Presbyterian way, according to its Form of Government, is to send up an overture or a memorial to the general assembly, urging the assembly to reverse its decision. Three years have intervened since the decision was rendered, but so far no such move has been made and there is little evidence that any will be made.

In addition, what is the League of Faith doing to reform the boards and agencies of the church which the league members have declared disloyal to the doctrinal standards of the church? No overtures have been made demanding that modernist literature be withdrawn, that only sound literature be distributed, that no compromising unions be made, that only those be elected to membership on the boards who will refuse to compromise with unbelief. No mass meetings are being held decrying the condition in the church and demanding its reform. Dr. J. A. MacCallum probably diagnosed the situation when he wrote,

> Fortunately, with the exception of one or two minor skirmishes, all is now quiet on the theological front. Of course we can never tell when the battle will break out again in all its ancient virulence but it looks as though we are in for an era of theological good-feeling. The conservatives are not so conservative, or at least not so militant, and the liberals are not so sure of themselves as they were a few years ago when Dr. Clarence Edward Macartney was the self-appointed

---

23   *Christianity Today* 9 (Spring 1939), 102.

knight of reaction. His occasional Cassandra calls may be as strident as ever but they have lost their sometime magic and in consequence his followers have been reduced to a weedy segment of their former battalions.[24]

The Presbyterian, which was designated as one of the two papers to help in the effort to reform the church, makes it quite apparent that Dr. MacCallum's judgment is not far wrong. That journal publishes articles written by men who are modernists as well as Bible-believers. The September 29, 1938 issue contained an impressive comparison of the Auburn Affirmation with the standards of the Presbyterian Church in the USA in parallel columns. The purpose of this and previous articles was to demonstrate how contrary is the Auburn Affirmation to the doctrines of the church. In the same issue of the magazine there was an article, "God, Youth and America," written by the Rev. Jesse H. Baird, D.D., a signer of the Auburn Affirmation, which the editor praised as follows: "Dr. Baird of our San Francisco Theological Seminary, San Anselmo, California, delivered this masterful address on the spiritual history of America at the Area Christian Endeavor Convention in July, where ten Western states were represented." With such contradictory testimony appearing in the same issue of *The Presbyterian*, which was conscripted to contend for the faith and whose editor was a vice-president of the League of Faith, there seems to be little hope of reform. In fact, it reveals that a proper conception of reform is sadly lacking. What is more, the attitude of those who are leading the so-called movement for reform has changed since the 1936 debacle.

In 1923 Dr. Macartney wrote, "The third way to control the great defection is by protest and appeal and ecclesiastical procedure. But from this method many turn away."[25] Now there seems to be a tendency to forget the ecclesiastical situation as a whole, except for an occasional verbal or written blast against modernism, and to hold to the conviction that the situation is quite hopeless and that the most important task is to hold the fort in the local church by preaching the gospel. Dr. Macartney evidenced this attitude when he wrote recently, "Therefore, I value less the whole ecclesiastical structure, and feel that more and more for the true witness to the gospel and the Kingdom of God we must

---

24   *The Presbyterian Tribune* 54 (March 16, 1939), 5.
25   Clarence E. Macartney, "The Great Defection," *The Presbyterian* 93 (September 20, 1923), 9.

depend upon the particular local church, the individual minister and the individual Christian."[26]

In the second place, the facts of church history do not augur well for the present "reform from within" cause. There is not a single instance in all of church history where a "reform from within" group has been victorious when once the church has become doctrinally corrupt in its ecclesiastical organization. The most outstanding example of an attempt to reform a corrupt church, and the one which almost parallels the present movement, is that which occurred in the Netherlands.

In 1834 the Rev. Hendrik De Cock was suspended from the ministry of the Netherlands Reformed Church because he criticized modernism within the church, so that De Cock and his congregation at Ulrum formed the mother church for a new and truly Reformed church in the Netherlands.[27] Gradually others were suspended from the ministry for the same reason. But some ministers who were themselves doctrinally sound remained in the church to reform it and formed a society for that purpose. They gave three reasons for remaining within the national church: (1) their main purpose was to preach the gospel of salvation to the lost; (2) the national church was still capable of reform; (3) the methods of those who withdrew were wrong.

Many years later Abraham Kuyper, who was to become one of the greatest theologians of the Netherlands, was born of parents who were members of the national church. After he was converted from liberalism to a belief in the Bible he saw the need for a theological faculty true to the faith. Under his leadership the Free University of Amsterdam was organized, which has become one of the truly great centers of Christian learning in Europe. But the tyranny of the national church became greater and many saw the hopelessness of reform from within, so that they withdrew from the church. In 1892 this group united with the church organized by Hendrik De Cock to form the great Reformed Churches of the Netherlands. The "reform from within" movement had failed miserably, and today it is the free Reformed Churches of the Netherlands to which Bible-believers look for comfort and aid in the fight for the faith.

Reform from within the Presbyterian Church in the USA seems doomed to failure not only because of the two main considerations

---

26   Clarence. E. Macartney, "Warm Hearts and Steady Faith," *The Christian Century* 56 (March 8, 1939), 317.

27   Paul Woolley, "What Have We Learned?" *Presbyterian Guardian* 2 (May 4, 1936), 45-46.

already discussed but also because there is not a single strictly orthodox seminary within the church. With this situation obtaining and with these leaders of reform mostly older men, from where are the Bible-believing ministers coming to fill their places and to carry on the conflict? In addition, there is the painful truth that every year scores of modernist and doctrinally indifferent ministers are being added to the roll to lead the church to a more liberal position.

No one would rejoice more than the former ministers and members of the Presbyterian Church in the USA, who have formed the Orthodox Presbyterian Church, if the "reform from within" group should succeed in reversing the 1936 decisions against the Independent Board, in gaining control of the boards and agencies of the church, and in placing orthodox professors in the theological seminaries of the church. But this seems impossible, not only because the reform movement has no organized plan, but also because the history of the Christian church seems aligned against it. It is strongly suspected that history will repeat itself and that the League of Faith has set a hopeless task before itself.

15
Whither Protestantism?

THE ASSERTION was made in the preface of this book that the Presbyterian Church in the USA and many Protestant churches of America in their corporate testimony have turned away from historic Christianity and are witnessing to another gospel known as modernism. The foregoing chapters have attempted to prove that judgment with respect to the Presbyterian Church in the USA. It is not within the province of this volume to present evidence in substantiation of the indictment concerning modernism in the other Protestant churches. On the other hand, how anyone who has the slightest knowledge of Christianity and its theology can listen to the sermons over the radio which are sponsored by the Federal Council of the Churches of Christ in America, read the contributions of ministers and theological professors of those churches in the denominational magazines, examine even superficially the literature which is being distributed by the boards and agencies, and listen to the teaching in the denominational colleges and theological seminaries and still believe that these churches are proclaiming the Christianity of the Bible and that gospel which was revived by the Protestant Reformation, is beyond comprehension. Modernism has won a sweeping victory, said Dr. Harry Emerson Fosdick, and he has never made a truer statement. The individual ministers in these churches who still believe and preach the true gospel of Jesus Christ as understood by all branches of Christendom for nineteen centuries are growing fewer each year. And with the theological seminaries by and large committed to modernism, this process will continue until such ministers are very few.

There are notable exceptions, however, among the large denominations. One of these is the Lutheran Church (Missouri Synod), which has a constituency of nearly one million and one of the largest Protestant theological seminaries, Concordia Theological Seminary, located in St. Louis. In the last few years one of its professors, the Rev. Walter A. Maier,

Ph.D., has been preaching sermons over the radio which have warmed the hearts of those who love the gospel. It almost makes one believe that the spirit of Martin Luther has come to life again. A number of the smaller church bodies, like the Christian Reformed Church, are also faithful to the gospel of the Bible. But, on the whole, the voice which Protestantism is raising in America today is not the voice of Christianity which is a condemnation of sin and a message of judgment to come, of salvation through the sacrificial atonement of Christ as a substitute for sinners, but the voice of modernism, which recognizes a divine spark in each man that only needs to be fanned into a flame and which calls on man to work out his own salvation.

Some one might ask, "What is modernism and how does it differ from Christianity?" At the outset it must be stated that the label, modernism, is question-begging and a misnomer. The religion which is called modernism is not new or up-to-date, as its name implies. It does not advance any twentieth-century discovery of religion which makes all other conceptions of Christianity *passé*. In fact, it is not a version nor even a perversion of Christianity, but a different religion. There are many kinds and degrees of modernism, but they have a common foundation. At the root is the denial of the supernaturalism of Christianity, a denial that God can and does intervene in His creation. In other words, its basis is naturalism.

Anyone acquainted with church history and Christian theology knows that such a manifestation of religion as modernism is not modern or new. While Jesus Christ was still upon this earth there were those who denied his miraculous powers and the resurrection from the dead. At one period in the fourth century, Athanasius stood almost alone in his steadfastness to the Christianity of the Bible. Spinoza of the seventeenth century denied the miraculous elements of Christianity because, he said, miracles were impossible and contrary to a proper idea of God. Then came the scientists of the nineteenth century who asserted that, according to their observations and experiments in hundreds and thousands of cases, God did not interpose in nature by supernatural power. Therefore he has never done so. In the field of biblical studies, but leading in the same direction, the theologians of Germany such as Schleiermacher, Ritschl, Baur, and others asserted that, according to their findings, the historical accuracy of the books of the Bible is not to be trusted. It is difficult to know what Christ said or did, they contended, because the writers of the Gospels contradict themselves, thereby proving that the

Bible is not a God-inspired document. In other words, unbelief has had many titles and has taken many forms, such as pantheism, deism, liberalism, and modernism, but they all resolve themselves into the same thing—naturalism.

Modernism, or unbelief, has entered the Protestant church in America in a very subtle way. The theological professors in America began to accept these modern "higher critical" views of the Bible and the naturalism of unbelieving science and to teach these ideas to the ministerial students in the seminaries. In turn, many ministers assimilated these views, preached them from the pulpits, and convinced the laymen, who were not learned in the knowledge of the Bible and Christianity, that modernism is the religion for this day. The colleges and universities aided in this process because they have accepted the dicta of modern science, which state that the world as it now exists is the result of natural processes. So today America, and for that matter most of the western world, is experiencing almost complete spiritual bankruptcy. At a time when the strong, authoritative message of the Christian church is needed to call the nations and men back to the God of the Bible, there is no such clarion call, but instead some feeble sputterings of confidence in the inherent goodness of man and the hope that somehow or other he will muddle through. Modernism has won a sweeping victory in the Christian church, no doubt, but it has also left the church feeble and spiritually decadent.

Laymen have begun to recognize this impotency of the church in the face of today's problems. The editors of *Fortune* magazine have written a respectful yet searching and thought-provoking indictment of the church's failure to lead the nation in spiritual things.

> Indeed, the pastors are not talking about the soul at all, they are talking about the flesh. . . . So long as the church pretends, or assumes to preach, absolute values, but actually preaches relative and secondary values, it will hasten this process of disintegration. We are asked to turn to the church for our enlightenment, but when we do so we find that the voice of the church is not inspired. . . . There is only one way out of the spiral. The way out is the sound of a voice, not our voice, but a voice coming from something not ourselves, in the existence of which we cannot disbelieve.[1]

The businessmen of this nation realize that even the economic and political welfare of America rests upon spiritual values, and that this spiritual leadership must be based upon absolute standards. The

---

1   Editorial, "War and Peace," *Fortune* (January 1940).

deplorable state of the church makes the church unable to answer this challenge in any effective way, because modernism, which is a religion of man and which speaks the voice of man, is in control. It is encouraging to those ministers who have been making this diagnosis of the church to find such corroboration among laymen.

What can be done about this condition in the Protestant church? Is one to believe that the situation is hopeless and beyond recovery? Some may have gathered the impression from the foregoing description that complete pessimism and despair must reign. Not at all. Some very definite and constructive steps can be taken which will help tremendously to alleviate the deplorable state of the church and bring it back to its place of power and usefulness in the life of America.

In the first place, one must have an historical perspective regarding the church and its various periods of spiritual apostasy and spiritual power before one can arrive at the proper solution to the present lamentable state. Such a long-range view not only will give a better understanding of the existing condition, but will also reveal what the church did in the past to recapture its power and God-given commission.

The low spiritual life of the Christian church today is not the first of its kind in history. In the middle ages the spiritual and moral corruption of the clergy and the doctrinal heresy which was being preached were like a plague which had struck the life of the church and its message. The immorality of the clergy was known to many, so that even the civil authorities were disgusted and called for a reform. The Roman church was selling indulgences which people thought would take away the guilt of their sins. The total effect of the preaching gave the impression and the assurance that man must do penance and works of merit in order to inherit eternal life. Superstition, idolatry, and ignorance held sway to such an extent that it seemed as though the Christianity of the Bible would be forgotten and trampled under foot.

But God raised up prophets in that day—Luther, Zwingli, Melanchthon, Calvin, Knox, and others who called the people back to the God of the Bible. These men had been chosen and enlightened by the Spirit of God to preach the true gospel and to warn the people that all have sinned and come short of the glory of God, that none is righteous, no, not one, and that everyone needs the forgiveness of sin, not through the purchase of indulgences but through the sacrifice of the divine Son of God upon the cross. This salvation by the sovereign grace of God alone, apart from the works of man, was heralded by the reformers. The

Bible was proclaimed the sole and final authority for faith and practice, the place where one can learn what he should believe about God, sin, and redemption. So rang out the preaching of those men of God. The Protestant Reformation revived the Christian church, returned it to its God-intended commission of preaching the gospel of the grace of God, and placed the church once more in a position of spiritual power and usefulness in the life of the nations.

Someone might object and say, "That situation was entirely different from the state of religion today. The attack on Christianity in this era is intellectual. No longer can one believe that the Bible is the Word of God and the authority for faith and practice, that one is saved from sin by the sacrifice of another, no matter how great he was. This is an age of reason and Christianity is *passé!*"

To this every true believer in the Lord Jesus can reply with a strong denial. At the same time, if men still object and contend that the attack on Christianity today is new and more devastating, one can turn the minds of these to another period in the church's life when man was loud in his boast of learning.

The deists of the seventeenth and eighteenth centuries, especially in England, also charged that men could no longer accept the Bible as the authority in religion, that human reason must be the determining factor. In fact, the deists went so far as to state that Christianity was founded on fiction. These men rejected revealed religion and fell back upon natural religion. Bishop Hoadly attacked the credibility of miracles; John Toland claimed that only what is rationally demonstrable is true; Matthew Tindal contended that man is thrown back upon reason as the basis for religion. These were the arguments of the intellectual enemies of Christianity in that day, and they are being repeated today.

The result of that attack of deism in the eighteenth century was the emergence of one of the classic periods of Christian apologetic. Sherlock, the Bishop of London, wrote an able defense of the resurrection of Jesus Christ which, along with all other miracles, had been ridiculed as impossible by Woolston. George Berkeley defended Christianity from a philosophic point of view and maintained that Christian belief is necessary to reason, for without it one cannot explain the universe. Bishop Butler, in his *Analogy of the Christian Religion*, answered particularly the arguments of John Toland that only what is rationally demonstrable is true. Bishop Butler accepted the position of theism and then built up the whole system of Christianity, making his work one of the greatest apologetics of Christian history up to that time.[2]

In addition to this intellectual defense of Christianity, evangelists like Whitefield and the Wesleys called the church to repentance and faith in Jesus Christ. The great movement in England under the guidance of these men produced new consecration to the gospel and zeal to publish the good tidings of the grace of God. It seemed as though a new breath of spiritual life had been infused into the church and its influence on the life of the people increased.

The attack on the Bible and on Christianity as the revealed and final religion is basically the same today. Almost identical arguments are being used. The modern "higher critical" view of the Bible, on the other hand, has been developed largely since the eighteenth century, but it is based upon the assumption that religion is natural in its origin. The New Testament account of Christianity is said to be faulty and contradictory, a collection of data by ordinary men who added to the plain religion of Jesus. Christianity, argues the modernist, is the simple gospel of brotherly love and kindness preached and exemplified by Jesus Christ, not the supernatural religion set forth by Paul the apostle. He added dogmas like the virgin birth and the resurrection of Christ which he had borrowed from the mystery religions of the East. "Back to Jesus and his simple gospel of good will," say the modernists. In other words, if the naturalistic basis of religion is true, then the supernatural elements of the Bible must be explained away. The records are false and untrustworthy.

The philosophic and scientific assault upon Christianity today is also fundamentally the same. Christianity as preached by the church for nineteen centuries is unreasonable and intellectually unsound because its supernaturalism is not demonstrable. All of the investigations of thousands of scientists in many experiments have not produced one bit of evidence that God has ever entered the universe in a supernatural way. Consequently, the supernaturalism of the gospel must have been borrowed from older mythical religions or conjured up in the minds of the credulous apostles.

As in the eighteenth century and the other periods of the church's history when men have attacked Christianity, so today able apologists and defenders of the faith are arising. The scholarly treatise, *The Origin*

---

2   J. W. C. Wand, *A History of the Modern Church* (London: Methuen and Co., 1930), 171-81.

of Paul's Religion, by J. Gresham Machen, refutes successfully the contention that Paul acquired his belief in the virgin birth, the Lord's Supper, the deity of Christ, and many other facts of Christianity from the mystery religions of the East. Dr. Machen proves that Paul's whole conception of Christianity including these doctrines, he received from Jesus himself. No one, according to competent conservative scholars, has undermined Dr. Machen's cogent reasoning and arguments or disproved his thesis. Many others, like him, have taken up the defense of Christianity.

Scientists today are not as certain of the "assured results" of science as they were twenty years ago. The dogmatism in support of modern scientific theories is diminishing. Furthermore, has modern science destroyed the supernatural basis of Christianity simply because experimentation has not revealed any evidence of divine intervention? Is man the measure of all things? Are a few thousand or even a million experiments sufficient proof that God has not and does not interpose himself in the universe to accomplish his purposes? No believer in Christianity is opposed to science as such, because it helps man to understand the ways and the wonders of God in creation. It is the unproved theories of science which are the conclusions of insufficient and partial knowledge to which strenuous objections must be raised. It is the crass naturalistic assumptions of many scientists, which take into consideration only an interpretation of the facts which excludes God, which are most unfair to a full knowledge of the truth. Faith, which alone can understand the eternal spiritual things, is entirely discounted and ruled out of these calculations.

The distinction of modern science between natural truth and spiritual truth, which gives the impression that there are two sets of truth, is entirely false. God is the author of all truth, spiritual and natural, so that one cannot contradict the other. If natural truth is separated from the spiritual, then one will receive only a partial and a distorted knowledge of the facts. One cannot comprehend the natural without a proper conception of God. Intelligent Christians urge more searching, more experimentation, and more scrutiny, for Christianity thrives on the light, but let the scientist not claim that his assumptions of naturalism are proven facts.

Philosophically, the answer to the assaults on Christianity is somewhat different and reinforced today. Apologetes like Dr. Cornelius Van Til of Westminster Theological Seminary maintain that one must base the philosophy of Christianity upon a belief in a personal God and the revelation of himself in the Bible. Kant's *Critique of Pure Reason* has shown that the proofs for the existence of God from pure reason as historically stated are not conclusive. And even if they were conclusive they would only prove the existence of a finite God. Far better and far sounder is it to presuppose the personal God of the Scriptures and to argue from that impregnable base.

Others have joined with Dr. Van Til in defending historic Christianity philosophically, and in demonstrating that no fact of the universe can be fully and rightly understood except as that fact is related to God. Only in the light of divine revelation in the Bible can man properly know God and the world. Such is Christianity's answer to skeptical philosophers.

In the light of the attacks on Christianity, what must Protestantism do today? How can it once more assume its important and essential place in the life of the people? How can Christianity become the first concern of the individual?

The church today must do what it has done in ages past; it must call the people back to faith in the Son of God as the Saviour of men and the only way to God, and direct their thoughts to the Bible as the only and final rule of faith and life. When this is done—and it must be done, for it is the only reasonable, and consistent view of life—then the church will regain its position of spiritual power, fulfill its divine commission of preaching the gospel of the grace of God, and become the means of restoring men and women to spiritual communion with God through Jesus Christ. The gospel is still the power of God unto salvation. It still has miraculous and divine efficacy to change the lives of men and women into saints of God. It still can make God the center of life from which all else radiates. And for those who by grace believe, it is doing that today.

The hope for this life and for the life to come is not the vitiated and emasculated gospel of modernism, but the gospel of genuine, supernatural Christianity. What possible comfort can a disillusioned, discouraged, or burdened man derive from the prattlings of this religion of modernism, which makes of God an impersonal something or suffused goodness? What assurance of salvation from sin and hope of life after death can it give a dying man, when it ridicules the atonement of Christ for sin and when it scoffs at personal immortality? This counterfeit gospel fails man at every point and in every crisis.

How different is the real gospel of Jesus Christ! To one who is burdened with trouble, Jesus pleads, "Come unto me, all ye that labor and are heavy laden and I will give you rest" (Matt 11:28). To one who is conscious of his sin and transgression against God and man, he says, "I came not to call the righteous, but sinners to repentance" (Mark 2:17). And, as one faces death or stands at the grave of a loved one, the Lord of Glory gives the assurance, "I am the resurrection and the life: he that believeth in me, though he were dead, yet shall he live: and whosoever liveth and believeth in me shall never die" (John 11:25-26). This gospel of grace meets man's every problem and sustains him in every crisis, even death itself.

And when one contemplates the state of society and civilization today, the failure and the futility of modernism become all the more apparent. The lawlessness of men and nations, the utter disregard for the higher values of life, the crumbling of the foundations of society, are due to the fact that men have rejected the infinite God of the Bible, the creator and sustainer of the universe, and have substituted for him a finite God of their own imaginings. Each man has become a law unto himself, each man does what is right in his own eyes. Nations have set up their own standards of right and wrong, and as a result there is moral chaos.

The Christianity of the Bible, on the other hand, condemns the lawlessness of men and nations as sin against a holy and righteous God. It proclaims absolute values of eternal worth and makes faith in God through Jesus Christ the foundation for every civilization. Only in such a gospel is there hope for this world.

God grant that a new and true intellectual renaissance will come, which will enable men to think straight and to begin that thinking with God. God hasten the day when this renaissance will be followed by a spiritual reformation which will revive his church and bring healing to the nations of the world. God grant that Protestants will see the true peril and realize the situation within their gates and thus be compelled to demand a return to genuine biblical Christianity on the part of the clergy and the church in its corporate testimony. When that takes place the Christian church will hold its rightful place in the world and will fulfill the command of the Lord, "Go ye therefore, and teach all nations, baptizing them in the name of the Father, and of the Son, and of the Holy Ghost" (Matt 28:19).

Appendix

Note 1

THE AUBURN AFFIRMATION

An Affirmation
Designed to safeguard the unity and liberty of the
Presbyterian Church in the United States of America[1]

Submitted for the consideration of its ministers and people

We, the undersigned, Ministers of the Presbyterian Church in the United States of America, feel bound, in view of certain actions of the General Assembly of 1923 and of persistent attempts to divide the church and abridge its freedom, to express our convictions in matters pertaining thereto. At the outset we affirm and declare our acceptance of the Westminster Confession of Faith, as we did at our ordinations, "as containing the system of doctrine taught in the Holy Scriptures." We sincerely hold and earnestly preach the doctrines of evangelical Christianity, in agreement with the historic testimony of the Presbyterian Church in the United States of America, of which we are loyal ministers. For the maintenance of the faith of our church, the preservation of its unity, and the protection of the liberties of its ministers and people, we offer this Affirmation.

The church's guarantees of liberty

(1) Concerning the interpretation of the Confession of Faith

I. By its law and its history, the Presbyterian Church in the United States of America safeguards the liberty of thought and teaching of its ministers. At their ordinations they "receive and adopt the Confession of this Church, as containing the system of doctrine taught in the Holy Scriptures." This the church has always esteemed a sufficient doctrinal subscription for its ministers. Manifestly it does not require their assent to the very words of the Confession, or to all of its teachings, or to interpretations of the Confession by individuals or church courts. The Confession of Faith itself disclaims infallibility. The authors

---

1   Reprinted from a copy received by William Garrison Hunter, II, October 29, 1934.

would not allow this to church councils, their own included: "All synods or councils since the apostles' times, whether general or particular, may err, and many have erred; therefore they are not to be made the rule of faith or practice, but to be used as a help in both" (Conf. XXXI, iii). The Confession also expressly asserts the liberty of Christian believers, and condemns the submission of the mind or conscience to any human authority: "God alone is lord of the conscience and hath left it free from the doctrines and commandments of men which are in anything contrary to his Word, or beside it, in matters of faith or worship. So that to believe such doctrines, or to obey such commandments out of conscience, is to betray true liberty of conscience; and the requiring of an implicit faith, and an absolute and blind obedience, is to destroy liberty of conscience, and reason also" (Conf. XX, ii).

The formal relation of American Presbyterianism to the Westminster Confession of Faith begins in the Adopting Act of 1729. This anticipated and provided for dissent by individuals from portions of the Confession. At the formation of the Presbyterian Church in the United States of America, in 1788, the Westminster Confession was adopted as the creed of the church; and at the same time the church publicly declared the significance of its organization in a document which contains these words: "There are truths and forms, with respect to which men of good characters and principles may differ. And in all these they think it the duty, both of private Christians and Societies, to exercise mutual forbearance towards each other" (Declaration of Principles, v).

Of the two parts into which our church was separated from 1837 to 1870, one held that only one interpretation of certain parts of the Confession of Faith was legitimate, while the other maintained its right to dissent from this interpretation. In the Reunion of 1870 they came together on equal terms, "each recognizing the other as a sound and orthodox body." The meaning of this, as understood then and ever since, is that office-bearers in the church who maintain their liberty in the interpretation of the Confession are exercising their rights guaranteed by the terms of the Reunion.

A more recent reunion also is significant, that of the Cumberland Presbyterian Church and the Presbyterian Church in the United States of America, in 1906. This reunion was opposed by certain members of the Presbyterian Church in the United States of America, on the ground that the two churches were not at one in doctrine; yet it was consummated. Thus did our church once more exemplify its historic policy of accepting theological differences within its bounds and subordinating them to recognized loyalty to Jesus Christ and united work for the kingdom of God.

(2) Concerning the interpretation of the Scriptures

With respect to the interpretation of the Scriptures the position of our church has been that common to Protestants. "The Supreme Judge," says the Confession of Faith, "by whom all controversies of religion are to be determined, and all decrees of councils, opinions of ancient writers, doctrines of men, and private spirits, are to be examined, and in whose sentence we are to rest, can be no other but the Holy Spirit speaking in the Scripture" (Conf. I, x). Accordingly our church has held that the supreme guide in the interpretation of the Scriptures is not, as it is with Roman Catholics, ecclesiastical authority, but the Spirit of God, speaking to the Christian believer. Thus our church lays it upon its ministers and others to read and teach the Scriptures as the Spirit of God through His manifold ministries instructs them, and to receive all truth which from time to time He causes to break forth from the Scriptures.

There is no assertion in the Scriptures that their writers were kept "from error." The Confession of Faith does not make this assertion; and it is significant that this assertion is not to be found in the Apostles' Creed or the Nicene Creed or in any of the great Reformation confessions. The doctrine of inerrancy, intended to enhance the authority of the Scriptures, in fact impairs their supreme authority for faith and life, and weakens the testimony of the church to the power of God unto salvation through Jesus Christ. We hold that the General Assembly of 1923, in asserting that "the Holy Spirit did so inspire, guide and move the writers of Holy Scripture as to keep them from error," spoke without warrant of the Scriptures or of the Confession of Faith. We hold rather to the words of the Confession of Faith, that the Scriptures "are given by inspiration of God, to be the rule of faith and life" (Conf. I, ii).

Authority under the constitution for the declaration of doctrine

II. While it is constitutional for any General Assembly "to bear testimony against error in doctrine," (Form of Govt. XII, v), yet such testimony is without binding authority, since the constitution of our church provides that its doctrine shall be declared only by concurrent action of the General Assembly and the presbyteries. Thus the church guards the statement of its doctrine against hasty or ill-considered action by either General Assemblies or presbyteries. From this provision of our constitution, it is evident that neither in one General Assembly nor in many, without concurrent action of the presbyteries, is there authority to declare what the Presbyterian Church in the United States of America believes and teaches; and that the assumption that any General Assembly has authoritatively declared what the church believes and teaches is groundless. A declaration by a General Assembly that any doctrine is "an essential doctrine" attempts to amend the constitution of the church in an unconstitutional manner.

Action of the General Assembly regarding the preaching in the first Presbyterian Church of New York City

III. The General Assembly of 1923, in asserting that "doctrines contrary to the standards of the Presbyterian Church" have been preached in the pulpit of the First Presbyterian Church of New York City, virtually pronounced a judgment against this church. The General Assembly did this with knowledge that the matter on which it so expressed itself was already under formal consideration in the Presbytery of New York, as is shown by the language of its action. The General Assembly acted in the case without giving hearing to the parties concerned. Thus the General Assembly did not conform to the procedure in such cases contemplated by our Book of Discipline, and, what is more serious, it in effect condemned a Christian minister without using the method of conference, patience and love enjoined on us by Jesus Christ. We object to the action of General Assembly in this case, as being out of keeping with the law and the spirit of our church.

The doctrinal deliverance of the General Assembly

IV. The General Assembly of 1923 expressed the opinion concerning five doctrinal statements that each one "is an essential doctrine of the Word of God and our standards." On the constitutional grounds which we have before described, we are opposed to any attempt to elevate these five doctrinal statements, or any of them, to the position of tests for ordination or for good standing in our church.

Furthermore, this opinion of the General Assembly attempts to commit our church to certain theories concerning the inspiration of the Bible, and the Incarnation, the Atonement, the Resurrection, and the Continuing Life and Supernatural Power of our Lord Jesus Christ. We all hold most earnestly to these great facts and doctrines; we all believe from our hearts that the writers of the Bible were inspired of God; that Jesus Christ was God manifest in the flesh; that God was in Christ, reconciling the world unto Himself, and through Him we have our redemption; that having died for our sins He rose from the dead and is our everliving Saviour; that in His earthly ministry He wrought many mighty works, and by His vicarious death and unfailing presence He is able to save to the uttermost. Some of us regard the particular theories contained in the deliverance of the General Assembly of 1923 as satisfactory explanations of these facts and doctrines. But we are united in believing that these are not the only theories allowed by the Scriptures and our standards as explanations of these facts and doctrines of our religion, and that all who hold to these facts and doctrines, whatever theories they may employ to explain them, are worthy of all confidence and fellowship.

Extent of the liberty claimed

V. We do not desire liberty to go beyond the teachings of evangelical Christianity. But we maintain that it is our constitutional right and our Christian duty within these limits to exercise liberty of thought and teaching, that we may more effectively preach the gospel of Jesus Christ, the Saviour of the World.

The spirit and purpose of this affirmation

VI. Finally, we deplore the evidences of division in our beloved church, in the face of a world so desperately in need of a united testimony to the gospel of Christ. We earnestly desire fellowship with all who like us are disciples of Jesus Christ. We hope that those to whom this Affirmation comes will believe that it is not the declaration of a theological party, but rather a sincere appeal, based on the Scriptures and our standards, for the preservation of the unity and freedom of our church, for which most earnestly we plead and pray.

Note 2

COMMITTEE FOR REORGANIZATION OF PRINCETON THEOLOGICAL SEMINARY

1. That the Assembly appoint a committee of eleven members of whom at least three shall be ruling elders of the Presbyterian Church in the United States of America who are learned in the law, said committee to be constituted by the continuance of the present committee and the appointment by the Moderator of six additional members, two of whom shall be members of the Board of Trustees of Princeton Seminary, and two of whom shall be members of the Board of Directors of Princeton Seminary, and two of whom shall be from the Church at large, with the further provision that three of the six new members of the committee shall be ministers and three of them ruling elders; that said committee proceed to confer with the Board of Trustees and the Board of Directors in obtaining such amendments to the Charter of the Seminary or such additional articles of incorporation, and preparing such ordinances or by-laws and taking such other action as they may be advised by counsel is necessary or proper to establish a single Board of Control for said Seminary, define the relationship and recognize the right of control of the General Assembly under the existing trusts, so as to assure the rights of the Presbyterian Church in the trust property and its control over the instruction of the Seminary; and to cooperate in preparing a complete plan for the educational work of the Seminary under the administration of the new Board and under the direction and control of the Assembly; that in all such conferences between said committee and said Trustees the present Board of Directors be requested to participate in an advisory capacity by the election by them for that purpose of a committee of five of their members. The enlarged committee herein authorized is hereby directed by the General Assembly to report to the next General Assembly for approval and adoption the proposed changes or additions to the Charter, and the new plan for the administration of the Seminary.

2. That pending this reorganization, the appointment of Professor J. Gresham Machen to the Chair of Apologetics and the appointment of Professor Oswald T. Allis to the Helena Chair of Semitics, be not confirmed and that the further consideration of these appointments be deferred until after the reorganization proposed in this report shall have been effected.

Note 3

RESOLUTION OF EXECUTIVE COMMITTEE FOR ESTABLISHMENT OF WESTMINSTER THEOLOGICAL SEMINARY

The following resolution was adopted unanimously:

Being convinced that the action of the General Assembly of 1929, establishing a new board of control for Princeton Theological Seminary, will inevitably make the institution conform to the present doctrinal drift of the

Church and so desert the distinctive doctrinal position which it is bound by the most solemn trust obligations to maintain, we believe that immediate steps should be taken for the establishment of a new theological seminary which shall continue the policy of unswerving loyalty to the Word of God and to the Westminster Standards for which Princeton Seminary has been so long and so honorably known.

Note 4

MINUTES OF THE MEETING OF THE BOARD OF TRUSTEES OF WESTMINSTER THEOLOGICAL SEMINARY OCTOBER 22, 1935

For the past six years Westminster Theological Seminary has been an institution "set for the defense and proclamation of the gospel." Its faculty have been exponents of the necessity of a militant setting forth of the doctrines of the Reformed Faith within and without the church as the bounden duty of every true Christian.

The Seminary has stood from the beginning for a vigorous prosecution of the battle against modernism in the ecclesiastical field. That was the issue on which the break occurred with the new Princeton Seminary.

The new Princeton Seminary permitted orthodox teaching in its classrooms but it discouraged in the members of the faculty the logical implications of such orthodox teaching in the presbyteries and General Assemblies and other councils of the Church. Hence certain members of the teaching staff left Princeton, and formed the nucleus of the Faculty of Westminster Seminary. From the beginning Westminster Seminary has stood for the belief that its classroom teaching is of little value unless it results in vigorously fostering a consistent program of reform in the Church.

The Seminary thus formed has prospered because it has hitherto remained true to the position which it was founded to maintain. Members of its faculty have entered vigorously into the ecclesiastical battle against modernism wherever God has put them. They have encouraged a similar attitude in the students. The consequence is that the institution has been greatly hated; but the consequence is also that it has been greatly blessed of God, and that it has the prayers and the support of those who stand in the vanguard of the evangelical forces in the Reformed churches throughout the world.

The question now is whether the Seminary shall continue in the front rank of the battle, or whether it shall lag in the rear; whether it shall continue to give a hearty God-speed to those who are consistently challenging the present modernist and indifferentist control of the Presbyterian Church in the U.S.A., or whether it shall, by implication at least, ask them to desist from their present activity and make their protest against modernism at best in word only and not in deed.

It is the latter policy which, we are compelled to hold, is now being advocated in the pages of *Christianity Today*. In view of the close connection in which this journal has always been regarded by its readers as standing with Westminster Seminary, and in view of the fact that its Editor, Dr. Samuel G. Craig, is a member of the Board of Trustees, the faculty feels compelled tc bring to the attention of the Board the fact that a serious division has been introduced into the affairs of the Seminary by the present editorial policy of that paper and by the present attitude of Dr. Craig.

If this policy of Dr. Craig dominates the Seminary, the Seminary will have lost the reason for its existence. It will simply have joined the ranks of those countless institutions and movements which have been begun as protests against unbelief or heresy and then, losing their first love, have sunk by insensible degrees into the very attitude of vacillation and compromise which they were founded to oppose. . . .

In response to this statement the Rev. Edwin H. Rian made the following motion:

In reply to the Faculty's special communication the Board declares that it is in sympathy with the aggressive stand of the Faculty in the present ecclesiastical crisis as agreeing with the purpose for which the Seminary was founded and deprecates the serious division which has been introduced into the affairs of the Seminary by the present policy and attitude of *Christianity Today.*

Before the vote was taken the following resolution was introduced by Dr. C. E. Macartney, not as a substitute motion but as a method to use in voting on the above motion:

RESOLVED: That in view of the grave importance of the motion now under discussion, and the absence from this stated meeting of eleven members of the Board, the question be put to a vote by ballots mailed to all members of the Board on Friday, October 25th, and that the President, Secretary, and Treasurer shall act as a Committee of Tellers, who shall announce the result of the vote to the members of the Board.

Should the vote show that a majority of the Board support the resolution by the Faculty, it is the sense of this meeting that those who have voted against the resolution should then withdraw from the Board. Likewise, that should the vote show that the majority of the Board oppose the resolution, that those constituting such majority withdraw from the Board, and leave the way clear for the continued witness of a Seminary which we believe was raised up of God as a witness to the Everlasting Gospel, and which has been so signally blessed by Him.

The Secretary of the Board is instructed to forward to all members of the Board a copy of the Faculty's resolution, the motion of Mr. Rian, and a copy of this resolution. Furthermore, that their Secretary in his communication call attention to that part of the resolution of the Faculty which declares the unalterable purpose of the majority of the Faculty to resign from the Seminary, should the Board of Trustees answer their resolution in the negative.

Note 5

STATEMENT OF BOARD OF TRUSTEES OF
WESTMINSTER THEOLOGICAL SEMINARY

The Board of Trustees of Westminster Theological Seminary announces that the Seminary will go forward in accordance with the policy favored by the Faculty, which it holds to be simply the policy which the institution has followed from the beginning and on the basis of which it has made its appeal for funds.

The Board expresses its warm admiration of the manner in which those members of the Board who could not support the Faculty in the present decision have sacrificed all personal considerations by resigning from the Board in order that the institution may continue, and it expresses its high appreciation of the services which they rendered during their period of office and its sincere regret that they cannot under the circumstances continue as members of the Board.

The Board also expresses its profound sense of the loss which the institution has sustained through the resignation of Dr. Oswald T. Allis, who has rendered distinguished service of quite incalculable value as Professor of Old Testament.

With regard to the future, the Board desires to emphasize the fact that in its judgment the present changes in its membership will not bring any innovations of policy but will simply insure the continuation of exactly the same policy as that which has been followed from the beginning and on the basis of which the appeal of the institution for support has been made. It has no intention whatever of forming any official connection with organizations like The Independent Board for Presbyterian Foreign Missions or the Presbyterian Constitutional Covenant Union; but the prevailing temper of its Trustees and Faculty will be to give hearty God-speed to those who are serving in the vanguard of any legitimate battle against modernism in the Presbyterian Church in the U.S.A.

Note 6

The Chairman of the Faculty issued this statement:

I have received through the courtesy of the newspapers a copy of the resignation of the Rev. A. A. MacRae, Ph.D., Assistant Professor of Old Testament in Westminster Theological Seminary. Professor MacRae labored faithfully in this institution and we are grateful for his past services.

The policy of Westminster Theological Seminary has been to carry on the traditions of loyalty to the Bible and the Reformed Faith which characterized the old Princeton Theological Seminary prior to its reorganization in 1929. There has been no change in this policy, and I regret that Professor MacRae no longer finds himself able to continue in accord with it.

His resignation follows a suggestion, made by certain persons, that Westminster Theological Seminary add to its faculty three members and to its Board of Trustees ten members, all of whom should be premillennialists. Such a basis has never been employed in the selection of members of the faculty or of trustees of Westminster Seminary. There is liberty on this point within the doctrinal standards of the Seminary and there have always been premillennialists on the Seminary's faculty and Board of Trustees. The sole basis for the selection of faculty members, however, is scholarship which gives the promise of contributing to the training of men utterly loyal to the Bible, the infallible Word of God, as set forth in the Westminster Standards. I trust that this basis of selection will never be changed.

The Seminary recognizes to the full the tremendous evils of intemperance. Its only concern is to proclaim the teaching of the Bible on this, as on all other questions. The Biblical teaching against intemperance is very emphatic but the Bible does not permit of a teaching which would make our Lord's example sinful.

The Seminary stands in the great tradition of Charles Hodge, B. B. Warfield, Robert Dick Wilson and J. Gresham Machen. Nothing will be allowed to move it from its loyalty to the Word of God.

(Signed) R. B. Kuiper,
Chairman of the Faculty,
Westminster Theological Seminary.

The students also came to the defense of the seminary:

We, the students of Westminster Theological Seminary, regret the resignation of Dr. Allan A. MacRae, who has been one of our honored instructors. We are at a loss to understand the charges included in his letter of resignation, made public in the press. The following statement was unanimously approved at a called meeting of the student body:

1. Westminster Seminary has not been taken over by "a small alien group without American Presbyterian background." All members of the faculty are in perfect accord with the Presbyterian faith as represented by Hodge, Warfield, and Machen; in fact, this was the reason for their appointment to the faculty.

2. Since the faculty has always been united in its teaching of the Presbyterian or Reformed Faith, it is absurd to charge that an "alien group" has tried to "enforce their own peculiar notions by crushing the broad evangelical point of view which in its earliest years made the Presbyterian Church in the U.S.A. a great reformed church." We emphatically assert that Westminster Seminary has consistently sought to teach only that which is set forth in the Word of God.

We wish to express publicly our high regard for the sound, biblical scholarship of the faculty. We rejoice in the humility with which they teach us, and in the freedom of interpretation they allow within the bounds of "the noble traditions which were once characteristic of the Presbyterian Church in the U.S.A."

3. The attack on "Modern Dispensationalism" was led by Dr. O. T. Allis, for many years teacher at Princeton Seminary and one of the founders of Westminster, who could not possibly have belonged to the alleged "alien group." This attack has never been intended as an attack on "Premillennialism."

4. We hope that no one will be misled by the assertion that "practically every member of the faculty has entered upon a vigorous defense of an asserted right to use intoxicating liquors–a defense occasioned by the fact that certain faculty members themselves use intoxicants." We as students can honestly assert that the faculty has neither taught nor practised anything out of accord with the historic Presbyterian position as based on the Word of God.

5. Dr. MacRae claims that only the "Premillennial" view of the Second Coming of Christ is biblical. This claim it is his privilege to make, since historically there has been granted the right to hold different interpretations of the events connected with the Second Coming of Christ among Bible-believing Christians in the American Presbyterian tradition. However, we do object to his intimation that certain of his colleagues who hold to another view do not strive to expound the Scriptures in a faithful and scholarly fashion.

It is our earnest prayer that all who love the Word of Christ and His Kingdom will give heed to this statement, and that the witness of Westminster Seminary may continue faithful to its foundation principles and may rise to new heights of influence, all to the honor and glory of God.

Signed, Robert Nicholas,
Pres. Student Association.
Edw. Heerema,
Chm., Formulating Comm.
April 26, 1937

Note 7

ACTION OF GENERAL ASSEMBLY OF PRESBYTERIAN CHURCH IN THE USA CONCERNING UNION WITH UNITED PRESBYTERIAN CHURCH OF NORTH AMERICA

That the Stated Clerk be directed to prepare and send to the Presbyteries for their action the following overture:

The Categorical Question on the Plan of Union:

Do you approve of the Union of the Presbyterian Church in the U.S.A. and the United Presbyterian Church of North America on the following basis:

(a) On the basis of the terms and provisions of the Plan of Union recommended to the respective General Assemblies of the said Churches, and herewith submitted by the General Assembly.

(b) The Union shall be effected upon the doctrinal basis of the Scriptures of the Old and New Testaments as the supreme standard, acknowledged as the inspired Word of God, the only infallible rule of faith and practice; and upon the subordinate standards of the Westminster Confession of Faith together with the amendments adopted in 1903 by the Presbyterian Church in the U.S.A.; and the Larger and Shorter Catechisms; all of which subordinate standards are recognized as agreeable to and founded upon the Scriptures.

(c) On the basis of the provisional Form of Government, the provisional Book of Discipline, and the provisional Directory for Worship, herewith submitted.

Pursuant to this action by the General Assembly, the Presbyteries of the Presbyterian Church in the U.S.A. are asked to express their approval or disapproval of this Overture, by giving a direct affirmative or negative answer thereto. In accordance with the provisions of Form of Government chapter XXIV "Of Amendments," this Overture shall not be obligatory on the Church, unless it shall be approved in writing by two-thirds of all the Presbyteries and agreed to and enacted by the General Assembly next ensuing and the written votes of the Presbyteries shall be returned to the General Assembly.

It is further ordered that the Stated Clerk of the Assembly shall transmit this Overture to the Presbyteries of the Presbyterian Church in the U.S.A. only if and when the General Assembly of the United Presbyterian Church of North America has ordered the submission of this Overture, entitled, "The Categorical Question on the Plan of Union," to its constituent Presbyteries, asking them to express their approval or disapproval of this Overture by giving a direct affirmative or negative answer thereto, in accordance with the Constitution of said Church applicable in this connection.

Note 8

ACTION OF GENERAL CONVENTION OF PROTESTANT EPISCOPAL CHURCH CONCERNING UNION WITH PRESBYTERIAN CHURCH IN THE USA

The General Convention of the Protestant Episcopal Church meeting in Cincinnati in October, 1937, made request of the Presiding Bishop that he convey to the authorities of the Presbyterian Church the following Resolution and Message:

I take pleasure therefore in presenting to you this information with the hope that it may have favorable action by the General Assembly of your Church. The Resolution reads as follows:

1. The General Convention of the Protestant Episcopal Church in the U.S. of A., acting with full realization of the significance of its proposal, hereby invites the Presbyterian Church in the U.S.A. to join with it in accepting the following declaration:

"The two churches, one in the faith of the Lord Jesus Christ, the Incarnate Word of God, recognizing the Holy Scriptures as the supreme rule of faith, accepting the two sacraments ordained by Christ, and believing that the visible unity of Christ's Church is the will of God, hereby formally declare their purpose to achieve organic union between their respective churches."

Upon the basis of these arguments it is hoped that the two Churches will take immediate steps toward the framing of plans whereby this end may be achieved.

With prayers for God's blessing upon the efforts made in His name toward the union of His Church on earth, I am,

Faithfully yours,

(Signed) James De Wolfe Perry,

Presiding Bishop

Note 9

ACTION OF GENERAL ASSEMBLY OF PRESBYTERIAN CHURCH IN THE USA CONCERNING UNION WITH PRESBYTERIAN CHURCH IN THE US

Whereas, One hundred and ninety-five Presbyteries have taken action on an Overture looking to organic union between the Presbyterian Church in the U.S.A. and the Presbyterian Church in the U.S., therefore, be it

Resolved, 1. That this Assembly has for many years stood ready and is now ready to enter into negotiations with a view to organic union with the Presbyterian Church in the U.S.

Resolved, 2. That this matter be committed to the General Assembly's Committee on Church Cooperation and Union, with instructions to enter into negotiations with the Presbyterian Church in the U. S. through a Committee appointed by the General Assembly of that Church, if it should deem it advisable to do so.

Resolved, 3. That these resolutions—together with the Overture, be telegraphed to the General Assembly of the Presbyterian Church in the U.S. in session at Birmingham, Alabama.

Note 10

DR. MACHEN'S PROPOSED OVERTURE CONCERNING FOREIGN MISSIONS

The Presbytery of New Brunswick respectfully overtures the General Assembly of 1933,

1. To take care to elect to positions on the Board of Foreign Missions only persons who are fully aware of the danger in which the Church stands and who are determined to insist upon such verities as the full truthfulness of Scripture, the virgin birth of our Lord, His substitutionary death as a sacrifice to satisfy Divine justice, His bodily resurrection and His miracles, as being essential to the Word of God and our Standards and as being necessary to the message which every missionary under our Church shall proclaim,

2. To instruct the Board of Foreign Missions that no one who denies the absolute necessity of acceptance of such verities by every candidate for the ministry can possibly be regarded as competent to occupy the position of Candidate Secretary,

3. To instruct the Board of Foreign Missions to take care lest, by the wording of the application blanks for information from candidates and from those who are asked to express opinions about them, or in any other way, the impression be produced that tolerance of opposing views or ability to progress in spiritual truth, or the like, is more important than an unswerving faithfulness in the proclamation of the gospel as it is contained in the Word of God and an utter unwillingness to make common cause with any other gospel whether it goes under the name of Christ or not,

4. To warn the Board of the great danger that lurks in union enterprises at home as well as abroad, in view of the widespread error in our day.

Note 11

JOHN McDOWELL'S STATEMENT CONCERNING MEMBERSHIP IN THE PRESBYTERIAN CHURCH IN THE USA

He stated:

On the other hand, if any minister, elder, deacon, or communicant decides to remain in the denomination, while they have a right to work for any changes in doctrine, in government or in work which they desire, they must work for these changes in harmony with the constitutional procedure; and while they are so working for them, they must be loyal to the doctrine, government and work of the Church as embodied in the local Church and in the Boards and Agencies of the General Assembly. The Presbyterian Church in the U.S.A. stands for liberty, but it must not be forgotten that it is liberty within the law and within loyalty.

Note 12

The Introductory Note and Summary of the Studies are as follows:

Introductory Note

Among the duties which chapter XXVI, section II, of the Form of Government assigns to the General Council is "to consider between annual meetings of the General Assembly cases of serious embarrassment or emergency concerning the benevolent and missionary work of the Church, and to provide direct relief." In view of this Constitutional requirement, the General Council has been compelled to take official notice of the action of certain ministers and laymen of the Presbyterian Church in organizing within the denomination an "Independent Board for Presbyterian Foreign Missions." This Board has been incorporated under the laws of the Commonwealth of Pennsylvania with Officers, Members, Executive Committee, General Secretary, Constitution and

By-Laws. Its purpose according to the charter, and a pamphlet being circulated by the Board throughout the Church, is to commission and send out missionaries, to establish mission stations, and to divert the missionary offerings of our churches from the Board of Foreign Missions of our Church to the Independent Board.

The organization of such a Board by officers and laymen of our Church to operate in precisely the same sphere which the General Assembly has assigned to its own Board of Foreign Missions, without the sanction of the Supreme Judicatory and entirely independent of its authority and jurisdiction, inevitably raises questions of great seriousness and importance to the members, the officers, and the judicatories of the entire Church. The unconstitutionality of such a Board, the particular action which presbyteries and sessions should adopt with reference to its officers and members, the source of responsibility under the Constitution for the conduct of the missionary work of the Church, and the extent of the control which the Church has over its judicatories and churches in the matter of their gifts to benevolent causes, are some of these questions which must be answered to insure the future peace and prosperity of the Church, and unity of effort in the great task of evangelizing the world.

The General Council has reached the unanimous opinion that there are two effective ways by which it can discharge its constitutional responsibilities "to provide direct methods of relief" in the existing situation. These are, (1) A Brief Summary of the action of the last General Assembly with reference to its endorsement of the Board of Foreign Missions; (2) A careful study of certain Constitutional questions relating to the missionary work of the Presbyterian Church under the following heads: I. The Authority of the Constitution of the Presbyterian Church; II. The Authority which the Constitution vests in the several judicatories of the Presbyterian Church; III. The Authority vested in the Constitution to conduct the missionary operations of the Church; IV. The Constitutional Authority of the Church over its missionary offerings. This Summary and Study are to be found in the pages which immediately follow and are respectfully submitted to the General Assembly for its information and guidance.

Summary

1. Missionary offerings are one of the ordinances enjoined in a particular church by the Constitution of the Presbyterian Church. The successive provisions of the Confession of Faith, the Form of Government, and the Directory for Worship, which have already been noted, make these missionary offerings just as really a part of the instituted worship of the Church as are prayer, preaching the Word of God, or the sacraments. A church member or an individual church that will not give to promote the officially authorized missionary program of the Presbyterian Church is in exactly the same position with reference to the Constitution of the Church as a church member or an individual church that would refuse to take part in the celebration of the Lord's

Supper or any of the prescribed ordinances of the denomination as set forth in chapter VII of the Form of Government.

2. In designating missionary offerings as an ordinance, the Constitution of the Presbyterian Church specifically enjoins all church judicatories, all church officers, and all individual churches to guide, direct, and make effectual through the authorized agencies of the Church the missionary offerings of all church members to the same extent as they are enjoined to perform the same office with reference to any other ordinance of the Church.

3. The missionary offerings of the Presbyterian Church must be restricted in their apportionment and distribution to those Boards created and maintained by the General Assembly for the spread of the Gospel, unless an expressed approval is granted by the judicatories of the Church to assign a portion of such offerings to other objects.

4. The General Assembly by virtue of its power to interpret authoritatively the Constitution and to superintend the concerns of the whole Church has consistently throughout its entire history defined with particularity the obligation of all those affiliated with the Church to fulfill all Constitutional provisions with reference to missionary offerings, and to support the authorized missionary work of the denomination in proportion to the ability of each.

5. The missionary offerings of the individual members of a particular Presbyterian church when made in connection with the worship of the congregation, or through any of the societies or organizations of the local church, are by the provisions of the Constitution under the jurisdiction of the denomination, and cannot be appropriated by any judicatory in whole or in part to any agency organized in antagonism to, or in rivalry with, any one or more of the authorized Boards of the Presbyterian Church in the United States of America.

Note 13

STATEMENT OF INDEPENDENT BOARD CONCERNING ITS ECCLESIASTICAL STATUS

The Independent Board for Presbyterian Foreign Missions is not an organization in the Presbytery of Philadelphia, or in the Synod of Pennsylvania, or in the Presbyterian Church in the U.S.A.

The term "Presbyterian" refers to church polity and, by extension, to doctrine. Its use is not confined to any church or to any part of the world. There are a large number of churches in our own country using the term, as for example, the Presbyterian Church in the U.S., the United Presbyterian Church, the Cumberland Presbyterian Church (Colored), the Reformed Presbyterian Church, General Synod, and the Associate Reformed Presbyterian Synod. Further, the name "Presbyterian" is widely used by independent institutions organized for charitable and other purposes throughout the world.

The Independent Board was formed for the purpose of sending out missionaries who would propagate the Presbyterian doctrine and organize, as opportunity might be afforded, churches along the lines of Presbyterian polity.

It is not of importance to the Independent Board whether its missionaries are members of the Presbyterian Church in the U.S.A. or not. What does matter, and matter tremendously, is that its missionaries and its members should be wholeheartedly in accord with Presbyterian doctrine, and believers in a Presbyterian system of church polity.

The Independent Board neither has, nor desires to have, any official relationship to the Presbyterian Church in the U.S.A.

Note 14

THE DELIVERANCE
on "The Independent Board for Presbyterian Foreign Missions" adopted by the 146th General Assembly of the Presbyterian Church in the USA, Cleveland, 1934.

The Presbyterian Church in the United States of America, in its solemn belief that, "there is no other way of salvation than that revealed in the Gospel" and, "that Christ hath commissioned His Church to go into all the world and make disciples of all nations," has consistently maintained throughout its entire history that as a Church, it is required and is admirably formed by its Constitution to become a great missionary society, and that specific provisions incorporated in said Constitution afford the best means for securing harmony of sentiment and unity of action on the part of its entire membership in the supreme task of extending the Kingdom of Christ throughout the whole earth.

In chapter XXXV of the Confession of Faith, therefore, and in repeated deliverances of the General Assembly, the truth is clearly set forth that the Presbyterian Church in its nature and organization is a missionary society whose object is to aid in the conversion of the world to Christ, and that every member of the Presbyterian Church is a member of the said society, and obligated by virtue of his membership, to contribute by his prayers, gifts and personal efforts, toward the accomplishments of this object. Further, Chapters XII and XVIII of the Form of Government, commit the responsibility for the superintendence and direction of the Presbyterian Church as a missionary society solely to the General Assembly to discharge in any way it may deem proper and efficient.

In the assumption of this responsibility, the General Assembly in the first fifty years of its existence, designated certain interdenominational and independent or voluntary societies as accredited agencies through which the missionary work of the denomination was to be accomplished. Finally, almost one hundred years ago, when many years of actual experience had clearly demonstrated the inefficacy of such agencies under a Presbyterian form of government, the General Assembly reached the decision, the constitutionality of which was never questioned, that all the missionary work of the Presbyterian

Church should be conducted by Boards or Agencies of the General Assembly, except for certain interdenominational work which in its judgment the Presbyterian Church could not undertake alone, and which the General Assembly itself would, therefore, agree to approve in specific deliverances.

Upon reaching this decision, the General Assembly immediately declared that the Presbyterian Church could best contribute to the great task of evangelizing the world through Boards created by the General Assembly, which are responsible to it alone, which are under its advice, review and absolute control, and which are required to exercise their sound discretion and judgment in deciding upon and in conducting the business entrusted to them.

From the day when that decision was made until the present hour, the General Assembly has endeavored scrupulously and faithfully to discharge the great responsibility thus laid upon it, in the unwavering and unvarying conviction that nothing further is needed to impart unity and vigor of effort to the missionary work of the whole Presbyterian Church, than the honest adherence to, and the loyal support of, those specific provisions governing that work which are set forth in the Constitution to which all persons consent when they become members of the Church, and which all church officers profess sincerely to receive, adopt and approve when they assume their office.

In emphasizing this responsibility of all church members and church officers under the Constitution, to engage actively in the spread of the Gospel through the officially designated Boards and Agencies of the Church, the General Assembly would most emphatically state that there is no arbitrary abridgement of personal liberty in the requirement of this duty of all who have affiliated themselves with the Presbyterian Church. As the judicatory of jurisdiction in all matters relating to missionary operations, it has never presumed to interfere with the rights or preferences of individual members to give their money or efforts to such missionary objects as they may choose.

On the contrary, it has always maintained that the right to control the property of the members of the Church, to assess the amount of their contributions, or to prescribe how they shall dispose of their money, is utterly foreign to the spirit of Presbyterianism. Every contribution on the part of an individual member of the Church must be purely voluntary. In fact, the Presbyterian Church itself is a voluntary association. All of its members voluntarily associate themselves with the Church, and maintain their affiliation with it no longer than they voluntarily choose to do so. All that they do for its support, therefore, is a voluntary donation, and there is no power which can compel them to contribute to any ecclesiastical object to which they are not willing to give.

In maintaining, however, this personal freedom of individual members, in their contributions to the Church, the General Assembly has never recognized any inconsistency in asserting with equal force, that there is a definite and sacred obligation on the part of every member of the Presbyterian Church to contribute to those objects designated by the authorized judicatory of the denomination.

When a church is organized under a written Constitution, which contains prescribed provisions as to giving for benevolent purposes, every member is in duty bound to observe those provisions with the same fidelity and care as he is bound to believe in Christ and to keep His commandments according to the doctrinal provisions set forth in that same Constitution.

Therefore, when the General Assembly, in accordance with specific provisions of the Constitution of the Church which empower it so to do, declares that it is the purpose of the Presbyterian Church to secure the proclamation of the Gospel in a prescribed way, by means of Boards and Agencies, which are created, controlled and maintained by it, then it is the definite obligation and sacred duty of each individual who is affiliated with any of its churches or judicatories to support those Boards and Agencies to the utmost of his ability. Certainly, if the Constitution declares that it is the duty of the General Assembly, which represents in one body all the particular churches of the denomination, to act in such matters, it must naturally follow that it is the duty of all those who compose those churches to unite in the action. There is, therefore, no abridgement of personal liberty when the Presbyterian Church demands of its members who have voluntarily attached themselves to it, and are thereby under its Constitution, to honor, sustain and extend the Church of their choice in the manner the Constitution itself prescribes.

This General Assembly has carefully reviewed the foregoing principles, specifically set forth in the Constitution of the Presbyterian Church, for the purpose of explaining the only remedy which appears to be applicable to a certain distressing and deplorable situation which during the past year has arisen within its jurisdiction, and which is revealed in a certain pamphlet being circulated throughout the Church, entitled "The Independent Board for Presbyterian Foreign Missions — A Statement as to its Organization and Program."

It is definitely stated in this pamphlet to which the names of certain ministers and laymen of the Presbyterian Church in the United States of America are appended, that an Independent Board for Presbyterian Foreign Missions, with officers, members, executive committee, general secretary, constitution and by-laws, and an established office in the city of Philadelphia, has been organized, and incorporated under the laws of the Commonwealth of Pennsylvania, which is not responsible to the General Assembly of the Presbyterian Church in the United States of America, or to any other ecclesiastical body, and whose purpose among other things is to commission and send out missionaries, to establish mission stations, and to seek "to encourage Presbyterian churches and individuals to support this Board," (see charter of "The Independent Board for Presbyterian Foreign Missions," Article 3, d), which will thereby divert the missionary offerings of our churches from the channels which the Presbyterian Church has made for them.

Such an attempt on the part of Presbyterian ministers and laymen, to exercise ecclesiastical and administrative functions without the sanction of the General Assembly, and in the precise sphere of missionary operations officially assigned by that judicatory to its own Board of Foreign Missions, is not only an usurpation of authority, but also a repudiation of the jurisdiction of the General Assembly, and of those terms of fellowship and communion contained in the Constitution of the Presbyterian Church which all solemnly and faithfully promised to observe when they assumed membership or office in the Church.

No organic body, whether it be a nation or a church, organized under a constitutional form of government, as is the Presbyterian Church in the United States of America, can tolerate such a defiance of lawful authority on the part of any of its constituents. Therefore, the General Assembly, as the Supreme judicatory of the Presbyterian Church, must insist that all those who have affiliated themselves with the Presbyterian Church and desire to remain in its fellowship, must be held strictly accountable to the agreements and the covenants which they have made with it and with each other. To admit of any other alternative would inevitably mean that similar independent movements prompted by the same disloyal and divisive spirit could be organized within individual churches, presbyteries and synods, throughout the entire denomination, creating eventually such anarchy and chaos as would be absolutely fatal to that law and order which has been the glory and strength of the Presbyterian Church from the very beginning of its existence.

In view of the principles herein set forth, the General Assembly would issue the following directions to its officers and judicatories:

1. That "The Independent Board for Presbyterian Foreign Missions" be and is hereby directed to desist forthwith from exercising any ecclesiastical or administrative functions, including the soliciting of funds, within the Synods, the Presbyteries, the particular churches and the mission stations of the Presbyterian Church in the United States of America.

2. That all ministers and laymen affiliated with the Presbyterian Church in the United States of America, who are officers, trustees or members of "The Independent Board for Presbyterian Foreign Missions," be officially notified by this General Assembly through its Stated Clerk, that they must immediately upon the receipt of such notification sever their connection with this Board, and that refusal to do so and a continuance of their relationship to the said Independent Board for Presbyterian Foreign Missions, exercising ecclesiastical and administrative functions in contravention of the authority of the General Assembly, will be considered a disorderly and disloyal act on their part and subject them to the discipline of the Church.

3. That the Presbyteries having in their membership ministers or laymen who are officers, trustees or members of "The Independent Board for Presbyterian Foreign Missions," be officially notified and directed by this General Assembly through its Stated Clerk to ascertain from said ministers and laymen within ninety days of the receipt of such notice as to whether they have complied with the above direction of the General Assembly, and in case of refusal, failure to respond or non-compliance on the part of these persons, to institute, or cause

to be instituted, promptly such disciplinary action as is set forth in the Book of Discipline.

4. That each Presbytery be and hereby is instructed to inform the ministers and sessions of the particular churches under its jurisdiction that it is the primary responsibility and privilege of all those affiliated with the Presbyterian Church in the United States of America to sustain to the full measure of their ability those Boards and Agencies which the General Assembly under its Constitutional authority has established and approved for the extension of the Kingdom of Christ at home and abroad.

The General Assembly profoundly deplores the existence of a situation within the Church which compels it to issue directions which may possibly result in the censure of certain persons affiliated with the Church. It firmly believes, however, that only by the issuance of such directions, can it be faithful to the solemn obligations committed to its sole jurisdiction by the Constitution of the Presbyterian Church in the United States of America.

Note 15

MEMORIAL OF PRESBYTERY OF PHILADELPHIA CONCERNING JURISDICTION OVER DR. MACHEN

Recognizing that it is both the right and the duty of a Presbytery to claim and exercise jurisdiction over all of its members, as well for their protection as for their correction, the Presbytery of Philadelphia finds itself obliged to take cognizance of and make solemn protest against the action of the Presbytery of New Brunswick in claiming jurisdiction and exercising discipline over Rev. Dr. J. Gresham Machen, subsequently to his reception by the Presbytery of Philadelphia on March 5, 1934. The Presbytery of Philadelphia holds that the said Dr. Machen, having been received by the Presbytery of Philadelphia, is subject to its own immediate jurisdiction. The Presbytery of Philadelphia therefore respectfully memorializes the Synod of New Jersey to reverse the above mentioned actions of the Presbytery of New Brunswick with reference to Dr. Machen and to declare them a nullity for the reason that the Presbytery of New Brunswick is without jurisdiction.

Note 16

PROTEST AGAINST RULING OF JUDICIAL COMMISSION OF NEW BRUNSWICK PRESBYTERY IN DR. MACHEN'S TRIAL

This defendant, through his counsel, respectfully and solemnly protests against the ruling of this Commission commencing, "The following matters—" etc., for these reasons:

(1) Because the matter of the signing of the document called the Auburn Affirmation, may have an important bearing upon the matters alleged against this defendant, and can not in fairness and justice, be ruled out, even before

evidence has been offered to show it is heretical and what that connection and bearing is.

(2) Because in paragraph 2 of its ruling, the Commission deprives this defendant of the right to reply concerning the truth of the charges made against him. In charge 3 and in charge 6, question 145, in the Larger Catechism is included. Under this question is set forth "giving false evidence." If this defendant is accused of giving false evidence he certainly by every consideration of fairness, justice and order, should be given the right to show that what he has said is not false but true.

(3) Because paragraph 3 of the ruling of the commission also deprives this defendant of the right to show that in matters of which he stands accused he has not offended against the Word of God, by reasons of the fact that he has spoken nothing but the truth.

(4) Because paragraph 4 of the ruling of the Commission amounts to a decision in advance not to determine whether this defendant has actually violated the law of the church as charged, but to hold him guilty even before hearing evidence or argument. No man is bound to obey an unconstitutional law. The decrees of synods and councils, one of which is the General Assembly of the Presbyterian Church in the U.S.A., are to be received only "if consonant to the Word of God." (Confession of Faith, chapter 31, section 2.) If this defendant is charged, (as he is charged), with not obeying an administrative order of the General Assembly, then he has the right to prove that the order is an illegal order. In charge 5 this defendant is accused of "rebellion against your superiors in the church and their lawful counsels, commands, and corrections, contrary to the Word of God, and to the rules and regulations of this church, founded thereupon." This charge places squarely upon the prosecution the burden of proving that the "counsels, commands and corrections" against which this defendant is alleged to be in rebellion, are lawful. The prosecution has already expressly agreed to assume this burden. By approving the charges and specifications as presented, this Commission has thus bound itself to listen to proof of the legality of the actions of the 146th General Assembly, and, in consequence, also to listen to the contention of this defendant that action was not lawful. Inasmuch as the guilt of this defendant depends wholly upon whether the commands of the General Assembly are lawful commands, it is plain that the Commission refuses in advance to listen to the only possible case of the defense in answer to the charges and specifications as drawn. In view of this fact, it is difficult to see just what further function the defense will have in these proceedings.

(5) Because in declaring that this Commission "cannot sit in judgment upon the acts or deliverances of a superior judicatory" and that such deliverances "stand," this Commission accepts as conclusive the action of the 146th General Assembly; therefore, it has determined in advance the guilt of this defendant, since the 146th General Assembly has declared that refusal to obey its action "will be considered a disorderly and disloyal act." Therefore, in ruling as it has,

this Commission has accepted the guilt of this defendant as a fact already determined by a superior judicatory, in judgment upon which it cannot sit.

This conclusion, the defense maintains, is contrary to the Confession of Faith, chapter 31, section 3, "All synods or councils since the apostles' times, whether general or particular, may err, and many have erred; therefore they are not to be made the rule of faith or practice, but to be used as a help in both."

(6) Because the Confession of Faith says, in chapter 20, section 2, "God alone is lord of the conscience, and hath left it free from the doctrines and commandments of men which are in any thing contrary to His Word, or beside it, in matters of faith or worship. So that to believe such doctrines, or to obey such commandments out of conscience, is to betray true liberty and conscience, and the requiring of an implicit faith, and an absolute and blind obedience, is to destroy liberty of conscience, and reason also."

If God alone is Lord of the conscience, and if a man is not bound to obey the commandments of men contrary to the Word of God, then if a man is accused it is his constitutional right to plead before the courts of his church that the commandment is contrary to the Word of God, and his plea ought to be heard because the constitution of his church gives him the right to disobey in such a case, for if the commandment is contrary to the Word of God he is no offender and should not be regarded as such.

(7) Since the ruling of this Commission has eliminated everything material to this case, we believe it has prejudiced the right of this defendant to make objection to testimony, to cross-examine witnesses, and has prejudiced the rights of this defendant in all subsequent proceedings. Respectfully submitted, counsel for the defendant.

Note 17

STATEMENT OF CANDIDATES FOR ORDINATION IN CHESTER PRESBYTERY CONCERNING FOREIGN MISSION BOARD

Mr. *Blackstone* said:

It is my firm intention to support the Boards and Agencies of the Presbyterian Church in the U.S.A. in so far as they themselves in their whole policy are loyal to the Constitution of the Church and the Word of God.

I wish it were possible for me in good conscience to say that I believe the present Board of Foreign Missions as now constituted to be wholly loyal to the constitution of the Church and the Word of God. With the evidence that I now have I cannot conscientiously affirm that I believe this Board to be wholly loyal to the constitution and the Word of God. However, my mind is open to receive any new facts and should I become convinced that this Board is wholly loyal to the Presbyterian Standards and the Word of God, I will give it my hearty and enthusiastic support.

Note 18

RECOMMENDATIONS OF SPECIAL COMMITTEE TO INVESTIGATE CHESTER AND PHILADELPHIA PRESBYTERIES

Following are the recommendations of the Commission:

1. "Putting away falsehood, speak ye truth, each one with his neighbor; for we are members one of another. Let no disintegrating speech proceed out of your mouth, but such as is good for building up, as the need may be, that it may give grace to them that hear. And grieve not the Holy Spirit of God in whom we were sealed unto the day of redemption. Let all bitterness, and wrath, and anger, and clamor, and railing be put away from you, with all malice; and be ye kind one to another, tender-hearted, forgiving each other, even as God also in Christ forgave you."

2. Conduct all sessions of Presbytery with decorum and Christian courtesy that becometh brethren who sit and deliberate in a court of Jesus Christ. "Let all things be done decently and in order."

3. Refrain from running to the public press and making a public scandal of your differences; and henceforth discipline according to the book those who persistently and disloyally continue the practice. Whether by enforcement of rules respecting private sessions or in some other effective manner, every effort should be made to prevent perverted accounts of Presbytery's affairs from being given to the press.

4. Discourage all caucuses and any other associations organized for political purposes to force through the Presbytery the will of this group or that group; and trust more in the Holy Spirit dwelling in the body of believers and making His will known in the corporate life of the Church. If any groups of ministers or elders persist in such political trickery they should be disciplined according to the book for inciting to schism in the body of Christ.

5. Respect the rights of minorities and see that they are represented in places of trust on committees and in the higher courts of the church. The light of truth has many colors in its spectrum and needs them all under the fusing power of the Holy Spirit. Institute forthwith the principle of rotary representation in Synod and General Assembly whereby churches as a general rule shall be represented in turn. This principle shall apply both to ministers and lay commissioners. The local church should be given the privilege of nominating the elder candidate or commissioner.

6. Create, if not already existing, a general council after the pattern laid down in the Constitution of our Church. This should absorb the functions now exercised by any executive or business committee.

7. Dignify the sacred office of the ministry by allowing ample time to elapse between licensure and ordination; pass a rule providing that the service of ordination shall always be held in the church to which the licentiate has been called, exception to the rule to be made only by a three-fourths vote of Presbytery; pass a further rule to prohibit licensure and ordination to take place at the same

meeting of Presbytery. In the examination of candidates for licensure or ordination the right of all members to ask any pertinent questions of the candidate that tend to satisfy Presbytery as to the qualifications of the candidate for the Gospel ministry in the Presbyterian Church in the U.S.A., shall be sustained.

8. Develop, perfect and trust more a strong Vacancy and Supply Committee that will watch over your vacant pulpits and counsel pastoral committees (this for Philadelphia). (For Chester:) Strengthen your Vacancy and Supply Committee so that it can and will watch over your vacant pulpits and counsel pastoral committees.

9. Now that our pension system operates so satisfactorily, the General Assembly and the four Boards having adopted a rule fixing seventy years as the age of retirement, Presbytery should seriously consider the adoption of a similar rule.

10. The Commission has been profoundly moved by the vision of tremendous opportunity in this metropolitan area of our Church and nation. We are mindful of the outstanding leadership given to our great church for so many generations from the Philadelphia area, the place of our beginnings. It is not primarily with the purpose of healing division, but with the ardent desire to see the great needs of the metropolitan area met, the glorious opportunities realized, and the Philadelphia center reclaim its rightful place in the leadership of our church that we make the following suggestions; entertain with open minds and prayerful hearts the proposal that the problem is so vast it demands and ought to command the resources of every individual Christian in this region. From this situation has sprung the suggestion for the realignment of the Presbyteries in this region, and the formation of a metropolitan presbytery. In connection with which suggestion a committee of Synod has already been appointed. Most parties are agreed that some such realignment will eventually be consummated. When all the facts are considered, we are forced to the conclusion that such a metropolitan presbytery would enable the Presbyterian forces in a much more adequate way to cope with the Kingdom task in this strategic center.

11. The Commission requests that special meetings of the Presbyteries be called, at which time the Commission will present this program for consideration and appropriate action.

12. Following the meetings of the Presbyteries transmit in writing to every minister and elder in the Presbyteries of Philadelphia and Chester this program, requesting their full cooperation in making it effective in both letter and spirit.

Note 19

FURTHER RECOMMENDATIONS OF SPECIAL COMMITTEE

A. The policy and program of the Church should be determined by ministers in full time service of the Church and their associated elders. It is significant that the Scottish and the Australian Presbyterian churches limit the voting and office holding membership of the Presbyteries to the pastors of its churches and those executives, and teachers of its accredited Theological Colleges, whom the General Assembly appoints as voting members in the Presbyteries.

B. A change in our constitution making it mandatory on the Presbytery in receiving as a candidate for licensure or ordination a graduate of a Theological School or Seminary not under the care of our Assembly, or a minister seeking membership by transfer from another denomination, to arrest the process and refer the question to the Synod's Committee on Licensure for recommendation. If Synod's Committee recommends that the applicant be not licensed or ordained, or received, Presbytery can proceed with the process only on a two-thirds vote.

Note 20

OVERTURE PROPOSED TO PHILADELPHIA PRESBYTERY CONCERNING BOARD OF CHRISTIAN EDUCATION

The Presbytery of Philadelphia respectfully overtures the General Assembly of 1936, 1. To take care to elect to the Board of Christian Education only persons who are aware of the danger in which the Church stands of losing its historic Christian witness, and who are determined to insist upon such verities as the full truthfulness of Scripture, the virgin birth of our Lord, His substitutionary death as a sacrifice to satisfy Divine justice, His bodily resurrection and His miracles as being essential to the system of doctrine to which the Presbyterian Church is committed by its Constitution, 2. To instruct the Board of Christian Education that no one who denies the absolute necessity of such loyalty to the Bible, and to the Confession of Faith shall serve on its staff, 3. To instruct the Board of Christian Education to publish only literature that is true to the historic witness of the Church, and to cease the publication of literature that departs from this witness, 4. To instruct the Board of Christian Education to cease cooperation with organizations or individuals that show by their publications or other activities that they are not insisting upon the full truthfulness of the Bible and upon the other evangelical verities.

Note 21

ADOPTING ACT OF PRESBYTERIAN CHURCH OF AMERICA

I. In order to continue what we believe to be the true spiritual succession of the Presbyterian Church in the U.S.A., which we hold to have been abandoned by the present organization of that body, and to make clear to all the world that we have no connection with the organization bearing that name, we, a company of ministers and ruling elders, having been removed from that organization in contravention (as we believe) of its constitution, or having severed our connection with that organization, or hereby solemnly declaring that we do sever our connection with it, or coming as ministers or ruling elders from other ecclesiastical bodies holding the Reformed Faith, do hereby associate ourselves together with all Christian people who do and will adhere to us, in a body to be known and styled as the Presbyterian Church of America.

II. We, a company of ministers and ruling elders, do hereby in our own name, in the name of those who have adhered to us, and by the warrant and authority of the Lord Jesus Christ, constitute ourselves a General Assembly of the Presbyterian Church of America.

III. We do solemnly declare (1) that the Scriptures of the Old and New Testament are the Word of God, the only infallible rule of faith and practice, (2) that the Westminster Confession of Faith and Catechisms contain the system of doctrine taught in the Holy Scriptures, and (3) that we subscribe to and maintain the principles of Presbyterian church government as being founded upon and agreeable to the Word of God.

All persons, before they shall be ordained or received as ministers or ruling elders or deacons, shall subscribe to the foregoing statement.

Note 22

INSTRUCTION TO CONSTITUTION COMMITTEE
OF PRESBYTERIAN CHURCH OF AMERICA

The Committee shall take as the basis of its consideration the particular form of the Westminster Confession of Faith and Catechisms which appear in the Constitution of the Presbyterian Church in the U.S.A., 1934 edition. The committee shall have the power to recommend the elimination, from that form of these Standards, of the changes made in the year of our Lord 1903, but it shall not have power to recommend any other changes. The committee shall also have power to recommend what relation this church shall bear to the Declaratory Statement of 1903.

Note 23

ACTION OF GENERAL ASSEMBLY OF PRESBYTERIAN CHURCH
OF AMERICA CONCERNING CHURCH PROPERTY RIGHTS

1. All particular churches now connected with the Presbyterian Church of America, and all particular churches which shall hereafter exist under its jurisdiction shall be entitled to hold, own and enjoy their own local properties, without any right of reversion to the Presbyterian Church of America whatsoever, save as is hereinafter provided.

2. The property of any particular church shall revert to the Presbyterian Church of America only if, as and when the said particular church shall become extinct. Dissolution of a particular church by any judicatory, or any other form of ecclesiastical action shall not be deemed as making a particular church extinct within the meaning of this act.

3. This act shall not be construed as limiting or abrogating the right of the judicatories of this church to exercise all constitutional and proper authority over the particular churches as spiritual bodies.

4. This act shall be deemed to possess, upon its adoption by this Assembly, full constitutional force and effect.

Note 24

PORTION OF COMPLAINT IN CIVIL SUIT REGARDING NAME PRESBYTERIAN CHURCH OF AMERICA

Part of the contentions of the Presbyterian Church in the USA, in the name suit are as follows:

By reason of the similarity between the name of the plaintiff church, to wit, "Presbyterian Church in the United States of America," and the name adopted by the defendant church, to wit, "Presbyterian Church of America," the said names will appear together in all church, business, city and telephone directories, whereby the public and the members of both plaintiff and defendant churches as well, will be likely to confuse the churches, offices, and agencies of the one church with those of the other. Telegraph, cable, postal and express agencies will be misled in the delivery of messages, letters and merchandise.

The similarity of names complained of will, and is intended to, cause confusion and uncertainty, and will, and is intended to, mislead the public and injure the plaintiff church and its work pecuniarily and otherwise. The acts done and threatened to be done by and on behalf of the defendant church are unfair and contrary to the principles of equity and good conscience and violate the rights of the plaintiff church in and to the use of its name and terminology not only in the State of Pennsylvania, but in all the states and territorial possessions of the United States and in foreign countries.

It is impracticable and impossible for the plaintiff church to recover in damages what it has suffered and is likely to suffer from the aforesaid acts done and threatened to be done by and on behalf of the defendant church. The plaintiff church is powerless to prevent the resulting injury to its property and enterprises, or to avoid the resulting loss in donations and financial support which may be diverted from it, which injuries are immediate, continuous and irreparable, and incapable of computation or estimate.

Note 25

PORTION OF JUDGES' RULING IN NAME SUIT

Part of the judge's ruling in the name suit is as follows:

1. The Presbyterian Church in the United States of America by long usage, ancient reputation, and general knowledge has a property right to its name which shall not be interfered with or disturbed. The defendant church bearing the name "Presbyterian Church of America" has adopted a name so similar to

that of the plaintiff as to be confusing and thereby hamper and impair the work of the plaintiff church, interfere with its orderly procedure and disturb the sources of support in its field of activity.

2. The Presbyterian Church of America . . . and all persons associated with them as members and officers of the defendant church, an unincorporated religious society, are enjoined from using or employing the name of "Presbyterian Church of America," or any other name of like import, or that is similar to or imitative of or a contractive of the name Presbyterian Church of the U.S.A., or the Presbyterian Church in the United States of America, or ever doing any act or thing calculated or designed to mislead the public or the members of the plaintiff church.

Note 26

OVERTURE ADOPTED BY GENERAL ASSEMBLY OF THE PRESBYTERIAN CHURCH OF AMERICA CONCERNING CHRISTIAN LIBERTY

The Third General Assembly of the Presbyterian Church of America has received an overture from the Presbytery of Philadelphia relative to the general subject of Christian Life and Conduct, and especially to the subject of the use of intoxicating beverages. The Assembly would make answer as follows:—

(1) We believe that the Westminster Standards speak with adequacy and force upon these subjects in the Confession of Faith, chapter XX, L.C. Questions 122-148, and S.C. 63-81: and in particular in the following passages.

C[onf]. XX. 2, 3—

"God alone is Lord of the Conscience, and hath left it free from the doctrines and commandments of men which are in anything contrary to his Word, or beside it, in matters of Faith or worship. So that to believe such commandments out of conscience, is to betray true liberty of Conscience, and the requiring of an implicit faith, and an absolute and blind obedience, is to destroy liberty of conscience, and reason also.

"They who upon pretence of Christian Liberty do practice any sin, or cherish any lust, do thereby destroy the end of Christian Liberty; which is, that, being delivered out of the hands of our enemies, we might serve the Lord without fear, in holiness and righteousness before him, all the days of our life."

Larger Catechism, Answer to question 136—

"The sins forbidden in the sixth Commandment are . . . all excessive passions, distracting cares, immoderate use of meat, drink, labor and recreation; provoking words: oppressions, quarreling, striking, wounding, and whatsoever else tends to the destruction of the life of any."

Answer to question 139—

"The sins forbidden in the seventh Commandment, besides the neglect of the duties required, are . . . idleness, gluttony, drunkenness, unchaste company, lascivious songs, books, pictures, dancing, stage-plays; and all other provocations to or acts of uncleanness either in ourselves or others."

(2) We do not feel that any situation has actually arisen within the Presbyterian Church of America, which calls for further statement.

Note 27

PROPOSED RESOLUTION OF REFORM OF THE INDEPENDENT BOARD

WHEREAS there are certain members of The Independent Board for Presbyterian Foreign Missions, including the President and Vice-President, whose practice in church government is that of Independency rather than of Presbyterianism, and who are therefore out of accord with the provisions of its charter and in particular with the following provisions:

III (a) The Corporation is formed for the purpose of establishing and conducting truly Biblical missions among all nations, in clear opposition to all forms of belief or practice which are contrary to the Bible or are indifferent to the necessity of acceptance of the doctrine that the Bible contains. Being convinced that the Confession of Faith and Catechisms of the Presbyterian Church in the U.S.A., in the form which they possessed in 1933, contain the system of doctrine taught in the Bible, the Corporation is to encourage the work of all missionaries who shall truly believe and cordially love and therefore endeavor to propagate and defend, in its genuineness, simplicity and fulness, that system of religious belief and practice which is now set forth in the Confession of Faith and Catechisms of the Presbyterian Church in the U.S.A., and which is involved in the fundamental principles of Presbyterian Church government; and thus to perpetuate and extend the influence of true evangelical piety and gospel order.

III (b) It is to act as an agency to receive and disburse funds to be used for foreign mission work which is true to the Bible and to the system of doctrine contained in the Westminster Confession of Faith and to the fundamental principles of Presbyterian church government.

III (c) It is to provide a Board under which missionaries who are true to the Bible and to the system of doctrine contained in the Westminster Confession of Faith and to the fundamental principles of Presbyterian church government can serve without compromise with any form of unbelief.

WHEREAS each member of the Board has subscribed to the following pledge:

"I hereby solemnly declare in the presence of God and of this Board (1) that I believe the Scriptures of the Old and New Testaments to be the Word of God, the only infallible rule of faith and practice, (2) that I sincerely receive and adopt the Confession of Faith of the Presbyterian Church in the U.S.A., in the form which it possessed in 1933, as containing the system of doctrine taught in the Holy Scriptures, (3) that, approving the charter of The Independent Board for

Presbyterian Foreign Missions, I will faithfully endeavor to carry into effect the articles and provisions of said Charter and to promote the great design of the Board," thus indicating his approval of the foregoing provisions of the Charter:

NOW THEREFORE BE IT RESOLVED that The Independent Board for Presbyterian Foreign Missions

(1) re-affirms its loyalty to the provisions of its Charter;

(2) rejects the Independent form of church government as contrary to its Charter;

(3) calls upon its members whose practice is not in accord with the principles of Presbyterian church governnent either forthwith to bring their practice into accord with the principles set forth in the Charter of the Board by ceasing to practice Independency thus fulfilling their pledge "to promote the great design of the Board," or to terminate their membership in The Independent Board for Presbyterian Foreign Missions.

I HEREBY ALSO GIVE FORMAL NOTICE that if, as and when the above resolution is passed, I shall request the Board to undertake an investigation of the doctrinal soundness of certain members.

When the board failed to pass this resolution eight members resigned and issued this letter:

To the Rev. Harold S. Laird:

Dear Mr. Laird:

In view of the decision of the Independent Board for Presbyterian Foreign Missions refusing to condemn independency in church government and to uphold its charter provisions favoring Presbyterian church government we believe that the usefulness of the Independent Board as an agency to promote the object for which it was founded, the conduct of truly Presbyterian foreign missions, is at an end.

We, therefore, present our resignation from the Board, effective immediately, Mr. Thompson also resigning as treasurer and Mr. Woolley as secretary.

Sincerely yours,
Paul Woolley
Ned B. Stonehouse,
Edwin H. Rian,
Murray F. Thompson,
Marguerite Montgomery,
Mary W. Stewart,
Mrs. Mildred Berry,
Mrs. J. B. Griggs.

Note 28

ACTION OF GENERAL ASSEMBLY OF
THE PRESBYTERIAN CHURCH OF AMERICA
CONCERNING THE INDEPENDENT BOARD

WHEREAS your committee feels that the Independent Board for Presbyterian Foreign Missions as it is now constituted is out of accord with the provisions of its charter and not consistent with the fundamental principles of Presbyterian Church government which are held by the Presbyterian Church of America, as evidenced by the fact that the practice of certain members of the Independent Board of Presbyterian Foreign Missions, including the President and Vice-President, in matters of church government is that of Independency rather than Presbyterianism, which practice was virtually endorsed by the majority on the Independent Board when, at its meeting May 31, 1937, said majority refused to insist that its members bring their practice into accord with the principles of true Presbyterian Church government, or else resign from said Board; and as further evidenced by the resignation from the Board of the following members, Mrs. J. B. Griggs, Miss Marguerite Montgomery, Mrs. A. L. Berry, Miss Mary W. Stewart, the Rev. Paul Woolley, the Rev. Ned B. Stonehouse, the Rev. Edwin H. Rian, and Murray F. Thompson, whose resignation reads as follows:

"In view of the decision of the Independent Board for Presbyterian Foreign Missions refusing to condemn Independency in church government and to uphold its charter provisions favoring Presbyterian church government, we believe that the usefulness of the Independent Board as an agency to promote the object for which it was founded, the conduct of truly Presbyterian Foreign Missions, is at an end.

"We therefore present our resignations from the Board effective immediately. . . ."

The General Secretary of the Board, the Rev. Charles J. Woodbridge, has resigned for the same reasons.

THEREFORE be it resolved that this General Assembly does not find itself able any longer to recommend the Independent Board for Presbyterian Foreign Missions as an agency for the propagation of the Gospel as set forth in the Westminster Standards.

Note 29

STATEMENT OF PURPOSE OF THE LEAGUE OF FAITH

The objects of the League of Faith as stated in its constitution are as follows:

1. To maintain loyalty to the Bible as the Word of God in opposition to denials of its full truthfulness.

2. To maintain the Reformed or Calvinistic system of doctrine as it is set forth in the Confession of Faith of the Presbyterian Church in the U.S.A. as it appears in 1931 in opposition to all plans of church union which could either break down that system or relegate it to a secondary place.

3. To oppose changes in the historic formula of creed subscription required of candidates for the ministry and the eldership.

4. To oppose the attack made by the document commonly called the "Auburn Affirmation" upon the doctrinal pronouncement of the General Assembly of 1923, and to insist, in opposition to that affirmation, that the full truth of the Scriptures, the Virgin Birth of Christ, the Substitutionary Atonement, the bodily Resurrection and Miracles of our Lord are essential doctrines of the Word of God and our Standards.

5. To warn men everywhere that salvation is to be obtained not by human merit or human effort to please God, but only through the redeeming work of our Lord and Saviour Jesus Christ as He is offered to us in the Gospel.

6. To encourage the vigorous defense and joyous propagation of the Gospel in its fullness as it is set forth in the Westminster Confession of Faith on the basis of Holy Scripture.

Index